STUDENT PRACTICE WORKBOOK

CALCULUS
GRAPHICAL, NUMERICAL, ALGEBRAIC
THIRD EDITION

Ross L. Finney

Franklin D. Demana
The Ohio State University

Bert K. Waits
The Ohio State University

Daniel Kennedy
Baylor School

PEARSON
Prentice Hall

Boston San Francisco New York
London Toronto Sydney Tokyo Singapore Madrid
Mexico City Munich Paris Cape Town Hong Kong Montreal

Pearson Prentice Hall™ is a trademark of Pearson Education, Inc.
Pearson® is a registered trademark of Pearson plc.
Prentice Hall® is a registered trademark of Pearson Education, Inc.

0-13-201411-4
3 4 5 6 7 8 9 10 BB 10 09 08 07

Contents

Chapter 1 Prerequisites for Calculus

1.1 Lines

Alternate Example 3 **Using the Point-Slope Equation**

Write the point-slope equation for the line that passes through the point $(-3, -2)$ with slope 2/3.

SOLUTION

The point-slope equation of a line is in the form $y = m(x - x_1) + y_1$. We substitute $x_1 = -3$, $y_1 = -5$, and $m = 2/3$ into this equation and obtain

$$y = \frac{2}{3}(x + 3) - 5 \quad \text{or} \quad y = \frac{2}{3}x - 3.$$

Exercises for Alternate Example 3

In Exercises 1–8, write the point-slope equation for each line whose slope and a point on it are given.

1. $(1, 2)$ and $m = -2$ **2.** $(-2, 11)$ and $m = -5$ **3.** $(0, -11)$ and $m = 3$ **4.** $(0, 3)$ and $m = 3$

5. $(0, 2)$ and $m = \frac{3}{11}$ **6.** $(1, -7)$ and $m = -5$ **7.** $\left(-\frac{3}{4}, -6\right)$ and $m = -\frac{4}{3}$ **8.** $(0, -11)$ and $m = -5$

Alternate Example 4 **Writing the Slope-Intercept Equation**

Write the slope-intercept equation for the line passing through $(5, -1)$ and $(2, -7)$.

SOLUTION

A line's slope passing through the points $P(x, y)$ and $P_1 = (x_1, y_1)$ is $m = \dfrac{y - y_1}{x - x_1}$. Replace the given coordinates in this formula:

$$m = \frac{-1 - (-7)}{5 - 2} = \frac{6}{3} = 2.$$

We can use this slope with either of the two given points in the point-slope equation. For $(x_1, y_1) = (5, -1)$, we obtain

$$y = 2(x - 5) - 1$$
$$y = 2x - 10 - 1$$
$$y = 2x - 11.$$

Exercises for Alternate Example 4

In Exercises 9–16, write the slope-intercept equation of the line passing through each pair of points.

9. $(2, -15)$ and $(0, -9)$ **10.** $(-1, 6)$ and $(-3, 16)$ **11.** $(3, -8)$ and $(-2, -23)$ **12.** $(2, -3)$ and $(-2, -7)$

13. $(3, 14)$ and $(-2, -11)$ **14.** $(0, 9)$ and $(1, 6)$ **15.** $(11, 0)$ and $(1, 10)$ **16.** $(0, 1)$ and $(2, -3)$

Alternate Example 6 **Writing Equations for Lines**

Write an equation for the line passing through the point (5, –3) that is **(a)** parallel, and **(b)** perpendicular to the line $L: y = -2x + 5$.

SOLUTION

The line $L: y = -2x + 5$ has slope –2.
(a) The slope of a line that is parallel to L is –2. The line $y = -2(x - 5) - 3$, or $y = -2x + 7$, passing through the point (5, –3) is parallel to L because its slope is –2.

(b) The slope of L is –2. A line that is perpendicular to L must have slope $\dfrac{1}{2}$ so that the

product of the slopes of two lines is –1. The line $y = \dfrac{1}{2}(x - 5) - 3$, or $y = \dfrac{1}{2}x - \dfrac{11}{2}$,

which passes through the point (5, –3), is perpendicular to L because its slope is 1/2.

Exercises for Alternate Example 6

In Exercises 17–23, write an equation for the line passing through the point (1, 3) that is **(a)** parallel, and **(b)** perpendicular to each given line L.

17. $L: y = x + 4$ **18.** $L: y = -x + 1$ **19.** $L: y = 4x + 5$ **20.** $L: y = 7x + 11$ **21.** $L: y = -2x - 1$

22. $L: y = 2x$ **23.** $L: y = -3x + 1$

Alternate Example 7 **Determining a Function**

The following table gives the values for the linear function $f(x) = mx + b$. Determine m and b.

x	$f(x)$
–2	$-\dfrac{9}{2}$
2	$\dfrac{7}{2}$
3	$\dfrac{11}{2}$

SOLUTION

The graph of f is a line. From the table we know that the following points are on the line:

$$\left(-2, -\frac{9}{2}\right), \left(2, \frac{7}{2}\right), \left(3, \frac{11}{2}\right).$$

Using the first two points, the slope m is

$$m = \frac{-\dfrac{9}{2} - \dfrac{7}{2}}{-2 - 2} = \frac{-8}{-4} = 2.$$

So $f(x) = 2x + b$. Because $f(-2) = -\dfrac{9}{2}$, we have

$$f(-2) = 2(-2) + b$$

$$-\frac{9}{2} = -4 + b$$

$$b = -\frac{1}{2}.$$

Thus, $m = 2$, $b = -\dfrac{1}{2}$, and $f(x) = 2x - \dfrac{1}{2}$.

We can use either of the other two points determined by the table to check our work.

Exercises for Alternate Example 7

In Exercises 24–30, each table gives the values for the linear function $f(x) = mx + b$. Determine m and b for each table.

24.

x	$f(x)$
1	–8
2	–5
3	–2

25.

x	$f(x)$
–2	11
–1	10
0	9

26.

x	$f(x)$
–2	–11
2	9
3	14

27.

x	$f(x)$
–3	–8
–2	–7
1	–4

28.

x	$f(x)$
–1	–1
–4	2
–6	4

29.

x	$f(x)$
2	–6
3	–3
5	3

30.

x	$f(x)$
1	4
2	9
2.4	11

■

1.2   Functions and Graphs

Alternate Example 3   **Defining Domain and Range of a Function**

Use a grapher to identify the domain and range, and then draw the graph of the function.

(a) $y = \sqrt{25 - x^2}$ **(b)** $y = x^{1/3}$

SOLUTION

(a) Figure 1.1a shows a graph of the function for $-5 \le x \le 5$ and $-2 \le y \le 5$, that is, the viewing window $[-5, 5]$ by $[-2, 5]$, with x-scale $= y$-scale $= 1$. The graph appears to be the upper half of a circle. The domain appears to be $[-5, 5]$. This observation is correct because we must have $25 - x^2 \ge 0$, or equivalently, $-5 \le x \le 5$. The range appears to be $[0, 5]$, which can also be verified algebraically.

(b) Figure 1.1b shows a graph of the function in the viewing window [–6, 6] by [–3, 3] with x-scale = y-scale = 1. The domain appears to be $(-\infty, \infty)$, which we can verify by observing that $x^{1/3} = \sqrt[3]{x}$. Also, the range is $(-\infty, \infty)$ by the same observation.

$y = \sqrt{25 - x^2}$

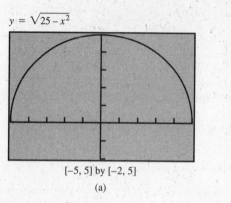

[–5, 5] by [–2, 5]

(a)

$y = x^{1/3}$

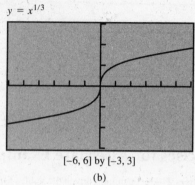

[–6, 6] by [–3, 3]

(b)

Figure 1.1 The graphs of (a) $y = \sqrt{25 - x^2}$ and (b) $y = x^{1/3}$.

Exercises for Alternate Example 3

In Exercise 1–7, use a grapher to identify the domain and range of each function, and then draw its graph.

1. (a) $y = \sqrt{1 - x^2}$ **2. (a)** $y = \sqrt{3 - x^2}$ **3. (a)** $y = \sqrt{49 - x^2}$ **4. (a)** $y = \sqrt{12 - x^2}$

   (b) $y = -x^{2/3}$ **(b)** $y = 2x^{1/3}$ **(b)** $y = -2x^{1/3}$ **(b)** $y = 3x^{2/3}$

5. (a) $y = \sqrt{16 - x^2}$ **6. (a)** $y = \sqrt{36 - x^2}$ **7. (a)** $y = \sqrt{48 - x^2}$

   (b) $y = -x^{1/2}$ **(b)** $y = 2x^{1/2}$ **(b)** $y = -3x^{1/2}$

Alternate Example 4   **Recognizing Even and Odd Functions**

A function $f(x)$ is even if $f(-x) = f(x)$ for all x in the function's domain.

A function $f(x)$ is odd if $f(-x) = -f(x)$ for all x in the function's domain.

$f(x) = -x^4$ Even function: $f(-x) = -(-x)^4 = -x^4 = f(x)$ for all x;

               Symmetric about y-axis (Figure 1.2a)

$f(x) = -x^4 + 2$ Even function: $f(-x) = -(-x)^4 + 2 = -x^4 + 2 = f(x)$ for all x;

               Symmetric about y-axis (Figure 1.2a)

$f(x) = -x$ Odd function: $f(-x) = -(-x) = x = -f(x)$ for all x;

               Symmetric about the origin (Figure 1.2b).

$f(x)$ $y = -x + 2$ Not odd: $f(-x) = -(-x) + 2$, but $-f(x) = x - 2$.

               The two are not equal.

               Not even: $f(-x) = -(-x) + 2$, but $f(x) = -x + 2$. $f(-x) \neq f(x)$

               for all $x \neq 0$ (Figure 1.2b)

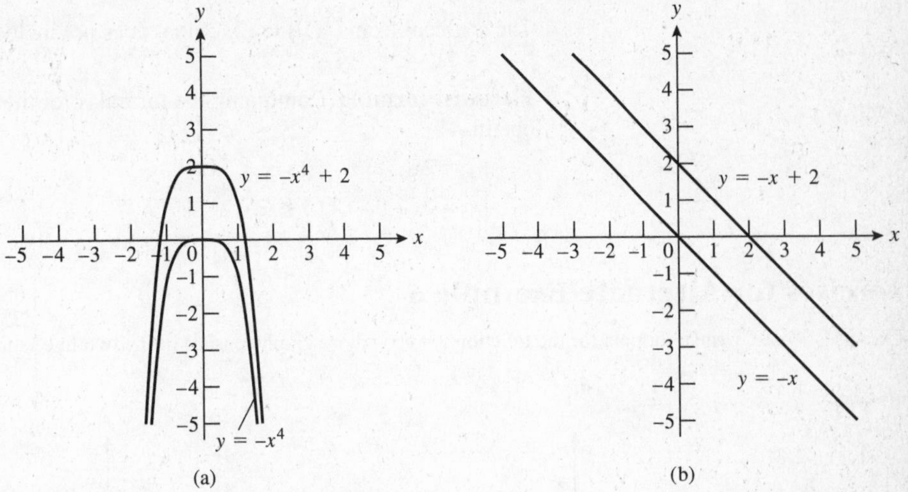

The graphs show:

$y = -x^4 + 2$

$y = -x^4$

(a)

$y = -x + 2$

$y = -x$

(b)

Figure 1.2 **(a)** When we add the constant term 2 to the function $y = -x^4$, the resulting function $y = -x^4 + 2$ is still symmetric about y-axis.

(b) When we add the constant term 2 to the function $y = -x$, the resulting function $y = -x + 2$ is no longer odd. The symmetry about the origin is lost.

Exercises for Alternate Example 4

In Exercises 8–14 recognize which function is even, odd, or neither.

8. $f(x) = -x^2$ **9.** $f(x) = -11x + 12$ **10.** $f(x) = -5x^3$ **11.** $f(x) = \dfrac{2}{x^2 - 9}$ **12.** $f(x) = x^5$

13. $f(x) = 5x + 9$ **14.** $f(x) = \sqrt[3]{x^2}$

■

Alternate Example 6 **Writing Formulas for Piecewise Functions**

Write a formula for the functions $y = f(x)$ whose graph consists of the two segments in Figure 1.3.

SOLUTION

We find the formulas for the segments from $(0, 0)$ to $(1, 2)$ and from $(1, 0)$ to $(2, 2)$ and piece them together.

Segment from (0, 0) to (1, 2) The line passing through the points with coordinates $(0, 0)$ and $(1, 2)$ has slope $m = \dfrac{2 - 0}{1 - 0} = 2$ and y-intercept $b = 0$. Its slope-intercept equation is $y = 2x$. The segment from $(0, 0)$ to $(1, 2)$ that does not include the points $(0, 0)$ and $(1, 2)$ is the graph of the function $y = 2x$ on the open interval $0 < x < 1$, namely,

$$y = 2x, \quad 0 < x < 1$$

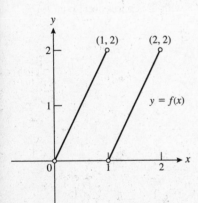

Figure 1.3 The segments do not contain any of the endpoints.

Segment from (1, 0) to (2, 2) The line passing through $(1, 0)$ and $(2, 2)$ has slope $m = \dfrac{2 - 0}{2 - 1} = 2$. Using this slope and one of the points given, say $(1, 0)$, the corresponding point-slope equation for the line is

$$y = 2(x - 1), \quad \text{or} \quad y = 2x - 2.$$

The segment from (1, 0) to (2, 2) that does not include the endpoints is the graph of
$$y = 2x - 2, \quad 1 < x < 2$$

Piecewise formula Combining the formulas for the two pieces of the function, we obtain
$$\begin{cases} y = 2x, & 0 < x < 1 \\ y = 2x - 2, & 1 < x < 2 \end{cases}$$

Exercises for Alternate Example 6

In Exercises 15–20, write a formula for the function $y = f(x)$ whose graph consists of the two line segments in each figure.

15.

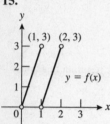

16.

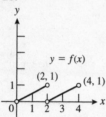

17.

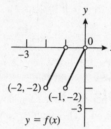

18.

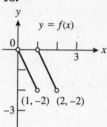

19.

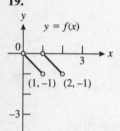

20.

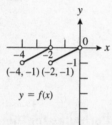

Alternate Example 8 **Composing Functions**

Find a formula for $f(g(x))$ if $g(x) = -x^3$ and $f(x) = 2x + 3$. Then find $f(g(-3))$.

SOLUTION

To find $f(g(x))$, we replace x in the formula $f(x) = 2x + 3$ with the expression given for $g(x)$.
$$f(x) = 2x + 3$$
$$f(g(x)) = 2[g(x)] + 3 = 2(-x^3) + 3 = -2x^3 + 3$$

We then find the value of $f(g(-3))$ by substituting -3 for x.
$$f(g(-3)) = -2(-3)^3 + 3 = 57$$

Exercises for Alternate Example 8

In Exercises 21–27, find a formula for $f(g(x))$ for each given pair of functions. Then find $f(g(x))$ for the indicted value of x.

21. $g(x) = 5x^3$ and $f(x) = 3x + 1$, for $x = -1$

22. $g(x) = -3x + 2$ and $f(x) = 4x^2$, for $x = 0$

23. $g(x) = 3x^5$ and $f(x) = 2x - 3$, for $x = -1$

24. $g(x) = -3x^3$ and $f(x) = 2x + 3$, for $x = -2$

25. $g(x) = 5x^2$ and $f(x) = 5x - 1$, for $x = -2$

26. $g(x) = 4x$ and $f(x) = -x^3$, for $x = 1$

27. $g(x) = x^4$ and $f(x) = -x - 3$, for $x = 5$

1.3 Exponential Functions

Alternate Example 1 **Graphing an Exponential Function**

Graph the function $y = 3(2^x) + 3$. State its domain and range.

SOLUTION

Figure 1.4 shows the graph of the function y. It appears that the domain is $(-\infty, \infty)$. The range is $(3, \infty)$ because $3(2^x) > 0$ for all x.

$y = 3(2^x) + 3$

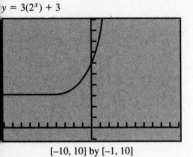

[–10, 10] by [–1, 10]

Figure 1.4 The graph of $y = 3(2^x) + 3$.

Exercises for Alternate Example 1

Graph each function. State its domain and range.

1. $y = 2^x - 1$ **2.** $y = 2(2^x) - 3$ **3.** $y = 3(3^x) - 1$ **4.** $y = -2^x + 4$ **5.** $y = 3^x - 6$

6. $y = -3(2^x) - 5$

Alternate Example 2 **Finding Zeros**

Find the zeros of $f(x) = 7 - 1.25^x$ graphically.

SOLUTION

Figure 1.5a suggests that f has a zero between $x = 8$ and $x = 9$ closer to 8. We can use our grapher to find that the zero is approximately 8.72 (Figure 1.5b)

$y = 7 - 1.25^x$

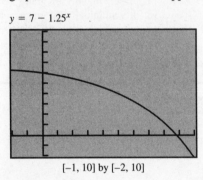

[–1, 10] by [–2, 10]

$y = 7 - 1.25^x$

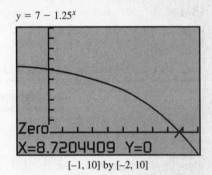

Zero
X=8.7204409 Y=0

[–1, 10] by [–2, 10]

Figure 1.5 (a) A graph of $f(x) = 7 - 1.25^x$.

(b) The use of the ZERO feature to approximate the zero of f.

Exercises for Alternate Example 2

In exercises 7–12, find the zeros of $f(x)$ graphically.

7. $f(x) = 2 - 1.20^x$ **8.** $f(x) = 1 - 1.15^x$ **9.** $f(x) = -4 + 1.25^x$ **10 .** $f(x) = -3 + 1.25^x$

11. $f(x) = 5 - 2.25^x$ **12.** $f(x) = 4 - 1.15^x$

Alternate Example 4 **Modeling Radioactive Decay**

Suppose the half-life of a certain radioactive substance is 12 days and that there are 8 grams present initially. When will there be only 1.5 grams of the substance remaining?

SOLUTION

Model The number of grams remaining after 12 days is

$$8\left(\frac{1}{2}\right) = 4.$$

The number of grams remaining after 24 days is

$$8\left(\frac{1}{2}\right)\left(\frac{1}{2}\right) = 2.$$

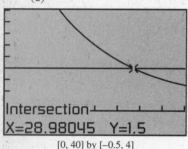

$y = 8\left(\frac{1}{2}\right)^{t/12}, y = 1.5$

Intersection
X=28.98045   Y=1.5
[0, 40] by [−0.5, 4]

Figure 1.6 Graph of $y_1 = 8\left(\frac{1}{2}\right)^{t/12}$
and $y_2 = 1.5$

The function $y = 8\left(\frac{1}{2}\right)^{t/12}$ models the mass in grams of the radioactive substance after t days.

Solve Graphically Figure 1.6 shows that the graphs of $y_1 = 8\left(\frac{1}{2}\right)^{t/12}$ and $y_2 = 1.5$ (for 1.5 grams) intersect when t is approximately 28.98.

Interpret There will be 1.5 grams of radioactive substance left after approximately 28.98 days, or about 28 days 23.5 hours.

Exercises for Alternate Example 4

In Exercise 13–18, each half-life of the radioactive substance is 20 days. The number of grams present initially is given. Determine when the indicated amount of the substance will remain.

13. present initially: 12 grams, remaining amount: 8 grams
14. present initially: 18 grams, remaining amount: 2 grams
15. present initially: 10 grams, remaining amount: 4 grams
16. present initially: 25 grams, remaining amount: 5 grams
17. present initially: 16 grams, remaining amount: 2 grams
18. present initially: 20 grams, remaining amount: 3 grams

1.4 Parametric Equations

Alternate Example 1 **Graphing Half a Parabola**

Describe the graph of the relation determined by $x = \sqrt{t}$, $y = 2t$, $t \geq 0$.

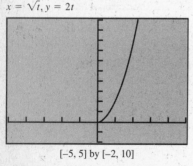

$x = \sqrt{t}, y = 2t$

[−5, 5] by [−2, 10]

Figure 1.7 You must choose a smallest and a largest value for t in parametric mode. Here, we chose 0 and 10, respectively.

SOLUTION

Set your calculator in parametric mode and enter $x_1 = \sqrt{t}$, $y_1 = 2t$. Press the GRAPH key. The graph being displayed appears to be the right half of the parabola $y = 2x^2$. Notice that there is no information about t on the graph itself. The curve appears to start from the point (0, 0), moving toward the upper right of the coordinate system.

Confirm Algebraically Both x and y are greater than or equal to zero, because $t \geq 0$.

Square both sides of $x = \sqrt{t}$.

$$x^2 = t$$

Substitute the equivalent of t in terms of x in $y = 2t$:

$$y = 2x^2$$

Thus, the relation is the function $f(x) = 2x^2$, where $x \geq 0$.

Exercises for Alternate Example 1

In Exercises 1–6, describe the graph of each relation that is determined by the parametric functions

1. $x = 2\sqrt{t}$, $y = 3t$, $t \geq 0$ **2.** $x = \sqrt{t}$, $y = -t$, $t \geq 0$ **3.** $x = 2t$, $y = \sqrt{t}$, $t \geq 0$ **4.** $x = \sqrt{t}$, $y = 5t$, $t \geq 0$

5. $x = -\sqrt{3t}$, $y = 2t$, $t \geq 0$ **6.** $x = \dfrac{t}{2}$, $y = -\sqrt{t}$, $t \geq 0$

Alternate Example 3 Graphing an Ellipse

Graph the parametric curve $x = 2\cos t$, $y = 3\sin t$, $0 \leq t \leq 2\pi$. Find the Cartesian equation for a curve that presents the same parametric curve. What portion of the graph of the Cartesian equation is traced by the parametric curve? Indicate the direction in which the curve is traced and the initial and terminal points, if any.

SOLUTION

Figure 1.8 suggests that the curve is an ellipse. To find the Cartesian equation, first solve the given equations for $\sin t$ and $\cos t$. Divide both sides of the first equation by 2 and the second equation by 3.

$$\cos t = \frac{x}{2}$$

$$\sin t = \frac{y}{3}$$

Square both sides of each equation.

$$\cos^2 t = \left(\frac{x}{2}\right)^2$$

$$\sin^2 t = \left(\frac{y}{3}\right)^2$$

Add the corresponding sides.

$$\cos^2 t + \sin^2 t = \left(\frac{x}{2}\right)^2 + \left(\frac{y}{3}\right)^2$$

Use the identity $\sin^2 t + \cos^2 t = 1$ in this equation.

$$\left(\frac{x}{2}\right)^2 + \left(\frac{y}{3}\right)^2 = 1$$

So, the parameterized curve lies along an ellipse with major axis endpoints $(0, \pm 3)$ and minor axis endpoints $(\pm 2, 0)$. As t increases from 0 to 2π, the point $(x, y) = (2\cos t, 3\sin t)$ starts at $(2, 0)$ and traces the entire ellipse once counterclockwise. Thus, $(2, 0)$ is both the initial point and the terminal point.

$x = 2\cos t$, $y = 3\sin t$

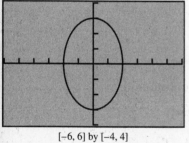

[−6, 6] by [−4, 4]

Figure 1.8 Graph of the parametric equation $x = 2\cos t$, $y = 3\sin t$ for $0 \leq t \leq 2\pi$.

Exercises for Alternate Example 3

In Exercises 7–12, graph each parametric curve. Find the Cartesian equation for each curve. What portion of the graph of the Cartesian equation is traced by the parametric curve?

7. $x = 6\cos t$, $y = 2\sin t$, $0 \leq t \leq 2\pi$ **8.** $x = 3\cos t$, $y = 4\sin t$, $0 \leq t \leq 2\pi$ **9.** $x = -5\sin t$, $y = \cos t$, $0 \leq t \leq 2\pi$

10. $x = 5\cos t$, $y = -2\sin t$, $0 \leq t \leq 2\pi$ **11.** $x = 3\cos t$, $y = -\sin t$, $0 \leq t \leq 2\pi$ **12.** $x = 2\sin t$, $y = 3\cos t$, $0 \leq t \leq 2\pi$

Alternate Example 4   Graphing a Line Segment

Draw and identify the graph of the parametric curve determined by

$$x = -2t, y = 3t + 1, 0 \le t \le 1.$$

SOLUTION

Figure (1.9) indicates that the graph of the function is a line segment with the endpoints (0, 1) and (–2, 4).

Confirm Algebraically Replacing the initial point of the graph, $t = 0$, in the given equations gives $x = 0$ and $y = 1$ as the coordinates of one endpoint. Replacing the terminal point $t = 1$ in the equations gives $x = -2$ and $y = 4$ as the coordinates of the other endpoint. Thus, the graph of the function is limited to the points (0, 1) and (–2, 4).

Now, divide both sides of $x = -2t$ by –2 to find t in terms of x.

$x = -2t, y = 3t + 1$

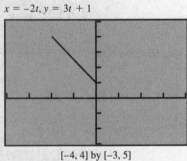

[–4, 4] by [–3, 5]

Figure 1.9 The graph of the line segment $x = -2t, y = 3t + 1, 0 \le t \le 1$ with trace on the initial point (0, 1).

$$t = -\frac{x}{2}$$

Substitute $-\dfrac{x}{2}$ for t in $y = 3t + 1$.

$$y = 3\left(-\frac{x}{2}\right) + 1$$

$$= -\frac{3}{2}x + 1$$

Therefore, the parametric curve traces the segment of the line $y = -\dfrac{3}{2}x + 1$ from the point (0, 1) to (–2, 4).

Exercises for Alternate Example 4

In Exercises 13–18, draw and identify the graph of the parametric curve determined by each pair of functions.

13. $x = 3t, y = 5t + 1, 0 \le t \le 1$ **14.** $x = 4t, y = 3t - 3, 0 \le t \le 1$ **15.** $x = 6t, y = 3t - 1, 0 \le t \le 1$

16. $x = 2t, y = -t + 1, 0 \le t \le 1$ **17.** $x = 4t + 1, y = t - 3, 0 \le t \le 1$ **18.** $x = 8t - 5, y = 4t + 4, 0 \le t \le 1$

Alternate Example 5   Parametrizing a Line Segment

Find a parametrization for the line segment with endpoints (2, –3) and (1, 4).

SOLUTION

Using (2, –3), we develop the parametric equations

$$x = 2 + at, y = -3 + bt.$$

If we solve these equations for t, and then equate the equivalents of t, we obtain an equation in terms of x and y, as shown below:

From the first equation, $x = 2 + at$,

$$x - 2 = at$$

$$t = \frac{x - 2}{a}$$

From the second equation, $y = -3 + bt$,

$$y + 3 = bt$$

$$t = \frac{y + 3}{b}$$

Equate the equivalents of t.

$$\frac{x-2}{a} = \frac{y+3}{b}$$

This line goes through the point $(2, -3)$ when $t = 0$ and goes through the point $(1, 4)$, when $t = 1$. We use the point $(1, 4)$ to determine a and b.

When $t = 1, x = 1$. So

$$1 = \frac{1-2}{a} \Rightarrow a = -1.$$

When $t = 1, y = 4$. So

$$1 = \frac{4+3}{b} \Rightarrow b = 7.$$

Therefore, with $a = -1$ and $b = 7$, we find that $x = 2 - t, y = -3 + 7t$ represents the parameterized equation of of the line $y = 7x + 11$ that is limited to the endpoints $(2, -3)$ and $(1, 4)$.

Exercises for Alternate Example 5

In Exercises 19–25, find a parametrization for each line segment with the given endpoints.

19. $(3, 7)$ and $(6, -2)$ **20.** $(2, 5)$ and $(-3, 6)$ **21.** $(2, 1)$ and $(1, 3)$ **22.** $(3, 1)$ and $(4, 5)$

23. $(3, -1)$ and $(-3, 2)$ **24.** $(2, -5)$ and $(5, 6)$ **25.** $(2, 6)$ and $(3, 2)$ ■

1.5 Functions and Logarithms

Alternate Example 2   Finding the Inverse Function

Show that the function $f(x) = 3x - 6$ is one-to-one and find its inverse function.

SOLUTION

The graph of given $f(x)$ is a line and its slope is 3. Therefore it is not horizontal, and every horizontal line intersects f exactly at one point. Therefore, f is a one-to-one function and has an inverse.

Step 1: Solve $y = 3x - 6$ for x:

$$y = 3x - 6$$
$$y + 6 = 3x$$
$$x = \frac{1}{3}y + 2$$

Step 2: Interchange x and y:

$$y = \frac{1}{3}x + 2$$

The inverse of the function $f(x) = 3x - 6$ is the function $f^{-1}(x) = \frac{1}{3}x + 2$. We can verify that both composites of f and f^{-1} are the identity function. To do so, find $f^{-1}(f(x))$ and $f(f^{-1}(x))$ as follows:

$$f^{-1}(f(x)) = \frac{1}{3}(3x - 6) + 2$$
$$= x - 2 + 2$$
$$= x$$

$$f(f^{-1}(x)) = 3\left(\frac{1}{3}x + 2\right) - 6$$
$$= x + 6 - 6$$
$$= x$$

Exercises for Alternate Example 2

In Exercises 1–7, show that each function $f(x)$ is one-to-one and find its inverse function.

1. $f(x) = -x - 11$ **2.** $f(x) = 3x - 15$ **3.** $f(x) = -11x + 6$ **4.** $f(x) = x^3 + 1$ **5.** $f(x) = 3x^2 - 15,\ x \geq 0$

6. $f(x) = x^2 - 6x + 9,\ x \geq 3$ **7.** $f(x) = \dfrac{1}{x^4},\ x > 0$

Alternate Example 4 **Using the Inverse Properties**

Solve for x: **(a)** $\ln x = 6t - 4$ **(b)** $e^{3x} = 100$

SOLUTION

(a) $\ln x = 6t - 4$ Given equation

$e^{\ln x} = e^{6t-4}$ Use the sides of the equation as exponents for two equal bases, e.

$x = e^{6t-4}$ We know that for any x, $e^{\ln x} = x$.

(b) $e^{3x} = 100$ Given equation

$\ln e^{3x} = \ln 100$ Take the natural logarithm of each side.

$3x \ln e = \ln 100$ Rule of exponents for logarithms.

$3x = \ln 100$ We know that $\ln e = 1$.

$x = \dfrac{1}{3} \ln 100$ Divide both sides by 3.

$x \approx 1.54$ Use calculator.

Exercises for Alternate Example 4

In Exercises 8–13, solve for x.

8. **(a)** $\ln x = t - 11$ **(b)** $e^{-3x} = 15$ **9.** **(a)** $\ln x = 11t + 12$ **(b)** $e^x = 14$ **10.** **(a)** $\ln x = t + 1$ **(b)** $e^{-2x} = 34$

11. **(a)** $\ln x = -11t - 12$ **(b)** $e^{5x} = 12$ **12.** **(a)** $\ln x = 3t - 6$ **(b)** $e^x = 18$ **13.** **(a)** $\ln x = 2t + 14$ **(b)** $e^{4x} = 22$

Alternate Example 5 **Graphing a Base a Logarithmic Function**

Graph $f(x) = \log_4 x$.

SOLUTION

We use the change of base formula to express $f(x)$ in terms of $\ln$.

$$f(x) = \log_4 x$$
$$= \frac{\ln x}{\ln 4}$$

Figure 1.10 represents the graph of $f(x)$.

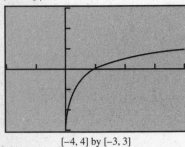

$y = \log_4 x$

$[-4, 4]$ by $[-3, 3]$

Figure 1.10 The graph of

$f(x) = \log_4 x$ using $f(x) = \dfrac{\ln x}{\ln 4}$.

Exercises for Alternate Example 5

In Exercises 14–21, graph each function.

14. $f(x) = \log_8 x$ **15.** $f(x) = 2\log_3 x$ **16.** $f(x) = \log_5 2x$ **17.** $f(x) = \log_6 x$ **18.** $f(x) = 2\log_7 x$

19. $f(x) = -4\log_4 x$ **20.** $f(x) = \log_5 2x$ **21.** $f(x) = \log_8 4x$ ■

Alternate Example 6 **Finding Time**

Sulmaz invests \$1800 in an account that earns 6.75% interest compounded annually. How long will it take the account to reach \$4320?

SOLUTION

If P dollars is deposited in an account with an annual interest rate of r compounded annually, then A, the total balance of the account (including principal and interest) after t years, is determined by $A = P(1 + r)^t$.

Model We desire the total amount in this account after t years to be \$4320. This amount is the result of $1800(1 + 0.0675)^t$. Equating these amounts yields

$$1800(1.0675)^t = 4320$$

Solve algebraically

$(1.0675)^t = 2.4$	Divide both sides by 1800.
$\ln(1.0675)^t = \ln 2.4$	Take logarithms of both sides.
$t(\ln 1.0675) = \ln 2.4$	Apply the exponent rules of logarithms to the left side.
$t = \dfrac{\ln 2.4}{\ln 1.0675}$	Divide both sides by ln 1.0675.
$t = 13.4$ years.	

That is, after about 13.4 years, or about 13 years and 5 months, the total amount in the account will be \$4320.

Exercises for Alternate Example 6

In Exercises 22–27, for each amount of investment compounded annually, calculate the time needed to reach the desired account balance including the principal and interest.

22. investment = \$2200, rate = 6.6%, desired account balance = \$3200

23. investment = \$3600, rate = 4.2%, desired account balance = \$3900

24. investment = \$4600, rate = 7.6%, desired account balance = \$5800

25. investment = \$2800, rate = 4.9%, desired account balance = \$3500

26. investment = \$3800, rate = 5.8%, desired account balance = \$6300

27. investment = \$4200, rate = 4.8%, desired account balance = \$6200 ■

1.6 Trigonometric Functions

Alternate Example 3 **Finding Trigonometric Values**

Find the trigonometric values of θ if $\cos\theta = -\dfrac{3}{5}$ and $\cot\theta > 0$.

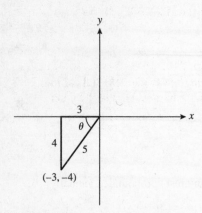

Figure 1.11 The angle θ in standard position

SOLUTION

Since $\cos\theta < 0$ and $\cot\theta > 0$, the angle θ is in the third quadrant, as shown in Figure 1.11. From this figure, using the definitions of trigonometric functions, we can conclude that $\sin\theta = -\dfrac{4}{5}$, $\tan\theta = \dfrac{4}{3}$, $\cot\theta = \dfrac{3}{4}$, $\csc\theta = -\dfrac{5}{4}$, and $\sec\theta = -\dfrac{5}{3}$.

Exercises for Alternate Example 3

In Exercises 1–6, find the trigonometric values of θ.

1. if $\cos\theta = -\dfrac{1}{5}$ and $\tan\theta > 0$

2. if $\sin\theta = -\dfrac{2}{7}$ and $\cos\theta < 0$

3. if $\cos\theta = \dfrac{1}{5}$ and $\cot\theta > 0$

4. if $\sin\theta = -\dfrac{5}{7}$ and $\cot\theta > 0$

5. if $\cos\theta = -\dfrac{3}{4}$ and $\cot\theta > 0$

6. if $\sin\theta = \dfrac{5}{13}$ and $\cos\theta > 0$

Alternate Example 4 Graphing a Trigonometric Function

Determine the **(a)** period, **(b)** domain, **(c)** range, and **(d)** draw the graph of the function $y = 2\sin(2x - \pi) - 2$.

SOLUTION

$y = 2\sin(2x - \pi) - 2$, $y = \sin x$

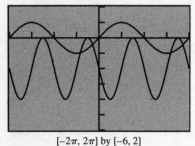

$[-2\pi, 2\pi]$ by $[-6, 2]$

Figure 1.12 The graph of $y = \sin x$ (thick curve) and the graph of $y = 2\sin(2x - \pi) - 2$ (thin curve).

The general form for the sine is $f(x) = A\sin\left[\dfrac{2\pi}{B}(x - C)\right] + D$, so we can rewrite the function as:

$$y = 2\sin\left[2\left(x - \dfrac{\pi}{2}\right)\right] - 2.$$

(a) The period can be determined by solving $\dfrac{2\pi}{B} = 2$ for B. This gives us $B = \pi$. Thus, the period is π.

(b) The domain is $(-\infty, \infty)$.

(c) The graph is a basic sine curve with the amplitude 2 that has been shifted down 2 units. Thus, the range is $[-4, 0]$.

(d) The graph has been shifted to the right $\pi/2$ units. As you can see in Figure 1.12, its graph is shown along the graph of $y = \sin x$. Notice that four periods of $y = 2\sin(2x - \pi) - 2$ are displayed.

Exercises for Alternate Example 4

In Exercises 7–12, determine the **(a)** period, **(b)** domain, **(c)** range, and **(d)** draw the graph of each function.

7. $y = 4\cos(5x - \pi) - 4$

8. $y = 2\sin(6x - \pi) - 1$

9. $y = -2\sin(4x - \pi) + 6$

10. $y = -\cos(3x + \pi) + 2$

11. $y = 5\sin(2x - \pi) - 6$

12. $y = 3\cos\left(\dfrac{x}{2} + \dfrac{\pi}{4}\right) + 3$

Alternate Example 7 **Finding Angles in Degrees and Radians**

Find the measures of $\sin^{-1}(0.78)$ in degrees and radians.

SOLUTION

Set the calculator in degree mode and enter $\sin^{-1}(0.78)$. The calculator then displays 51.26, which means 51.26 degrees. Now, set the calculator in radian mode and enter $\sin^{-1}(0.78)$. The calculator displays 0.89. You can check that $51.26 \cdot \dfrac{\pi}{180} \approx 0.89$

Exercises for Alternate Example 7

In Exercises 13–20, find the measures of each angle in degrees and radians.

13. $\cos^{-1}(-0.75)$ **14.** $\tan^{-1}(3)$ **15.** $\sin^{-1}(-0.65)$ **16.** $\sin^{-1}(0.05)$ **17.** $\cos^{-1}(0.85)$

18. $\tan^{-1}(-12)$ **19.** $\sin^{-1}(-0.88)$ **20.** $\tan^{-1}(-2.25)$

Alternate Example 8 **Using Inverse Trigonometric Functions**

Solve for x.

(a) $\sin x = 0.82$ in $0 \le x \le 2\pi$

(b) $\tan x = -3$ in $-\infty < x < \infty$

SOLUTION

(a) Notice that $x = \sin^{-1}(0.82) \approx 0.96$ is in the second quadrant , so 0.96 is one solution to this equation. Since $\sin(\pi - x) = \sin x$, then $\pi - 0.96 \approx 2.18$ is another solution to x, which is in the first quadrant. Thus, two solutions within the given interval are

$$x = \sin^{-1}(0.82) = 0.96 \text{ radian and } \pi - \sin^{-1}(0.82) \approx 2.18$$

(b) The angle $x = \tan^{-1}(-3) \approx -1.25$ radians is in the fourth quadrant and is

the only solution to this equation within the interval $-\dfrac{\pi}{2} < x < \dfrac{\pi}{2}$, where $\tan x$ is one-to-

one. Since $\tan x$ is periodic with π, the solutions to this equation are of the form $\tan^{-1}(-3) + k\pi \approx -1.25 + k\pi$, where k is any integer.

Exercises for Alternate Example 8

In Exercises 21–27, solve each equation for x.

21. (a) $\sin x = 0.12$ in $0 \le x \le 2\pi$ **22. (a)** $\cos x = 0.43$ in $0 \le x \le 2\pi$

(b) $\cot x = 7$ in $-\infty < x < \infty$ **(b)** $\tan x = 5$ in $-\infty < x < \infty$

23. (a) $\sin x = 0.55$ in $0 \le x \le 2\pi$ **24. (a)** $\sin x = 0.56$ in $0 \le x \le 2\pi$

(b) $\cot x = -8$ in $-\infty < x < \infty$ **(b)** $\tan x = 6$ in $-\infty < x < \infty$

25. (a) $\sin x = 0.27$ in $0 \le x \le 2\pi$ **26. (a)** $\cos x = 0.84$ in $0 \le x \le 2\pi$

(b) $\cot x = 3$ in $-\infty < x < \infty$ **(b)** $\cot x = 12$ in $-\infty < x < \infty$

27. (a) $\cos x = 0.56$ in $0 \le x \le 2\pi$

(b) $\tan x = 4$ in $-\infty < x < \infty$

Chapter 2

Limits and Continuity

2.1 Rates of Change and Limits

Alternate Example 2 **Finding an Instantaneous Speed**

A rock breaks loose from the top of a tall cliff. What is the speed of its fall at the instant $t = 4$?

SOLUTION

Solve Numerically Experiments show that a dense solid object dropped from rest to fall freely near the surface of the earth will fall

$$y = 16t^2$$

feet for the first t seconds. The average speed of the rock over any given time interval is the distance traveled, Δy, divided by the length of the interval Δt.

To find instantaneous speed, we can calculate the average speed of the rock over the interval from time $t = 4$ to any slightly later time $t = 4 + h$, where $\Delta t = h$ as

$$\frac{\Delta y}{\Delta t} = \frac{16(4+h)^2 - 16(4)^2}{h} \qquad (1)$$

We cannot use this formula to calculate the speed at the exact instant $t = 4$ because that would require taking $h = 0$, and $\frac{0}{0}$ is undefined. However, we can get a good idea of what is happening at $t = 4$ by evaluating the formula at values of h close to 0. When we do, we see a clear pattern (Table 2.1).

As h approaches 0, the average speed approaches the limiting value 128 ft/sec.

Confirm Algebraically If we expand the numerator of equation (1) and simplify, we find that

$$\frac{\Delta y}{\Delta t} = \frac{16(4+h)^2 - 16(4)^2}{h}$$

$$= \frac{16(16 + 8h + h^2) - 256}{h} \qquad \text{Expand the numerator.}$$

$$= \frac{256 + 128h + 16h^2 - 256}{h} \qquad \text{Distribute.}$$

$$= \frac{128h + 16h^2}{h} \qquad \text{Simplify the numerator.}$$

$$= \frac{h(128 + 16h)}{h} \qquad \text{Factor the numerator.}$$

$$= 128 + 16h$$

Table 2.1 Average Speeds Over Short Time Intervals Starting at $t = 4$

$$\frac{\Delta y}{\Delta t} = \frac{16(4+h)^2 - 16(4)^2}{h}$$

Length of Time Interval, h(sec)	Average Speed for Interval $\Delta y / \Delta t$ (ft/sec)
1	144
0.1	129.6
0.01	128.16
0.001	128.016
0.0001	128.0016
0.00001	128.00016

For values of h different from 0, the expressions on the right and left are equivalent and the average speed is $128 + 16h$ ft/sec. We can now see why the average speed is $128 + 16(0) = 128$ ft/sec as h approaches 0.

Exercises for Alternate Example 2

A rock breaks loose from the top of a tall cliff. In Exercises 1–8, what is the speed of its fall at each given instant?

1. $t = 1$ **2.** $t = 3$ **3.** $t = 5$ **4.** $t = 6$ **5.** $t = 7$ **6.** $t = 8$ **7.** $t = 9$ **8.** $t = 10$ ■

Alternate Example 5   Using the Product Rule

Determine $\displaystyle\lim_{x \to 0} \frac{3\tan x}{x}$.

SOLUTION

Solve Graphically The graph of $f(x) = \dfrac{3\tan x}{x}$ in Figure 2.1 suggests that the limit exists and is about 3.

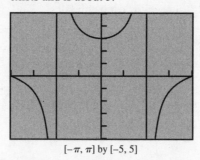

$[-\pi, \pi]$ by $[-5, 5]$

Figure 2.1 The graph of $f(x) = \dfrac{3\tan x}{x}$ suggests that $f(x) \to 3$ as $x \to 0$.

Confirm Analytically In Exercise 75 in Section 2.1, we learn that $\displaystyle\lim_{x \to 0} \frac{\sin x}{x} = 1$.

In order to apply this conclusion to the given problem, rewrite the fraction as follows:

$$\lim_{x \to 0} \frac{3\tan x}{x} = \lim_{x \to 0} 3\left(\frac{\sin x}{x}\right)\left(\frac{1}{\cos x}\right) \qquad \tan x = \frac{\sin x}{\cos x}$$

$$= 3\lim_{x \to 0}\left(\frac{\sin x}{x}\right) \cdot \lim_{x \to 0}\left(\frac{1}{\cos x}\right) \qquad \text{Constant Multiple Rule and Product Rule}$$

$$= 3(1)\left(\frac{1}{\cos 0}\right)$$

$$= 3(1)(1)$$

$$= 3$$

Exercises for Alternate Example 5

In Exercises 9–16, determine each limit.

9. $\displaystyle\lim_{x \to 0} \frac{-2\tan x}{x}$ **10.** $\displaystyle\lim_{x \to 0} \frac{\tan x}{4x}$ **11.** $\displaystyle\lim_{x \to 0} 2\sin x \cos x$ **12.** $\displaystyle\lim_{x \to 0} \frac{3\sin 4x}{x}$ **13.** $\displaystyle\lim_{x \to 0} \frac{\sin 7x}{4x}$

14. $\displaystyle\lim_{x \to 0} \frac{x}{\sin x}$ **15.** $\displaystyle\lim_{x \to 0} x \cot 4x$ **16.** $\displaystyle\lim_{x \to 0} \frac{a\tan x}{bx}$

■

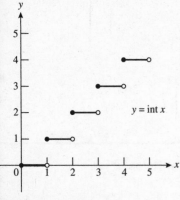

Figure 2.2 At each integer, the greatest integer function $y = $ int x has different right-hand and left-hand limits.

Alternate Example 7 **Function Values Approach Two Numbers**

Find $\lim\limits_{x \to 4^+}$ int x and $\lim\limits_{x \to 4^-}$ int x .

SOLUTION

The function $f(x) = $ int $x = [x]$ for any x associates an integer that is equal to x or less than x. As we can see in Figure 2.2, the greatest integer function $f(x) = $ int x has different right-hand and left-hand limits at each integer. As you see in the figure, when x approaches 4 from the right, $f(x)$ approaches 4, and when x approaches 4 from the left, $f(x)$ approaches 3. That is, $\lim\limits_{x \to 4^+}$ int $x = 4$ and $\lim\limits_{x \to 4^-}$ int $x = 3$.

Exercises for Alternate Example 7

In Exercises 17–23, find left and right limits for each function.

17. $\lim\limits_{x \to 11^+}$ int x and $\lim\limits_{x \to 11^-}$ int x

18. $\lim\limits_{x \to 7^+}$ int x and $\lim\limits_{x \to 7^-}$ int x

19. $\lim\limits_{x \to 9^+}$ int x and $\lim\limits_{x \to 9^-}$ int x

20. $\lim\limits_{x \to 21^+}$ int x and $\lim\limits_{x \to 21^-}$ int x

21. $\lim\limits_{x \to (-5)^+}$ int x and $\lim\limits_{x \to (-5)^-}$ int x

22. $\lim\limits_{x \to (-21)^+}$ int x and $\lim\limits_{x \to (-21)^-}$ int x

23. $\lim\limits_{x \to 14^+}$ int x and $\lim\limits_{x \to 14^-}$ int x

Alternate Example 9 **Using the Sandwich Theorem**

Show that $\lim\limits_{x \to 0}\left[x^4 \sin\left(\dfrac{1}{x}\right) \right] = 0.$

SOLUTION

We know that the values of the sine function lie between -1 and 1, inclusively. Thus, it follows that

$$\left| x^4 \sin\left(\frac{1}{x}\right) \right| = \left| x^4 \right| \cdot \left| \sin\frac{1}{x} \right|$$

$$\leq \left| x^4 \right| \cdot 1$$

$$= x^4$$

and

$$-x^4 \leq x^4 \sin\frac{1}{x} \leq x^4$$

Because $\lim\limits_{x \to 0}\left(-x^4\right) = \lim\limits_{x \to 0}\left(x^4\right) = 0$, the Sandwich Theorem yields

$$\lim\limits_{x \to 0}\left[x^4 \sin\left(\frac{1}{x}\right) \right] = 0.$$

The graphs in Figure 2.3 support this result.

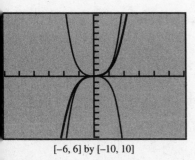

[–6, 6] by [–10, 10]

Figure 2.3 The graphs of $y_1 = -x^4$, $y_2 = x^4$, and $y_3 = \sin 1/x$. Notice that $y_3 \leq y_2 \leq y_1$.

Exercises for Alternate Example 9

In Exercises 24–29, using the Sandwich Theorem, find each limit.

24. $\lim\limits_{x\to 0}\left[x^6\sin\left(\dfrac{1}{x}\right)\right]$ **25.** $\lim\limits_{x\to 0}\dfrac{\sin 3x}{x}$ **26.** $\lim\limits_{x\to 0}\left[x^2\cos\left(\dfrac{1}{x}\right)\right]$ **27.** $\lim\limits_{x\to 0}\dfrac{1-\cos x}{x}$

28. $\lim\limits_{x\to 0}\dfrac{\sin 11x}{11x}$ **29.** $\lim\limits_{x\to 0}\dfrac{\sin 7x}{x}$

2.2 Limits Involving Infinity

Alternate Example 3   **Using Properties of Limits as** $x\to\pm\infty$

Find $\lim\limits_{x\to\infty}\dfrac{8x-\sin 3x}{x}$.

SOLUTION

Notice that

$$\frac{8x-\sin 3x}{x}=\frac{8x}{x}-\frac{\sin 3x}{x}$$

Note that $\dfrac{\sin 3x}{x}$ can be rewritten as

$$=8-3\left(\frac{\sin 3x}{3x}\right)$$

$3\left(\dfrac{\sin 3x}{x}\right)$ in order to arrive at the

$\dfrac{\sin u}{u}$ form.

Thus,

$$\lim_{x\to\infty}\frac{8x-\sin 3x}{x}=\lim_{x\to\infty}8-\lim_{x\to\infty}3\left(\frac{\sin 3x}{3x}\right)\quad\text{Sum Rule}$$

$$=8-0\qquad\qquad\text{Known values}$$

$$=8$$

Exercises for Alternate Example 3

In Exercises 1–6, find each limit.

1. $\lim\limits_{x\to\infty}\dfrac{4x-\sin 4x}{4x}$ **2.** $\lim\limits_{x\to\infty}\dfrac{3+\sin x}{x}$ **3.** $\lim\limits_{x\to\infty}\dfrac{3x+\sin x^2}{x^2}$ **4.** $\lim\limits_{x\to\infty}\dfrac{-4x+5\sin 3x}{x}$

5. $\lim\limits_{x\to\infty}\dfrac{x-\sin 3x}{6x}$ **6.** $\lim\limits_{x\to\infty}\dfrac{9-\sin x}{2x}$

Alternate Example 5   **Finding Vertical Asymptotes**

Determine vertical asymptotes of $f(x)=\cot x$.

SOLUTION

The graph of the function $f(x)=\cot x=\dfrac{\cos x}{\sin x}$ has infinitely many vertical asymptotes, one at each point where the $\sin x$ is zero. If a is any multiple of π, then

$$\lim_{x\to a^+}\cot x=\infty\ \text{ and }\ \lim_{x\to a^-}\cot x=-\infty\ \text{ as suggested by Figure 2.4.}$$

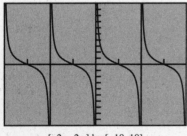

$[-2\pi,\,2\pi]$ by $[-10,\,10]$

Figure 2.4 The graph of $f(x)=\cot x$ has vertical asymptotes at $\ldots,\ -2\pi,\ -\pi, 0,\ \pi,\ 2\pi,\ldots$

Exercises for Alternate Example 5

n Exercises 7–14, determine the vertical asymptotes of each function.

7. $f(x) = \dfrac{\sin x}{1 - \cos x}$ **8.** $f(x) = \dfrac{x^2 + 11}{x - 2}$ **9.** $f(x) = \dfrac{3\sin x}{1 + \cos x}$ **10.** $f(x) = \dfrac{4 - \cos x}{1 - 2\sin x}$

11. $f(x) = \dfrac{x - 7}{4x^2 - 1}$ **12.** $f(x) = \dfrac{1}{\sin x - 1}$ **13.** $f(x) = \dfrac{\cos^2 x}{1 + 2x}$ **14.** $f(x) = \dfrac{3x - 11}{x^4 - 1}$

Alternate Example 6 **Modeling Functions for | x | Large**

Let $f(x) = 5x^4 - 4x^3 + 6x^2 - 3x + 2$ and $g(x) = 5x^4$. Show that while f and g are quite different for numerically small values of x, they are virtually identical for $|x|$ large.

SOLUTION

Solve Graphically The graphs of f and g (Figure 2.5a), quite different near the origin, are virtually identical on a larger scale. (Figure 2.5b).

Confirm Analytically We can test the claim that g models f for numerically large values of x by examining the ratio of the two functions as $x \to \pm\infty$. We find that

$$\lim_{x \to \pm\infty} \frac{f(x)}{g(x)} = \lim_{x \to \pm\infty} \frac{5x^4 - 4x^3 + 6x^2 - 3x + 2}{5x^4}$$

$$= \lim_{x \to \pm\infty} \left(\frac{5x^4}{5x^4} - \frac{4x^3}{5x^4} + \frac{6x^2}{5x^4} - \frac{3x}{5x^4} + \frac{2}{5x^4} \right)$$

$$= \lim_{x \to \pm\infty} \left(1 - \frac{4}{5x} + \frac{6}{5x^2} - \frac{3}{5x^3} + \frac{2}{5x^4} \right)$$

$$= 1$$

convincing evidence that f and g behave alike for $|x|$ large.

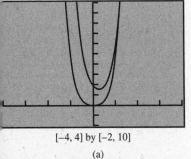

[–4, 4] by [–2, 10]

(a)

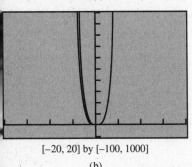

[–20, 20] by [–100, 1000]

(b)

Figure 2.5 The graphs of f and g, are (a) distinct for small $|x|$, and (b) nearly identical for $|x|$ large.

Exercises for Alternate Example 6

In Exercises 15–20, verify that functions $f(x)$ and $g(x)$ are identical for $|x|$ large.

15. $f(x) = 11x^7 - 6x^6 - 7x^3 + 11x^2 - 3x + 14$ and $g(x) = 11x^7$ **16.** $f(x) = -3x^6 - x^3 + 8x^2 - x + 4$ and $g(x) = -3x^6$

17. $f(x) = 2x^5 - 3x^4 - x^3 + x^2 - 7x + 21$ and $g(x) = 2x^5$ **18.** $f(x) = \dfrac{x^2 - 3}{2x + 4}$ and $g(x) = \dfrac{x}{2}$

19. $f(x) = \dfrac{x^3 - x^2 + 10}{3x^2 - 4x}$ and $g(x) = \dfrac{x}{3}$ **20.** $f(x) = \dfrac{x + 2}{x^2 + 6x + 4}$ and $g(x) = \dfrac{1}{x}$

Alternate Example 8 **Finding End Behavior Models**

Let $f(x) = 2x - e^{-x}$. Show that $g(x) = 2x$ is a right end behavior model for f while $h(x) = -e^{-x}$ is the left end behavior model for f.

SOLUTION

On the right,

$$\lim_{x \to \infty} \frac{f(x)}{g(x)} = \lim_{x \to \infty} \frac{2x - e^{-x}}{2x}$$

$$= \lim_{x \to \infty} \left(\frac{2x}{2x} - \frac{e^{-x}}{2x} \right)$$

$$= \lim_{x \to \infty} \left(1 - \frac{e^{-x}}{2x} \right)$$

$$= 1 \qquad\qquad \text{Because both } e^{-x} \text{ and } x \text{ approach 0 as } x \to \infty, \lim_{x \to \infty} \frac{e^{-x}}{x} = 0.$$

On the left,

$$\lim_{x \to -\infty} \frac{f(x)}{h(x)} = \lim_{x \to -\infty} \frac{2x - e^{-x}}{-e^{-x}}$$

$$= \lim_{x \to -\infty} \left(\frac{2x}{-e^{-x}} - \frac{e^{-x}}{-e^{-x}} \right)$$

$$= \lim_{x \to -\infty} \left(-2xe^{x} + 1 \right)$$

$$= \lim_{x \to -\infty} \left(-2xe^{x} \right) + 1$$

$$= 0 + 1 \qquad\qquad \text{It can be shown that } \lim_{x \to -\infty} \left(-2xe^{x} \right) = 0 \text{ using a}$$

$$= 1 \qquad\qquad\qquad \text{graphing calculator.}$$

The graph in Figure 2.6 supports these end behavior conclusions.

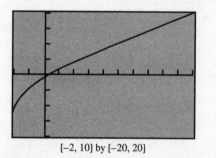

[−2, 10] by [−20, 20]

Figure 2.6 The graph of $f(x) = 2x - e^{-x}$ looks like the graph of $g(x) = 2x$ to the right of the y-axis, and like the graph of $h(x) = -e^{-x}$ to the left of the y-axis.

Exercises for Alternate Example 8

In Exercises 21–26, find a right end behavior model $g(x)$ and a left end behavior model $h(x)$ for the function $f(x)$.

21. $f(x) = -2x - e^{-x}$ **22.** $f(x) = -x + 2e^{-x}$ **23.** $f(x) = x^2 - 3e^x$ **24.** $f(x) = x^3 - \sin x$

25. $f(x) = -3x^2 + e^x$ **26.** $f(x) = ax + be^{-x}$

2.3 Continuity

Alternate Example 1 **Investigating Continuity**

Find the points at which the function f in Figure 2.7 is continuous, and the points at which f is discontinuous.

SOLUTION

From the graph it is clear that f is not continuous at every point of its domain because the graph has breaks. The function f is continuous at every point of its domain [0, 7] except at $x = 2$ and $x = 4.5$. At these points there are breaks in the graph. Note the relationship between the limit of f and the value of f at each point of the function's domain.

Points at which f is continuous:

At $x = 0$, $\lim_{x \to 0^+} f(x) = f(0)$.

At $x = 7$, $\lim_{x \to 7^-} f(x) = f(7)$.

At $0 < c < 7$, $c \neq 2, 4.5$, $\lim_{x \to c} f(x) = f(c)$.

Points at which f is discontinuous:

At $x = 2$, $\lim_{x \to 2} f(x)$ does not exist.

At $x = 4.5$, $\lim_{x \to 4.5} f(x) = 3$, but $f(4.5) = 5 \neq \lim_{x \to 4.5} f(x)$.

At $c < 0$ or $c > 7$, these points are not in the domain of f.

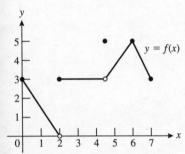

Figure 2.7 The function $f(x)$ is continuous on [0, 7] except at $x = 2$ and $x = 4.5$.

Exercises for Alternate Example 1

In Exercises 1–6, find the points at which the graph of the function f is continuous, and the points at which f is discontinuous.

1.
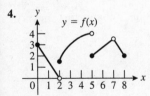

2.
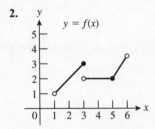

3.
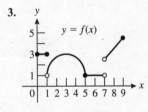

4.
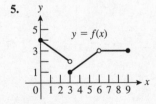

5.
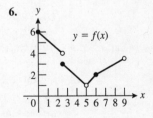

6.

Alternate Example 2   **Finding Points of Continuity and Discontinuity**

Find the points of continuity and discontinuity of the function $f(x) = \begin{cases} 2, & x \geq 0 \\ x+1, & x < 0 \end{cases}$

(Figure 2.8).

SOLUTION

For the function to be continuous at $x = c$, the limit as $x \to c$ must exist and must equal the value of the function at $x = c$. The given function is discontinuous at $x = 0$ because

$$\lim_{x \to 0^-} f(x) = 1 \text{ and } \lim_{x \to 0^+} f(x) = 2,$$

so the limit as $x \to 0$ does not exist.

The given function is continuous at every other real number. For example,

$$\lim_{x \to 1} f(x) = 2 \text{ and } \lim_{x \to 1} f(1) = 2,$$

so $\lim_{x \to 1} f(x) = f(1)$.

Similarly, $\lim_{x \to -2} f(x) = -1 f(-2)$.

In general, if $-\infty < c < 0$ and $0 < c < \infty$,

$$\lim_{x \to c} f(x) = f(c).$$

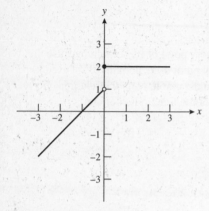

Figure 2.8 The function

$f(x) = \begin{cases} 2, & x \geq 0 \\ x+1, & x < 0 \end{cases}$ is continuous at

every real number $\neq 0$.

Exercises for Alternate Example 2

In Exercises 7–12, find the points of continuity and discontinuity of the function $f(x)$.

7. $f(x) = \dfrac{1}{(x+3)^2}$ **8.** $f(x) = \dfrac{x+1}{x^2-1}$ **9.** $f(x) = \dfrac{x}{|x|}$ **10.** $f(x) = \sec x$

11. $f(x) = \dfrac{x^2}{x}$ **12.** $f(x) = \sqrt{3x-2}$

Alternate Example 4   **Using Composite of Continuous Functions**

Show that $y = \left| \dfrac{x^2 \cos x}{x^2 + 5} \right|$ is continuous.

SOLUTION

The graph (Figure 2.9) of $y = \left| \dfrac{x^2 \cos x}{x^2 + 5} \right|$ suggests that the function is continuous at every value of x. By letting

$$g(x) = |x| \text{ and } f(x) = \frac{x^2 \cos x}{x^2 + 5},$$

we see that y is the composite $g \circ f$.

We know that the absolute value function g is continuous. The function f is continuous by the Properties of Continuous Functions. Their composite is continuous by the Theorem of Composite Continuous Functions.

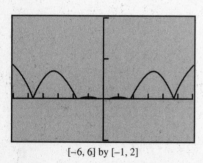

[−6, 6] by [−1, 2]

Figure 2.9 The graph suggests that

$y = \left| \dfrac{x^2 \cos x}{x^2 + 5} \right|$ is continuous.

Exercises for Alternate Example 4

In Exercises 13–18, show that the functions are continuous.

13. $y = \left| \dfrac{x^2 + 4x + 4}{x^2 + 4} \right|$

14. $y = \left| \dfrac{-x^2 \cos x}{x^4 + 2} \right|$

15. $y = \sqrt{x^2 + 2x + 1}$

16. $y = \cos\left(x^2 + 1\right)$

17. $y = \sqrt[3]{\cos\left(x^2 + 1\right)}$

18. $y = \left| \dfrac{-3x \cos x}{3x^2 + 1} \right|$

Alternate Example 5 **Using the Intermediate Value Theorem for Continuous Functions**

Is there any real number that is 5 less than its fifth power?

SOLUTION

We answer this question by applying the Intermediate Value Theorem in the following way. Any such number must satisfy $x = x^5 - 5$ or, equivalently, $x^5 - x - 5 = 0$. The function $f(x) = x^5 - x - 5$ is continuous at any real number and its zero exists. As the graph of $f(x)$ in Figure 2.10 suggests, there is a zero for f between $x = 1$ and $x = 2$. Thus, there is a number that is 5 less than its fifth power.

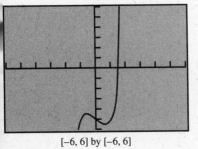

[–6, 6] by [–6, 6]

Figure 2.10 The graph of $f(x) = x^5 - x - 5$.

We can use the Intermediate Value Theorem to show this result analytically. For $f(x) = x^5 - x - 5$, $f(1) = -5$ and $f(2) = 25$. The Intermediate Value Theorem states that a continuous function on a closed interval $[a, b]$ takes on every value between $f(a)$ and $f(b)$. Since $-5 < 0 < 25$, there must be some number c between 1 and 2 for which $f(c) = 0$.

Exercises for Alternate Example 5

In Exercises 19–25, determine which real number exists.

19. A real number that is 6 less than its sixth power

20. A real number that is 4 less than its square

21. A real number that is 8 less than its eighth power

22. A real number that is 10 more than its tenth power

23. A real number that is 7 less than its seventh power

24. A real number that is 5 more than its cube

25. A real number that is 3 more than its fourth power

2.4 Rates of Change and Tangent Lines

Alternate Example 3 **Finding Slope and Tangent Line**

Find the slope of the parabola $y = x^2 + 1$ at the point $P(2, 5)$. Write an equation for the tangent to the parabola at this point.

SOLUTION

We begin with a secant line through $P(2, 5)$ and a nearby point $Q(2 + h, (2 + h)^2 + 1)$ on the curve (Figure 2.11).

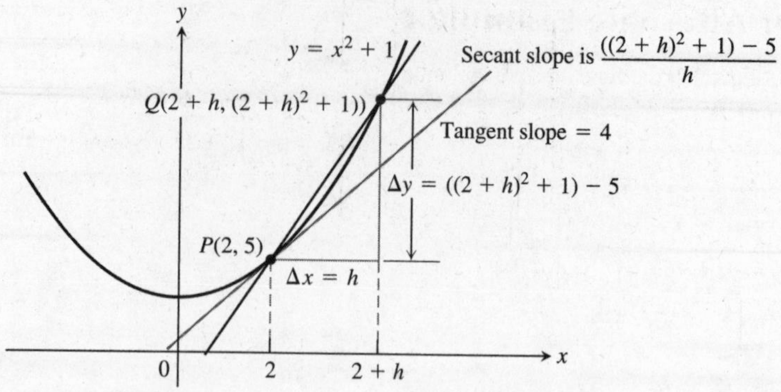

Figure 2.11 Finding the slope of the tangent to the parabola $y = x^2 + 1$ at $P(2, 5)$.

We then write an expression for the slope of the secant line and find the limiting value of this slope as Q approaches P along the curve.

$$\text{secant slope} = \frac{\Delta y}{\Delta x}$$

$$= \frac{\left[(2 + h)^2 + 1\right] - 5}{h}$$

$$= \frac{h^2 + 4h + 4 + 1 - 5}{h}$$

$$= \frac{h^2 + 4h}{h}$$

$$= h + 4$$

The limit of secant slope as Q approaches P along the curve is

$$\lim_{Q \to P}\left(\text{secant slope}\right) = \lim_{h \to 0}(h + 4) = 4.$$

Thus, the slope of the parabola at P is 4.

The tangent to the parabola at P is the line passing through $P(2, 5)$ with slope $m = 4$. Using the point-slope equation, the equation of the tangent line is

$$y - 5 = 4(x - 2)$$
$$y = 4x - 8 + 5$$
$$y = 4x - 3.$$

Exercises for Alternate Example 3

In Exercises 1–8, find the slope of the parabola y at the point P. Then, write an equation for the tangent to the parabola at this point.

1. $y = -x^2 + 1$, $P(-3, -8)$.   **2.** $y = 2x^2 - 1$, $P(2, 7)$.   **3.** $y = 3x^2 - 2$, $P(1, 1)$.   **4.** $y = -4x^2 + 5$, $P(-2, -11)$.

5. $y = x^2 + 5$, $P(-1, -6)$.   **6.** $y = -x^2 - 3$, $P(-2, -7)$.   **7.** $y = x^2 + 6$, $P(-1, 7)$.   **8.** $y = -x^2 + 4$, $P(-3, -5)$. ■

Alternate Example 4   Exploring Slope and Tangent

Let $f(x) = -\dfrac{3}{2x}$.

(a) Find the slope of the curve at $x = a$.

(b) Where does the slope equal $3/32$?

(c) What happens to the tangent to the curve at the point $(a, -3/2a)$ for different values of a?

SOLUTION

(a) The slope at $x = a$ is

$$\lim_{h \to 0} \frac{f(a + h) - f(a)}{h} = \lim_{h \to 0} \frac{-\dfrac{3}{2(a + h)} - \left[-\dfrac{3}{2a}\right]}{h}$$

$$= \lim_{h \to 0} \frac{-\dfrac{3}{2(a + h)} + \dfrac{3}{2a}}{h}$$

$$= \lim_{h \to 0} \frac{\dfrac{-3a + 3(a + h)}{2a(a + h)}}{h}$$

$$= \lim_{h \to 0} \frac{\dfrac{3h}{2a(a + h)}}{h}$$

$$= \lim_{h \to 0} \left(\frac{1}{h} \cdot \frac{3h}{2a(a + h)}\right)$$

$$= \lim_{h \to 0} \frac{3}{2a(a + h)}$$

$$= \frac{3}{2a^2}.$$

(b) The slope will be 3/32 if

$$\frac{3}{2a^2} = \frac{3}{32}$$

$$a^2 = 16 \qquad \text{Multiply each side by } 32a^2.$$

$$a = \pm 4$$

The curve has slope $\dfrac{3}{32}$ at two points $\left(-4, \dfrac{3}{8}\right)$ and $\left(4, -\dfrac{3}{8}\right)$ (Figure 2.11).

(c) The slope $3/(2a^2)$ is always positive for any value of a. As , the slope approaches $+\infty$ and tangent becomes increasingly steep. We see this again as $a \to 0^-$. As a moves away from the origin in either direction, the slope approaches 0 and the tangent becomes increasingly horizontal

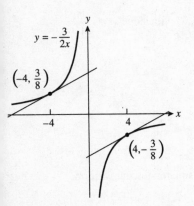

Figure 2.12 The two tangent lines to $f(x) = -\dfrac{3}{2x}$ having slope $\dfrac{3}{32}$.

Exercises for Alternate Example 4

In Exercises 9–14, **(a)** Find the slope of f at $x = a$. **(b)** Where is the slope equal to p? **(c)** What happens to the tangent to the curve at the point $(a, f(a))$?

9. $f(x) = \dfrac{6}{5x}$, $p = -\dfrac{6}{125}$

10. $f(x) = -\dfrac{1}{2x}$, $p = \dfrac{1}{98}$

11. $f(x) = 7 + x^2$, $p = 4$

12. $f(x) = x^3$, $p = 27$

13. $f(x) = x^2 + 2x + 1$, $p = 0$

14. $f(x) = \dfrac{3}{x^2}$, $p = -\dfrac{3}{4}$

Alternate Example 5 **Finding a Normal Line**

Write an equation for the normal to the curve $f(x) = x^2 - 3$ at $x = 2$.

SOLUTION

The slope of the tangent to the curve at $x = 2$ is

$$\lim_{h \to 0} \frac{f(2 + h) - f(2)}{h} = \lim_{h \to 0} \frac{\left((2 + h)^2 - 3\right) - 1}{h} \qquad f(2+h) = (2+h)^2 - 3$$

$$\text{and } f(2) = 2^2 - 3 = 1$$

$$= \lim_{h \to 0} \frac{h^2 + 4h + 4 - 4}{h} \qquad \text{Expand.}$$

$$= \lim_{h \to 0} \frac{h^2 + 4h}{h} \qquad \text{Simplify the numerator.}$$

$$= \lim_{h \to 0} \frac{h(h + 4)}{h} \qquad \text{Factor the numerator.}$$

$$= \lim_{h \to 0} (h + 4)$$

$$= 4$$

Thus, the slope of the normal is $-\dfrac{1}{4}$, the negative reciprocal of 4. The normal to the curve at $(2, f(2)) = (2, 1)$ is the line passing through $(2, 1)$ with slope $m = -\dfrac{1}{4}$.

$$y - 1 = -\frac{1}{4}(x - 2)$$

$$y = -\frac{1}{4}x + \frac{1}{2} + 1$$

$$y = -\frac{1}{4}x + \frac{3}{2}$$

You can support this result by drawing the graphs in a square viewing window.

Exercises for Alternate Example 5

In Exercises 15–22, write an equation for the normal to the curve $f(x)$ at the given x.

15. $f(x) = -x^2 + 5$ at $x = 1$.

16. $f(x) = 2x^2 - 1$ at $x = 2$.

17. $f(x) = \dfrac{1}{2x}$ at $x = -1$.

18. $f(x) = -x^3 + 3$ at $x = 2$.

19. $f(x) = \dfrac{3}{x^2}$ at $x = -1$.

20. $f(x) = x^2 + 2x + 1$ at $x = 0$.

21. $f(x) = \dfrac{6}{5x}$ at $x = -1$.

22. $f(x) = -4x^2 - 2$ at $x = 1$.

Alternate Example 6 **Investigating Free Fall**

A rock breaks loose from the top of a tall cliff. Find the speed of this falling rock at $t = 3$ sec.

SOLUTION

The position function for the rock is $f(t) = 16t^2$. The average speed of the rock over the interval between $t = 3$ and $t = 3 + h$ sec was

$$\frac{f(3 + h) - f(3)}{h} = \frac{16(3 + h)^2 - 16(3^2)}{h}$$

$$= \frac{16h^2 + 96h + 16(3^2) - 16(3^2)}{h}$$

$$= \frac{16h(h + 6)}{h}$$

$$= 16(h + 6)$$

The rock's speed at the instant $t = 3$ was

$$\lim_{h \to 0} 16(h + 6) = 96 \text{ ft/sec}$$

Exercises for Alternate Example 6

In Exercises 23–30, find the instantaneous speed of a falling rock at each given instant time t.

23. $t = 2$ sec   **24.** $t = 4$ sec   **25.** $t = 5$ sec   **26.** $t = 6$ sec   **27.** $t = 7$ sec   **28.** $t = 8$ sec

29. $t = 9$ sec   **30.** $t = 10$ sec

Chapter 3 — Derivatives

3.1 Derivative of a Function

Alternate Example 1 **Applying the Definition**

Differentiate (that is, find the derivative of) $f(x) = 2x^2$.

SOLUTION

Applying the definition, we have

$$f'(x) = \lim_{h \to 0} \frac{f(x+h) - f(x)}{h}$$

$$= \lim_{h \to 0} \frac{2(x+h)^2 - 2x^2}{h} \qquad \text{Apply the definition of the derivative to } f(x) = 2x^2.$$

$$= \lim_{h \to 0} \frac{\left(2x^2 + 4hx + 2h^2\right) - 2x^2}{h} \qquad \text{Expand } 2(x+h)^2.$$

$$= \lim_{h \to 0} \frac{2h(2x+h)}{h} \qquad \text{Like terms combined and } 2h \text{ is factored out.}$$

$$= \lim_{h \to 0} 2(h + 2x)$$

$$= 4x$$

Exercises for Alternate Example 1

In Exercises 1–8, apply the definition of derivative to find $f'(x)$.

1. $f(x) = 3x - 1$ **2.** $f(x) = x^2 - 6$ **3.** $f(x) = -4x^3 - 5x$ **4.** $f(x) = x^3 + 8$ **5.** $f(x) = 5x^2 - 4$

6. $f(x) = 2x + x^2$ **7.** $f(x) = 6x^3 - 11$ **8.** $f(x) = x^2 + 2x - 1$

Alternate Example 2 **Applying the Alternate Definition**

Differentiate $f(x) = \sqrt{x - 1}$ using the alternate definition.

SOLUTION

At the point $x = a$,

$$f'(a) = \lim_{x \to a} \frac{f(x) - f(a)}{x - a}$$

$$= \lim_{x \to a} \frac{\sqrt{x - 1} - \sqrt{a - 1}}{x - a} \qquad \text{Apply the definition of derivative to } f(x).$$

$$= \lim_{x \to a} \frac{\sqrt{x - 1} - \sqrt{a - 1}}{x - a} \cdot \frac{\sqrt{x - 1} + \sqrt{a - 1}}{\sqrt{x - 1} + \sqrt{a - 1}} \qquad \text{Rationalize the numerator.}$$

$$= \lim_{x \to a} \frac{x - 1 - a + 1}{\left(x - a\right)\left(\sqrt{x - 1} + \sqrt{a - 1}\right)} \qquad \text{Multiply the factors in the numerator.}$$

$$= \lim_{x \to a} \frac{x - a}{\left(x - a\right)\left(\sqrt{x - 1} + \sqrt{a - 1}\right)} \qquad \text{Combine like terms .}$$

$$= \lim_{x \to a} \frac{1}{\left(\sqrt{x - 1} + \sqrt{a - 1}\right)} \qquad \text{Divide by } (x - a).$$

$$= \frac{1}{2\sqrt{a - 1}} \qquad \text{Take the limit.}$$

Applying this formula to an arbitrary $x > 1$ in the domain of f identifies the derivative as the function $f'(x) = \dfrac{1}{2\sqrt{x - 1}}$ with the domain $(1, \infty)$.

Exercises for Alternate Example 2

In Exercise 9–16, use the alternate definition to find the derivative of the given function.

9. $f(x) = \dfrac{1}{2x}$ **10.** $f(x) = \sqrt{x^2 - 1}$ **11.** $f(x) = x^2 + 5x + 4$ **12.** $f(x) = x^3 - x$ **13.** $f(x) = 4 - x^2$

14. $f(x) = \dfrac{3}{x^2}$ **15.** $f(x) = -3\sqrt{2x - 1}$ **16.** $f(x) = 7 - 3x$

Alternate Example 4 **Graphing *f* from *f* ′**

Sketch the graph of a function f that has the following properties:

i. $f(2) = -1$

ii. the graph of f', the derivative of f, is shown in Figure 3.1.

iii. f is continuous for all x.

SOLUTION

To satisfy property (i), we begin with the point $(2, -1)$. To satisfy property (ii), we consider what the graph of the derivative tells us about slopes. To the left of $x = 2$, the graph has a constant slope of $-\dfrac{3}{2}$; therefore, we draw a line with slope $-\dfrac{3}{2}$ to the left of $x = 2$ that passes through the point $(2, -1)$.

To the right of $x = 2$, the graph has a constant slope of $\frac{1}{2}$. There are infinitely many such lines but only one, the one that meets the left side of the graph at $(2, -1)$, will satisfy the continuity requirement. The resulting graph is shown in Figure 3.2.

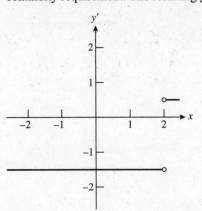

Figure 3.1 The graph of the derivative of f.

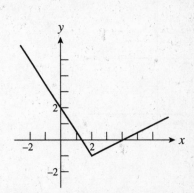

Figure 3.2 The graph of f constructed from the graph of f' and two other conditions.

Exercises for Alternate Example 4

In Exercises 17–22, sketch the graph of a function f that has the given properties.

17. i. $f(1) = -1$
 ii. the graph of f' is shown in Figure 3.3.
 iii. f is continuous for all x.

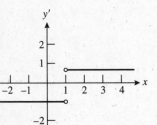

Figure 3.3

18. i. $f(2) = -2$
 ii. the graph of f' is shown in Figure 3.4.
 iii. f is continuous for all x.

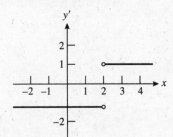

Figure 3.4

19. i. $f(2) = -2$
 ii. the graph of f' is shown in Figure 3.5.
 iii. f is continuous for all x.

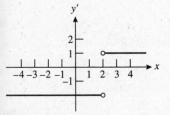

Figure 3.5

20. i. $f(-3) = -2$
 ii. the graph of f' is shown in Figure 3.6.
 iii. f is continuous for all x.

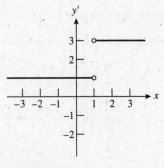

Figure 3.6

21. i. $f(-1) = 2$
  ii. the graph of f' is shown in Figure 3.7.
  iii. f is continuous for all x.

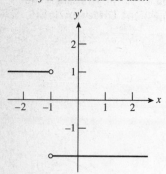

Figure 3.7

22. i. $f(2) = -1$
  ii. the graph of f' is shown in Figure 3.8.
  iii. f is continuous for all x.

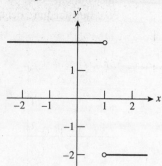

Figure 3.8

 Alternate Example 6 **One-Sided Derivatives Can Differ at a Point**

Show that the following function has left-hand and right-hand derivatives at $x = 0$, but no derivative there. (Figure 3.9).

$$y = \begin{cases} 2x^2 & x \le 0 \\ 3x & x > 0 \end{cases}$$

SOLUTION

We verify the existence of the left-hand derivative:

$$\lim_{h \to 0^-} \frac{2(0 + h)^2 - 2(0^2)}{h} = \lim_{h \to 0^-} \frac{2h^2}{h}$$

$$= 0$$

We verify the existence of the right-hand derivative:

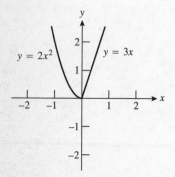

Figure 3.9 A function with different one-sided derivatives at $x = 0$.

$$\lim_{h \to 0^-} \frac{3(0 + h) - 3(0)}{h} = \lim_{h \to 0^-} \frac{3h}{h}$$

$$= 3$$

Since the left-hand derivative equals zero and the right-hand derivative equals 3, the derivatives are not equal at $x = 0$. The function does not have a derivative at $x = 0$.

Exercises for Alternate Example 6

In Exercises 23–28, show that each function has left-hand and right-hand derivatives at the given x, but no derivative there.

23. $y = \begin{cases} -x^2 & x \le 2 \\ x - 6 & x > 2 \end{cases}$; $x = 2$

24. $y = \begin{cases} x^2 - 1 & x \le -1 \\ x + 1 & x > -1 \end{cases}$; $x = -1$

25. $y = \begin{cases} 1 - x^2 & x \le 0 \\ 3x + 1 & x > 0 \end{cases}$; $x = 0$

26. $y = \begin{cases} x^2 & x \le 1 \\ 3x - 2 & x > 1 \end{cases}$; $x = 1$

27. $y = \begin{cases} 25x^2 & x \le 0 \\ x & x > 0 \end{cases}$; $x = 0$

28. $y = \begin{cases} 2 - x^2 & x \le -1 \\ -3x - 2 & x > -1 \end{cases}$; $x = -1$

3.2 Differentiability

Alternate Example 1   **Finding Where a Function Is Not Differentiable**

Find all points in the domain of $f(x) = |x + 6| + 1$, where f is not differentiable.

SOLUTION

The graph of this function is the same as that of $y = |x|$, translated 6 units to the left and 1 unit up. This puts the corner at the point $(-6, 1)$, so this function is not differentiable at $x = -6$.

At every other point, the graph is (locally) a straight line and f has derivative $+1$ or -1 (again just like $y = |x|$).

Exercises for Alternate Example 1

In Exercises 1–8, find all points in the domain of $f(x)$ where f is not differentiable.

1. $f(x) = |x - 3| + 4$

2. $f(x) = \begin{cases} \dfrac{x^2}{2} & x \geq 2 \\ x & x < 2 \end{cases}$

3. $f(x) = |x + 4| - 2$

4. $f(x) = |x - 2| - 6$

5. $f(x) = |x + 7| + 9$

6. $f(x) = 3x - |2x|$

7.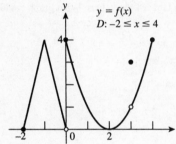

8.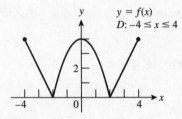

Alternate Example 2   **Computing a Numerical Derivative**

Compute NDER $(x^2, 3)$.

SOLUTION

Using $h = 0.001$ in the formula NDER $f(a) = \dfrac{f(a + 0.001) - f(a - 0.001)}{0.002}$,

$$\text{NDER } (x^2, 3) = \frac{(3 + 0.001)^2 - (3 - 0.001)^2}{0.002}$$

$$= 6$$

Exercises for Alternate Example 2

In Exercises 9–14, compute each numerical derivative.

9. NDER $(3x^3, 1)$

10. NDER $(-2x^2, 2)$

11. NDER $(3x^4 + x^3, -5)$

12. NDER $(x - x^3, 4)$

13. NDER $(-3x^4, -1)$

14. NDER $(x^{1/3}, 1)$

Alternate Example 4 **Graphing a Derivative Using NDER**

Let $f(x) = \ln(x + 1)$. Use NDER to graph $f'(x)$. Can you guess what function $f'(x)$ is by analyzing its graph?

SOLUTION

The graph is shown in Figure 3.10a. The shape of the graph suggests, and the table of values supports, the conjecture that this is a graph of $y = \dfrac{1}{x + 1}$. We will prove in Section 3.9 (using analytical methods) that this is indeed the case.

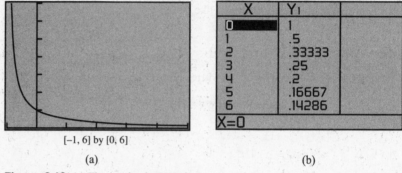

[−1, 6] by [0, 6]

(a)   (b)

Figure 3.10 (a) The graph of NDER ln $(x + 1)$ and (b) a table of the values. What graph could this be?

Exercises for Alternate Example 4

In Exercises 15–20, use NDER to graph $f'(x)$ Can you guess what function $f'(x)$ is by analyzing its graph?

15. $f(x) = \ln(x - 3)$ **16.** $f(x) = \sin x$ **17.** $f(x) = 3 + \ln x$ **18.** $f(x) = \dfrac{x^3}{3}$ **19.** $f(x) = |x|$

20. $f(x) = x^2 + 7x$

3.3 Rules of Differentiation

Alternate Example 1 **Differentiating a Polynomial**

Find $\dfrac{dp}{dt}$ if $p = t^4 - 5t^3 + t^2 - 12$.

SOLUTION

The Sum and Difference Rule states that $\dfrac{d}{dx}(u \pm v) = \dfrac{du}{dx} \pm \dfrac{dv}{dx}$ if u and v are differentiable functions of x.

Using this rule, we can differentiate the polynomial term-by-term, applying the rule for a derivative as a constant function, the power rule, and the constant multiple rule as we go.

$$\frac{dp}{dt} = \frac{d}{dt}(t^4) - \frac{d}{dt}(5t^3) + \frac{d}{dt}(t^2) - \frac{d}{dt}(12) \qquad \text{Sum and Difference Rule}$$

$$= 4t^3 - 5 \cdot 3t^2 + 2t + 0 \qquad\qquad\qquad \text{Constant and Power Rule}$$

$$= 4t^3 - 15t^2 + 2t$$

Exercises for Alternate Example 1

In Exercise 1–8, find $p'(t)$.

1. $p(t) = 4t^5 - 2t^4 + 6t^3 + 5t + 43$

2. $p(t) = -6t^4 + t^3 + 11t^2 + t - 21$

3. $p(t) = t^5 - t^4 + t^3 - t^2 + 3t + 19$

4. $p(t) = 11t^5 - 2t^4 + 11t^3 + 14t^2 + t + 12$

5. $p(t) = 12t^5 - 14t^4 + 9t^3 + 6t^2 + t - 3$

6. $p(t) = 13t^5 - 2t^4 + 6t^3 + 5t^2 + 5t + 4$

7. $p(t) = 19t^5 - 2t^4 + 6t^3 + 5t^2 + 8t - 45$

8. $p(t) = t^5 - 2t^4 + 6t^3 + 5t^2 + 11t + 4$ ■

Alternate Example 4   **Differentiating a Product**

Find $f'(x)$ if $f(x) = (x^2 - 3)(x^4 + 2)$.

SOLUTION

The Product Rule states that $\dfrac{d}{dx}(uv) = u\dfrac{dv}{dx} + v\dfrac{du}{dx}$ if u and v are differentiable functions of x.

From the Product Rule with $u = x^2 - 3$ and $v = x^4 + 2$, we find

$$
\begin{aligned}
f'(x) &= \frac{d}{dx}\left[(x^2 - 3)(x^4 + 2)\right] \\
&= (x^2 - 3)(4x^3) + (x^4 + 2)(2x) \\
&= 4x^5 - 12x^3 + 2x^5 + 4x \\
&= 6x^5 - 12x^3 + 4x
\end{aligned}
$$

Exercises for Alternate Example 4

In Exercise 9–16, find $f'(x)$.

9. $f(x) = (x^2 - 1)(x + 21)$

10. $f(x) = (x^3 - 4)(x^4 - 3)$

11. $f(x) = (3x - 3)(x^2 + 2)$

12. $f(x) = (x - 3)(x^5 + 8)$

13. $f(x) = (4x^2 + 1)(2x^4 - 2)$

14. $f(x) = (2x^2 + 2)(3x^4 - 1)$

15. $f(x) = (3x - 3)(x - 1)$

16. $f(x) = (4x^2 - x)(x - 1)$ ■

Alternate Example 7   **Using the Power Rule**

Find an equation for the line tangent to the curve

$$
y = \frac{x^2 - 1}{3x}
$$

at the point $(1, 0)$. Support your answer graphically.

SOLUTION

The Power Rule for both positive and negative integer powers of x states that

$$
\frac{d}{dx}\left(x^n\right) = nx^{n-1} \quad \text{if } x \neq 0.
$$

The Quotient Rule states that $\dfrac{d}{dx}\left(\dfrac{u}{v}\right) = \dfrac{v\dfrac{du}{dx} - u\dfrac{dv}{dx}}{v^2}$ if u and v are differentiable functions of x and $v \neq 0$.

We could find the derivative by Quotient Rule, but it is easier to first rewrite the function as a sum of two powers of x.

$$\frac{dy}{dx} = \frac{d}{dx}\left(\frac{x^2}{3x} - \frac{1}{3x}\right)$$

$$= \frac{d}{dx}\left(\frac{1}{3}x - \frac{1}{3}x^{-1}\right)$$

$$= \frac{1}{3} + \frac{1}{3}x^{-2}$$

The slope at $x = 1$ is

$$\frac{dy}{dx}\bigg|_{x=1} = \left[\frac{1}{3} + \frac{1}{3}(1)^{-2}\right]$$

$$= \frac{2}{3}$$

The line passing through $(1, 0)$ with slope $m = \frac{2}{3}$ is

$$y - 0 = \frac{2}{3}(x - 1)$$

$$y = \frac{2}{3}x - \frac{2}{3}$$

We graph $y = \frac{x^2 - 1}{3x}$ and $y = \frac{2}{3}x - \frac{2}{3}$ (Figure 3.11), observing that the line appears to be tangent to the curve at $(1, 0)$. Thus, we have graphical support that our computations are correct.

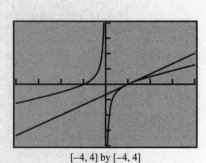

[−4, 4] by [−4, 4]

Figure 3.11 The line $y = \frac{2}{3}x - \frac{2}{3}$ appears to be tangent to the graph of $y = \frac{x^2 - 1}{3x}$ at the point $(1, 0)$.

Exercises for Alternate Example 7

In Exercises 17–22, find an equation for the line tangent to the curve $f(x)$ at the given point.

17. $y = \frac{x^2 + 2}{-x}$ at $(2, -3)$

18. $y = \frac{x^2 + 1}{-4x}$ at $\left(3, -\frac{5}{6}\right)$

19. $y = \frac{2x^2 - 1}{5x}$ at $\left(1, \frac{1}{5}\right)$

20. $y = \frac{x^3 + 4}{x^2}$ at $(-1, 3)$

21. $y = \frac{3x^2 - 1}{x}$ at $(1, 2)$

22. $y = \frac{6x^2 - 4}{5x^2}$ at $(2, 1)$

Alternate Example 8   Finding Higher Order Derivatives

Find the first five derivatives of $y = x^4 - 4x^3 + x^2 + 7x - 11$

SOLUTION

The first five derivatives are:

First derivative: $y' = 4x^3 - 12x^2 + 2x + 7$

Second derivative: $y'' = 12x^2 - 24x + 2$

Third derivative: $y''' = 24x - 24$

Fourth derivative: $y^{(4)} = 24$

Fifth derivative $y^{(5)} = 0.$

This function has derivatives of all orders, the fifth and higher order derivatives all being zero.

Exercises for Alternate Example 8

In Exercises 23–30, find the fifth derivative of *y*.

23. $y = x^5 - 4x^4 + 4x^3 + 11x^2 - 7x$

24. $y = 3x^6 - 2x^4 + x^3 + 7x - 99$

25. $y = x^7 - 4x^4 + x^3 + 7x^2 - 12x$

26. $y = 4x^5 - 11x^3 + 21x^2 + x - 31$

27. $y = x^7 - 31x^4 + 21x^2 + 12x - 25$

28. $y = x^8 - x^4 + x^2 + 4x - 19$

29. $y = x^{-2} + 3x^4$

30. $y = \dfrac{x^2 + 2}{x^2}$

■

3.4 Velocity and Other Rates of Change

Alternate Example 1 **Enlarging a Circle**

(a) Evaluate the rate of change of *A*, the area of a circle at *r* = 7 and *r* = 12.

(b) If *r* is measured in feet and *A* is measured in square feet, what units would be appropriate for $\dfrac{dA}{dr}$.

SOLUTION

The area of a circle is related to its radius by the equation $A = \pi r^2$.

(a) The (instantaneous) rate of change of *A* with respect to *r* is

$$\frac{dA}{dr} = \frac{d}{dr}\left(\pi r^2\right)$$
$$= \pi(2r)$$
$$= 2\pi r.$$

At *r* = 7, the rate is 14π (about 43.98). At *r* = 12, the rate is 24π (about 75.40).

(b) The appropriate units for $\dfrac{dA}{dr}$ are square feet (of area) per foot (of radius).

Exercises for Alternate Example 1

In Exercises 1–8, (a) Evaluate the rate of change of *A*, the area of a circle at given *r*. (b) What units would be appropriate for measuring $\dfrac{dA}{dr}$?

1. *r* = 2 and *r* = 4, *A* is measured in square centimeters and *r* is measured in centimeters.

2. *r* = 3 and *r* = 5, *A* is measured in square yards and *r* is measured in yards.

3. *r* = 6 and *r* = 8, *A* is measured in square miles and *r* is measured in miles.

4. *r* = 7 and *r* = 9, *A* is measured in square inches and *r* is measured in inches.

5. *r* = 10 and *r* = 11, *A* is measured in square millimeters and *r* is measured in millimeters.

6. *r* = 12 and *r* = 14, *A* is measured in square kilometers and *r* is measured in kilometers.

7. *r* = 16 and *r* = 17, *A* is measured in square meters and *r* is measured in meters.

8. *r* = 22 and *r* = 25, *A* is measured in square feet and *r* is measured in feet.

Alternate Example 4 **Modeling Vertical Motion**

A dynamite blast rock propels a heavy rock straight up with a launch velocity of 192 ft/sec (about 130.91 mph) (Figure 3.12a). It reaches a height of $s = 192t - 16t^2$ after *t* seconds.

(a) How high does the rock go?

(b) What is the velocity and speed of the rock when it is 512ft above the ground on the way up?

(c) What is the acceleration of the rock at any time *t* during its flight (after the blast)?

(d) When does the rock hit the ground?

SOLUTION

In the coordinate system we have chosen, s measures height from the ground up, so velocity is positive on the way up and negative on the way down.

(a) The instant when the rock is at its highest point is the one instant during the flight when the velocity is 0. At any time t, the velocity is

$$v = \frac{ds}{dt}$$

$$= \frac{d}{dt}\left(192t - 16t^2\right)$$

$$= 192 - 32t \ \text{ft/sec.}$$

The velocity is 0 when $192 - 32t = 0$ or at $t = 6$ sec.

The maximum height is the height of the rock at $t = 6$ sec. That is,

$$s_{max} = s(6)$$

$$= 192(6) - 16(6^2)$$

$$= 576 \ \text{ft.}$$

See Figure 3.12b.

(b) To find the velocity when the height is 512 ft, we determine the values of t for which $s(t) = 512$ ft.

$$s(t) = 192t - 16t^2 = 512$$
$$16t^2 - 192t + 512 = 0$$
$$16(t^2 - 12t + 32) = 0$$
$$t^2 - 12t + 32 = 0$$
$$(t - 4)(t - 8) = 0$$
$$t = 4 \ \text{sec} \quad \text{or} \quad t = 8 \ \text{sec.}$$

The velocity of the rock at each of these times is

$$v(4) = 192 - 32(4)$$

$$= 64 \ \text{ft/sec.}$$

$$v(8) = 192 - 32(8)$$

$$= -64 \ \text{ft/sec.}$$

At both instants, the speed of the rock is 64 ft/sec.

(c) At any time during its flight after the exploration, the rock's acceleration is

$$a = \frac{dv}{dt}$$

$$= \frac{d}{dt}\left(192 - 32t\right)$$

$$= -32 \ \text{ft/sec}^2.$$

The acceleration is always downward. When the rock is rising, it is slowing down; when it is falling, it is speeding up.

(d) The rock hits the ground at the positive time for which $s = 0$. The equation $192t - 16t^2 = 0$ has two solutions: $t = 0$ and $t = 12$. The blast initiated the flight of the rock from the ground level at $t = 0$. The rock returned to the ground 12 seconds later.

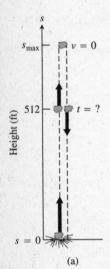

(a)

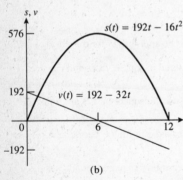

(b)

Figure 3.12 (a) The rock in Alternate Example 4.
(b) The graphs of s and v as functions of time t, showing that s is largest when $v = ds/dt = 0$. (The graph of s is not the path of the rock; it is a plot of height as a function of time.)

Exercises for Alternate Example 4

In Exercises 9–11, a dynamite blast rock propels a heavy rock straight up with a launch velocity of $v(t)$ ft/sec. It reaches a height of s after t seconds. In Exercises 12–14, a rock is thrown vertically upward from the surface of the moon at velocity of $v(t)$ m/sec. For each exercise, answer the following questions.

(a) How high does the rock go?

(b) What is the velocity of the rock when it is h ft above the ground on the way up?

(c) What is the acceleration of the rock at any time t during its flight (after the blast)?

(d) When does the rock hit the ground?

9. $s(t) = 144t - 16t^2$, $h = 224$ ft

10. $s(t) = 128t - 16t^2$, $h = 208$ ft

11. $s(t) = 152t - 16t^2$, $h = 240$ ft

12. $s(t) = 32t - 0.8t^2$, $h = 240$ m

13. $s(t) = 48t - 0.8t^2$, $h = 400$ m

14. $s(t) = 52t - 0.8t^2$, $h = 600$ m ■

Alternate Example 5 **Studying Particle Motion**

A particle moves along a line so that its position at any time $t \geq 0$ is given by the function $s(t) = t^2 - 6t + 2$, where s is measured in meters and t is measured in seconds.

(a) Find the displacement of the particle during the first 3 seconds.

(b) Find the average velocity of the particle during the first 5 seconds.

(c) Find the instantaneous velocity of the particle when $t = 6$.

(d) Find the acceleration of the particle when $t = 6$.

(e) Describe the motion of the particle. At what values of t does the particle change directions?

(f) Use parametric graphing to view the motion of the particle on the horizontal line $y = 3$.

SOLUTION

(a) We can find that $s(0) = 2$ and $s(3) = -7$. The displacement is given by $s(3) - s(0) = -7 - 2 = -9$. This value means that the particle is 9 units left of where it started.

(b) The average velocity we seek is

$$\frac{s(5) - s(0)}{5 - 0} = \frac{-3 - 2}{5} = \frac{-5}{5} = -1 \text{ m/sec.}$$

(c) The velocity $v(t)$ at any time t is $v(t) = \dfrac{ds}{dt} = 2t - 6$. So, $v(6) = 6$ m/sec.

(d) The acceleration $a(t)$ at any time t is $a(t) = \dfrac{dv}{dt} = 2$ m/sec^2. So, $a(6) = 2$.

(e) The graphs of $s(t) = t^2 - 6t + 2$ for $t \geq 0$ and its derivative $v(t) = 2t - 6$ shown in Figure 3.13 will help us analyze the motion.

For $0 \leq t < 3$, $v(t) > 0$, so the particle is moving left. Notice that $s(t)$ is decreasing. The particle starts ($t = 0$) at $s = 2$ and moves left arriving at the origin when $t = 0.35$ and $t = 5.65$. The particle continues moving to the left until it reaches the point where $s = -7$ at $t = 3$.

At $t = 3$, $v(t) = 0$, so the particle is at rest.

For $t > 3$, $v(t) > 0$, so the particle is moving to the right. Notice that $s(t)$ is increasing. In this interval, the particle starts at $s = -7$ moving to the right for the rest of time.

The particle changes direction at $t = 3$, when $v = 0$.

(f) Enter X1T $= T^2 - 6T + 2$, Y1T $= 3$ in parametric mode and graph in the window of $[-4, 4]$ by $[-2, 6]$ with Tmin $= 0$, Tmax $= 10$ (it really should be ∞), and Xscl $=$ Yscl $= 1$. (Figure 3.14). By using TRACE you can follow the path of the particle.

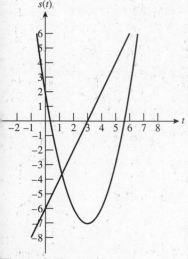

Figure 3.13 The graph of $s(t) = t^2 - 6t + 2$, $t \geq 0$ and its derivative $v(t) = 2t - 6$, $t \geq 0$.

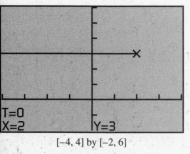

$[-4, 4]$ by $[-2, 6]$

Figure 3.14 The graph of X1T $= T^2 - 6T + 2$ and Y1T $= 3$ in parametric mode.

Exercises for Alternate Example 5

In Exercises 15–20, a particle moves along a line so that its position at any time $t \geq 0$ is given by the function $s(t)$, where s is measured in meters and t is measured in seconds.

(a) Find the displacement of the particle during the first 2 seconds.

(b) Find the average velocity of the particle during the first 4 seconds.

(c) Find the instantaneous velocity of the particle when $t = 7$.

(d) Find the acceleration of the particle when $t = 7$.

(e) Describe the motion of the particle. At what values of t does the particle change directions?

15. $s(t) = t^2 - 3t + 1$ **16.** $s(t) = t^2 - 6t + 5$ **17.** $s(t) = -t^2 + 9t - 4$ **18.** $s(t) = -t^2 + 11t - 9$

19. $s(t) = t^3 - 7t^2 + 14t - 8$ **20.** $s(t) = -t^3 + 8t^2 - 20t + 16$

Alternate Example 7   **Marginal Cost and Marginal Revenue**

Suppose it costs

$$c(x) = x^3 - 8x^2 + 20x$$

dollars to produce x radiators when 7 to 9 radiators are produced, and that

$$r(x) = x^3 - 6x^2 + 15x$$

gives the dollar revenue from selling x radiators. Your shop currently produces 9 radiators a day. Find the marginal cost and marginal revenue.

SOLUTION

The marginal cost of producing one more radiator a day when 9 are being produced is $c'(9)$.

$$c'(x) = \frac{d}{dx}\left(x^3 - 8x^2 + 20x\right)$$
$$= 3x^2 - 16x + 20$$
$$c'(9) = 3(81) - 16(9) + 20$$
$$= 243 - 144 + 20$$
$$= 119 \text{ dollars}$$

The marginal revenue is

$$r'(x) = \frac{d}{dx}\left(x^3 - 6x^2 + 15x\right)$$
$$= 3x^2 - 12x + 15$$

So,

$$r'(9) = 3(81) - 12(9) + 15$$
$$= 243 - 108 + 15$$
$$= 150 \text{ dollars.}$$

Exercises for Alternate Example 7

In Exercises 21–23, suppose that the cost in dollars to produce x radiators is $c(x)$, and that $r(x)$ gives the revenue, in dollars, from selling x radiators. Find the marginal cost and marginal revenue when 10 radiators are produced by using the cost and revenue functions given in each exercise.

21. $c(x) = x^3 - 10x^2 + 18x$ and $r(x) = x^3 - 8x^2 + 16x$

22. $c(x) = x^3 - 12x^2 + 18x$ and $r(x) = x^3 - 7x^2 + 12x$

23. $c(x) = x^3 - 14x^2 + 19x$ and $r(x) = x^3 - 10x^2 + 14x$

In Exercises 24–26 you are given a revenue function $r(x)$ that represents the weekly revenue, in dollars, from selling x items produced by a certain company. In each case answer the following:

a) Draw a graph of r. What value of x makes sense in this problem situation?

b) Find the marginal revenue when x items are sold.

c) Use the function $r'(x)$ to estimate the increase in revenue that will result from increasing sales from 2 items per week to 3 items per week.

d) Find the limit of $r'(x)$ as $x \to \infty$. How would you interpret this number?

24. $r(x) = 200 + 100\left(2 - \dfrac{2x^2 + 3}{x^2 + 1}\right)$

25. $r(x) = 1000\left(1 - \dfrac{x^2 + 3x + 2}{x^3 + 4x}\right)$

26. $r(x) = 50\left(\dfrac{x^3 + x + 1}{200x^2 + 3}\right)$ ■

3.5 Derivatives of Trigonometric Functions

Alternate Example 1 **Revisiting Differentiation Rules**

Find the derivatives of **(a)** $y = x^3 \cos x$ and **(b)** $y = \dfrac{\sin x}{2 - \cos x}$.

SOLUTION

(a) $\dfrac{dy}{dx} = x^3 \dfrac{d}{dx}(\cos x) + (\cos x)\dfrac{d}{dx} x^3$

$\qquad = x^3(-\sin x) + (\cos x)(3x^2)$

$\qquad = -x^3 \sin x + 3x^2 \cos x$

(b) $\dfrac{dy}{dx} = \dfrac{\left(2 - \cos x\right)\dfrac{d}{dx}(\sin x) - (\sin x)\dfrac{d}{dx}\left(2 - \cos x\right)}{(2 - \cos x)^2}$

$\qquad = \dfrac{\left(2 - \cos x\right)(\cos x) - (\sin x)\left(\sin x\right)}{(2 - \cos x)^2}$

$\qquad = \dfrac{2\cos x - \cos^2 x - \sin^2 x}{(2 - \cos x)^2} \qquad \cos^2 x + \sin^2 x = 1$

$\qquad = \dfrac{2\cos x - 1}{(2 - \cos x)^2}$

Exercises for Alternate Example 1

In Exercises 1–6, find the derivative of y.

1. $y = x^4 \cos x$

2. $y = \dfrac{-\sin x}{\cos x}$

3. $y = -3x^2 \cos x$

4. $y = \dfrac{3\sin x}{\cos x - 3}$

5. $y = \dfrac{\tan x + 2x^3}{\sec x - x^3}$

6. $y = \dfrac{\sin x}{1 + \cot x}$ ■

Alternate Example 3   A Couple of Jerks

Two bodies moving in simple harmonic motion have the following position functions:

(a) $s(t) = 3\cos t$

(b) $s(t) = 2\sin t - \cos t$

Find the jerks of the bodies at time t.

SOLUTION

We know that the jerk is equal to the derivative of acceleration. Thus,

(a) $v(t) = \dfrac{ds}{dt}$

$\qquad = \dfrac{d}{dt}(3\cos t)$

$\qquad = -3\sin t$

$\quad a(t) = \dfrac{dv}{dt}$

$\qquad = \dfrac{d}{dt}(-3\sin t)$

$\qquad = -3\cos t$

$\quad j(t) = \dfrac{da}{dt}$

$\qquad = \dfrac{d}{dt}(-3\cos t)$

$\qquad = 3\sin t$

(b) $v(t) = \dfrac{ds}{dt}$

$\qquad = \dfrac{d}{dt}(2\sin t - \cos t)$

$\qquad = 2\cos t + \sin t$

$\quad a(t) = \dfrac{dv}{dt}$

$\qquad = \dfrac{d}{dt}(2\cos t + \sin t)$

$\qquad = -2\sin t + \cos t$

$\quad j(t) = \dfrac{da}{dt}$

$\qquad = \dfrac{d}{dt}(-2\sin t + \cos t)$

$\qquad = -2\cos t - \sin t$

Exercises for Alternate Example 3

In Exercises 7–14, find the jerk of each body with simple harmonic motion $s(t)$ at the time t

7. $s(t) = -\cos t$ **8.** $s(t) = \sin t - 3\cos t$ **9.** $s(t) = 3 + 3\cos t$ **10.** $s(t) = \sin t - \cos t$ **11.** $s(t) = 3 - 3\cos t$

12. $s(t) = -3\cos t + 5$ **13.** $s(t) = 3 - 2\cos t$ **14.** $s(t) = 4\cos t + 4$

Alternate Example 4 **Finding Tangent and Normal Lines**

Find equations for the lines that are tangent and normal to the graph of

$$f(x) = \frac{\tan x}{3x}$$

at $x = 4$. Support graphically.

SOLUTION

Solve Numerically Since we will be using a calculator approximation for $f(4)$ anyway, that is a good place to use NDER.

We compute $\dfrac{\tan 4}{3(4)}$ (approximately 0.0965) on the calculator and store it as k. The slope of the tangent line at $(4, k)$ is

$$\text{NDER}\left(\frac{\tan x}{3x}, 4\right),$$

which we compute and store as m (approximately 0.1709). The equation of the tangent line is

$$y - k = m(x - 4)$$
$$y = mx - 4m + k.$$

Only after we have found m and $k - 4m$ do we round the coefficients, giving the tangent line as

$$y = 0.17x - 4(0.17) + 0.10$$
$$= 0.17x - 0.58$$

The equation of the normal line is

$$y - k = -\frac{1}{m}(x - 4)$$

$$y = -\frac{1}{m}x + \frac{4}{m} + k$$

Again, we wait until the end to round the coefficients, giving the normal line as

$$y = -\frac{x}{0.17} + \frac{4}{0.17} + 0.10$$

$$y = -5.88x + 23.62$$

Support Graphically Figure 3.15, showing the original function and the tangent and normal lines, supports our computations.

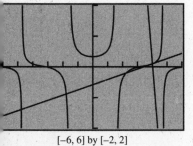

[−6, 6] by [−2, 2]

Figure 3.15 Graphic support for Alternate Example 4.

Exercises for Alternate Example 4

In Exercises 15–20, find equation for the lines that are tangent and normal to the graph of $f(x)$ at given x. Check your answers graphically.

15. $f(x) = 3\sin x$ at $x = \dfrac{\pi}{3}$

16. $f(x) = \dfrac{\cos x}{x}$ at $x = \dfrac{\pi}{2}$

17. $f(x) = \sin x \cos x$ at $x = \dfrac{\pi}{2}$

18. $f(x) = \sin x \cos x$ at $x = \pi$

19. $f(x) = \dfrac{\sin x}{3x}$ at $x = \dfrac{\pi}{2}$

20. $f(x) = \dfrac{\cos x}{2x}$ at $x = \dfrac{\pi}{3}$

■

Alternate Example 5 **A Trigonometric Second Derivative**

Find y'' if $y = \csc x$.

SOLUTION

$$y = \csc x$$
$$y' = -\csc x \cot x$$
$$y'' = \left[\frac{d}{dx}(-\csc x)\right]\cot x + (-\csc x)\left[\frac{d}{dx}\cot x\right]$$
$$= -(-\csc x \cot x)\cot x - \csc x(-\csc^2 x)$$
$$= \csc x \cot^2 x + \csc^3 x$$

Exercises for Alternate Example 5

In Exercises 21–26, find y''.

21. $y = \sec x$ **22.** $y = \sin x \sec x$ **23.** $y = \sec^2 x - \tan^2 x$ **24.** $y = \dfrac{1 - \cos x}{\sin x}$ **25.** $y = x^2 \tan x$

26. $y = \dfrac{\cos x}{x}$

3.6 Chain Rule

Alternate Example 2 **Relating Derivatives**

Calculate the derivative of $y = 4x^6 + 28x^3 + 49$ using composite functions.

SOLUTION

The polynomial $y = 4x^6 + 28x^3 + 49 = (2x^3 + 7)^2$ is the composite of the functions $y = u^2$ and $u = 2x^3 + 7$. Calculating derivatives, we see that

$$\frac{dy}{du} \cdot \frac{du}{dx} = (2u)(6x)$$
$$= 2(2x^3 + 7)(6x^2)$$
$$= 24x^5 + 84x^2$$

Also,

$$\frac{dy}{dx} = \frac{d}{dx}\left(4x^6 + 28x^3 + 49\right)$$
$$= 24x^5 + 84x^2$$

Once again,

$$\frac{dy}{dx} = \frac{dy}{du} \cdot \frac{du}{dx}$$

Exercises for Alternate Example 2

In Exercise 1–8, use the given substitution and the Chain Rule to find dy/dx.

1. $y = x^6 + 10x^3 + 25,\ u = x^3 + 5$ **2.** $y = 25x^6 - 10x^3 + 1,\ u = 5x^3 - 1$ **3.** $y = \cos^3 x,\ u = \cos x$

4. $y = \cos(x^3),\ u = x^3$ **5.** $y = 2x\sin(3x),\ u = 3x$ **6.** $y = \sqrt{3x^2 + 2x + 1},\ u = 3x^2 + 2x + 1$

7. $y = \left(x + \dfrac{1}{x}\right)^{30},\ u = x + \dfrac{1}{x}$ **8.** $y = \tan(\cos x),\ u = \cos x$

Alternate Example 3   Applying the Chain Rule

An object moves along the x-axis so that its position at any given time $t \geq 0$ is defined by $x(t) = \cos(t^2 + 5)$. Find the velocity of the object as a function of t.

SOLUTION

We know that the velocity is $\dfrac{dx}{dt}$. In this instance, x is a composite function: $x = \cos(u)$ and $u = t^2 + 5$. We have

$$\frac{dx}{du} = -\sin(u) \qquad\qquad x = \cos(u)$$

$$\frac{du}{dt} = 2t \qquad\qquad u = t^2 + 5$$

By the Chain Rule,

$$\frac{dx}{dt} = \frac{dx}{du} \cdot \frac{du}{dt}$$
$$= -\sin u \cdot 2t$$
$$= -\sin(t^2 + 5)(2t)$$
$$= -2t \sin(t^2 + 5)$$

Exercises for Alternate Example 3

In Exercise 9–16, $s(t)$ defines the position of an object that moves along the x-axis at any given time $t \geq 0$. Find the velocity of the object as a function of t.

9. $s(t) = \cos(t^2 + 8)$

10. $s(t) = \sin(2t^2 + 1)$

11. $s(t) = \cos(t^2 + t)$

12. $s(t) = 4\cos(3t) + 3t \sin 4$

13. $s(t) = \tan(\pi/4 + 2t)$

14. $s(t) = \cot(\pi t + \sec t)$

15. $s(t) = (t^2 + t)\sin^2 t$

16. $s(t) = \sin(\sin(6t))$ ∎

Alternate Example 5   A Three Link "Chain"

Find the derivative of $g(t) = \tan(3 + \cos 3t)$.

SOLUTION

Notice that tan is a function of $(3 + \cos 3t)$, while $\cos 3t$ is a function of $3t$, which is itself a function of t. Therefore, by the Chain Rule,

$$g'(t) = \frac{d}{dt}\Big(\tan(3 + \cos 3t)\Big)$$

$$= \sec^2(3 + \cos 3t) \cdot \frac{d}{dt}(3 + \cos 3t) \qquad \text{Derivative of } \tan u \text{ with } u = 3 + \cos 3t.$$

$$= \sec^2(3 + \cos 3t)\left(0 - \sin 3t\left(\frac{d}{dt}(3t)\right)\right) \qquad \text{Derivative of } 3 + \cos 3t \text{ with } u = 3t.$$

$$= \sec^2(3 + \cos 3t)(-\sin 3t) \cdot 3$$
$$= -3(\sin 3t)\sec^2(3 + \cos 3t)$$

Exercises for Alternate Example 5

In Exercises 17–24, find the derivative of $g(t)$.

17. $g(t) = \left(3t^2 + 1\right)^{-1/2}$

18. $g(t) = \cot^5\left(2t + 1\right)^3$

19. $g(t) = \left(\csc^3\left(t^4\right)\right)^8$

20. $g(t) = \sqrt{1 + \sqrt{1 + \sqrt{t}}}$

21. $g(t) = \dfrac{1}{1 + 1/t}$

22. $g(t) = \sqrt[3]{1 + \tan^2(\pi t)}$

23. $g(t) = 2\sin(3 + 3\sin 6t)$

24. $g(t) = \left(2t + \tan\left(\dfrac{\pi}{t}\right)\right)^{-2}$ ∎

Alternate Example 7 **Finding Slope**

(a) Find the slope of the line tangent to the curve $y = \cos^5 x$ at the point where $x = \dfrac{\pi}{6}$.

(b) Show that the slope of every line tangent to the curve $y = \dfrac{3}{(3-x)^3}$ is positive.

SOLUTION

(a) $\dfrac{dy}{dx} = 5\cos^4 x \left(\dfrac{d}{dx} \cos x \right)$ Power Rule with $u = \cos x, n = 5$

$\qquad = -5(\sin x)\left(\cos^4 x \right)$

The tangent line has slope

$$\left. \dfrac{dy}{dx} \right|_{x=\pi/6} = -5 \left(\sin \dfrac{\pi}{6} \right)\left(\cos^4 \dfrac{\pi}{6} \right)$$

$$= -5 \left(\dfrac{1}{2} \right)\left(\dfrac{\sqrt{3}}{2} \right)^4$$

$$= -\dfrac{45}{32}.$$

(b) $\dfrac{dy}{dx} = \dfrac{d}{dx} 3(3-x)^{-3}$

$\qquad = -9(3-x)^{-4} \dfrac{d}{dx}(3-x)$

$\qquad = -9(3-x)^{-4}(-1)$

$\qquad = \dfrac{9}{(3-x)^4}$

At any point on the curve, $x \neq 3$ and the slope of the tangent line is

$$\dfrac{dy}{dx} = \dfrac{9}{(3-x)^4},$$

which is positive since it is the quotient of two positive values.

Exercises for Alternate Example 7

In Exercises 25–30, **(a)** Find the slope of the line tangent to the curve y at the given point x. **(b)** Show that the slope of a line tangent to the curve y is either negative for all values of x or positive for all values of x in the domain of y.

25. **(a)** $y = \cos^3 x$ at $x = \pi$ **(b)** $y = \dfrac{1}{(5-x)^3}$ **26.** **(a)** $y = 2\sin^2 x$ at $x = \dfrac{\pi}{6}$ **(b)** $y = \dfrac{1}{(1-3x)^5}$

27. **(a)** $y = -\cos^4 2x$ at $x = \dfrac{\pi}{4}$ **(b)** $y = \dfrac{4}{(2-x)^5}$ **28.** **(a)** $y = -3\cos x$ at $x = \dfrac{\pi}{3}$ **(b)** $y = \dfrac{-4}{(1-x)}$

29. **(a)** $y = 4\cos x$ at $x = \dfrac{\pi}{4}$ **(b)** $y = \dfrac{4}{(1-2x)^3}$ **30.** **(a)** $y = \cos 5x$ at $x = \dfrac{\pi}{5}$ **(b)** $y = \dfrac{6}{(1-5x)}$

3.7 Implicit Differentiation

Alternate Example 1 **Differentiating Implicitly**

Find $\dfrac{dy}{dx}$ if $y^3 = 3x$.

SOLUTION

To find $\dfrac{dy}{dx}$, we simply differentiate both sides of the equation $y^3 = 3x$ with respect to x, treating y as a differentiable function of x and applying the Chain Rule:

$$y^3 = 3x$$

$$\frac{d}{dx}y^3 = \frac{d}{dx}3x$$

$$3y^2\frac{dy}{dx} = 3$$

$$\frac{dy}{dx} = \frac{3}{3y^2}$$

$$= \frac{1}{y^2}.$$

Exercises for Alternate Example 1

In Exercises 1–8, find $\dfrac{dy}{dx}$ for each y.

1. $y^2 = -3x$ **2.** $y^3 = 4x^2$ **3.** $y^2 + 25x^2 = 0$ **4.** $xy^3 = -32x$ **5.** $2xy - 7x = 4$ **6.** $y = \dfrac{x}{x+2y}$

7. $2x^3\dfrac{dy}{dx} + 2x^2 y = 4x^3 - y$ **8.** $\dfrac{dy}{dx}\cot x - x\cos = x^2\dfrac{dy}{dx} + y$ ■

Alternate Example 3 **Solving for *dy/dx***

Show that the slope $\dfrac{dy}{dx}$ is defined at every point on the graph of $4y = x^2 - \cos y$.

SOLUTION

First we need to know $\dfrac{dy}{dx}$, which we find by implicit differentiation:

$$4y = x^2 - \cos y$$

$$\frac{d}{dx}(4y) = \frac{d}{dx}\left(x^2 - \cos y\right) \qquad \text{Differentiate both sides with respect to } x.$$

$$\frac{d}{dx}(4y) = \frac{d}{dx}\left(x^2\right) - \frac{d}{dx}(\cos y)$$

$$4\frac{dy}{dx} = 2x + (\sin y)\frac{dy}{dx} \qquad \text{Treat } y \text{ as a function of } x \text{ and use the Chain Rule.}$$

$$4\frac{dy}{dx} - (\sin y)\frac{dy}{dx} = 2x \qquad \text{Collect terms with } dy/dx$$

$$\left(4 - \sin y\right)\frac{dy}{dx} = 2x \qquad\qquad \text{Factor out } \frac{dy}{dx}.$$

$$\frac{dy}{dx} = \frac{2x}{4 - \sin y} \qquad\qquad \text{Solve for } \frac{dy}{dx}.$$

The formula for $\frac{dy}{dx}$ is defined at every point (x, y), except for those at which $\sin y = 4$.

Since $\sin y$ cannot be greater than 1, this never happens.

Exercises for Alternate Example 3

In Exercises 9–14, show that the slope $\frac{dy}{dx}$ is defined at every point on the graph of each equation.

9. $-3y = 5x^2 + \sin y$ **10.** $11y = -4x^2 - 3\sin y$ **11.** $5y = -x^2 - 3\cos y$ **12.** $7y = -4x^2 + 2\sin y - 6$

13. $4y = -x^2 - 3\cos y + 2$ **14.** $4y = -2x^2 - 3\cos y$

Alternate Example 5 Finding a Second Derivative Implicitly

Find $\dfrac{d^2 y}{dx^2}$ if $3x^4 + 4y^2 = 121$.

SOLUTION

To start, we differentiate both sides of the equation with respect to x in order to find $y' = \dfrac{dy}{dx}$.

$$\frac{d}{dx}\left(3x^4 + 4y^2\right) = \frac{d}{dx}(121)$$

$$12x^3 + 8yy' = 0$$

$$3x^3 + 2yy' = 0$$

$$2yy' = -3x^3$$

$$y' = \frac{-3x^3}{2y}, \qquad \text{where } y \neq 0$$

We now apply the Quotient Rule to find y''.

$$y'' = \frac{d}{dx}\left(\frac{-3x^3}{2y}\right)$$

$$= \frac{-18x^2 y + 6x^3 y'}{4y^2}$$

$$= \frac{-18x^2 y}{4y^2} + \frac{6x^3 y'}{4y^2}$$

$$= -\frac{9x^2}{2y} + \frac{3x^3}{2y^2}(y')$$

Finally, substitute $y' = \dfrac{-3x^3}{2y}$ to express y'' in terms of x and y, when $y \neq 0$.

$$y'' = -\frac{9x^2}{2y} + \frac{3x^3}{2y^2}\left(-\frac{3x^3}{2y}\right)$$

$$= -\frac{9x^2}{2y} - \frac{9x^6}{4y^3}, \qquad \text{where } y \neq 0$$

Exercises for Alternate Example 5

In Exercise 15–20, find $\dfrac{d^2y}{dx^2}$ for each equation.

15. $4x^2 - y^2 = -40$ **16.** $x^3 - 4y^2 = 9$ **17.** $2x^5 + 3y = -11$ **18.** $5x - 4y^2 = 33$ **19.** $x^3 - y^2 = 4$

20. $8x + 4y^2 = 12$

Alternate Example 6   Using the Rational Power Rule

Find **(a)** $\dfrac{d}{dx}\sqrt{x-3}$, **(b)** $\dfrac{d}{dx}\left(x^{3/5}\right)$, and **(c)** $\dfrac{d}{dx}(\sin x)^{-2/3}$.

Solution

(a) $\dfrac{d}{dx}\sqrt{x-3} = \dfrac{d}{dx}(x-3)^{1/2}$

$$= \frac{1}{2}(x-3)^{1/2-1}\cdot \frac{d}{dx}(x-3)$$

$$= \frac{1}{2}(x-3)^{-1/2}\cdot 1$$

$$= \frac{1}{2\sqrt{x-3}}.$$

Notice that $\sqrt{x-3}$ is defined for $x \geq 3$, but $\dfrac{1}{2\sqrt{x-3}}$ for $x > 3$ only.

(b) $\dfrac{d}{dx}\left(x^{3/5}\right) = \dfrac{3}{5}\left(x^{3/5-1}\right)$

$$= \frac{3}{5}\left(x^{-2/5}\right)$$

$$= \frac{3}{5\sqrt[5]{x^2}}.$$

The original function is defined for all real numbers, but the derivative is undefined at $x = 0$.

(c) $\dfrac{d}{dx}\left(\sin x\right)^{-2/3} = -\dfrac{2}{3}\left(\sin x\right)^{-2/3-1} \cdot \dfrac{d}{dx}\left(\sin x\right)$

$\qquad\qquad = -\dfrac{2}{3}\left(\sin x\right)^{-5/3} \cdot \left(\cos x\right)$

$\qquad\qquad = -\dfrac{2\cos x}{3\sin x\sqrt[3]{\sin^2 x}}.$

The derivative is undefined for $k\pi$, where k is an integer.

Exercises for Alternate Example 6

In Exercises 21–26, find the indicated derivative .

21. $\dfrac{d}{dx}\sqrt{4x-1}$

22. $\dfrac{d}{dx}(-\sin x)^{5/3}$

23. $\dfrac{d}{dx}\sqrt{x^3}$

24. $\dfrac{d}{dx}\dfrac{2x}{\sqrt{3x^2-2x+1}}$

25. $\dfrac{d}{dx}\left(\cot 2x\right)^{3/8}$

26. $\dfrac{d}{dx}\left(x^2\sqrt{x+1}\right)$

27. $\dfrac{d}{dx}\left[\cos\left(x^2+\pi\right)\right]^{4/5}$

28. $\dfrac{d}{dx}\left[\left(6-x^3\right)^{3/5}\right]$

3.8 Derivatives of Inverse Trigonometric Functions

Alternate Example 1 **Applying the Formula**

Find the derivative of $y = \sin^{-1} 2x$.

SOLUTION

We know that if $y = \sin^{-1} u$, then $\dfrac{dy}{dx} = \dfrac{1}{\sqrt{1-u^2}} \cdot \dfrac{du}{dx}$

Thus,

$\dfrac{dy}{dx} = \dfrac{d}{dx}\left(\sin^{-1} 2x\right)$

$\qquad = \dfrac{1}{\sqrt{1-(2x)^2}}\left(\dfrac{d}{dx}2x\right)$

$\qquad = \dfrac{2}{\sqrt{1-4x^2}}$

Exercises for Alternate Example 1

In Exercises 1–6, find the derivative of y.

1. $y = \sin^{-1} 2t$

2. $y = 8\sin^{-1}\dfrac{1}{x}$

3. $y = t\sin^{-1} t^2$

4. $y = \sin^{-1}\sqrt{x}$

5. $y = \sin^{-1}(4x-5)$

6. $y = \sin^{-1}(5-3x)$

Alternate Example 2 **A Moving Particle**

A particle moves along the *x*-axis so that its position at any time $t \geq 0$ is $x(t) = \tan^{-1}\sqrt{2t + 1}$. What is the velocity of the particle when $t = 24$?

SOLUTION

$$v(t) = \frac{d}{dt}x$$

$$= \frac{d}{dt}\tan^{-1}\sqrt{2t + 1}$$

$$= \frac{1}{1 + \left(\sqrt{2t+1}\right)^2}\left(\frac{d}{dt}\sqrt{2t+1}\right)$$

$$= \frac{1}{1 + 2t + 1} \cdot \frac{2}{2\sqrt{2t+1}}$$

$$= \frac{1}{2(1 + t)}\left(\frac{1}{\sqrt{2t+1}}\right)$$

When $t = 24$, the velocity is

$$v(24) = \frac{1}{2(1 + 24)}\left(\frac{1}{\sqrt{2(24) + 1}}\right)$$

$$= \frac{1}{350}.$$

Exercises for Alternate Example 2

In Exercises 7–12, $x(t)$ defines the position of an object moving along the *x*-axis at any time $t \geq 0$. Find the velocity of the object at the indicated value of *t*.

7. $x(t) = \tan^{-1}3t$ at $t = 3$

8. $x(t) = \tan^{-1}(t - 1)$ at $t = 2$

9. $x(t) = \sin^{-1}\sqrt{t}$ at $t = 1/4$

10. $x(t) = \sin^{-1}\left(\frac{t}{3}\right)$ at $t = 2$

11. $x(t) = \sec^{-1}(t^2/4)$ at $t = 3$

12. $x(t) = \sec^{-1}\sqrt{t}$ at $t = 9$

Alternate Example 3 **Using the Formula**

Find $\dfrac{dy}{dx}$ if $y = \sec^{-1}(4x^3)$.

SOLUTION

We know that if $y = \sec^{-1}u$, then $\dfrac{dy}{dx} = \dfrac{1}{|u|\sqrt{u^2 - 1}}\left(\dfrac{du}{dx}\right)$, $|u| > 1$. Thus,

$$\frac{dy}{dx} = \frac{1}{\left|4x^3\right|\sqrt{\left(4x^3\right)^2 - 1}}\left(\frac{d}{dx}\left(4x^3\right)\right)$$

$$= \frac{12x^2}{\left|4x^3\right|\sqrt{\left(4x^3\right)^2 - 1}}$$

$$\frac{dy}{dx} = \frac{12x^2}{4x^2 |x| \sqrt{\left(4x^3\right)^2 - 1}}$$

$$= \frac{3}{|x| \sqrt{16x^6 - 1}}$$

Exercises for Alternate Example 3

In Exercises 15–20, find $\dfrac{dy}{dx}$, the derivative of y.

13. $y = \sec^{-1}(7x^2)$

14. $y = \csc^{-1}\left(\dfrac{x^4}{16}\right), x \ge 2$

15. $y = \cot^{-1}(2x^2 - 1)$

16. $y = \tan^{-1}\sqrt{x+1} + \sin^{-1}\left(\dfrac{x}{2}\right)$

17. $y = \sec^{-1}(x^4 + 2x^2)$

18. $y = \cos^{-1}\sqrt{1-x^2}, |x| \le 1$

Alternate Example 4   **A Tangent Line to the Arccotangent Curve**

Find an equation for the line tangent to the graph of $y = \cot^{-1} 2x$ at $x = -2$.

SOLUTION

First, we note that

$$\cot^{-1}(-4) = \frac{\pi}{2} - \tan^{-1}(-4) = 2.8966$$

because we know that

$$\cot^{-1} x = \frac{\pi}{2} - \tan^{-1} x.$$

The slope of the tangent line is the value of y at $x = -2$.

$$\frac{dy}{dx} = -\frac{1}{1 + (2x)^2}\left(\frac{d}{dx}(2x)\right)$$

$$= -\frac{2}{1 + 4x^2}$$

If the slope is m, then

$$m = \frac{dy}{dx}\bigg|_{x=-2}$$

$$= -\frac{2}{1 + 4x^2}\bigg|_{x=-2}$$

$$= -\frac{2}{1 + 4(-2)^2}$$

$$= -\frac{2}{17} \approx -0.1176$$

So, the tangent line has equation

$$y - 2.8966 = -0.1176\,(x + 2).$$

Exercises for Alternate Example 4

In Exercise 19–24, find an equation for the line tangent to the graph of y at given x.

19. $y = \cot^{-1} 3x$ at $x = 3$

20. $y = \tan^{-1} x$ at $x = -\sqrt{3}$

21. $y = \sec^{-1} 5x$ at $x = -1$

22. $y = \csc^{-1}\left(\dfrac{x}{3}\right)$ at $x = \dfrac{6}{\sqrt{3}}$

23. $y = \sin^{-1}(x+1)$ at $x = -\dfrac{1}{2}$

24. $y = \cot^{-1} 6x$ at $x = 1$

Derivatives of Exponential and Logarithmic
3.9 Functions

Alternate Example 1 **Using the Formula**

Find $\dfrac{dy}{dx}$ if $y = e^{(x-x^3)}$.

SOLUTION

Let $u = x - x^3$. Then $y = e^u$. Therefore,

$$\frac{dy}{dx} = e^u \frac{du}{dx}$$

$$= \left(1 - 3x^2\right) e^{(x-x^3)}.$$

Exercises for Alternate Example 1

In Exercises 1–8, Find $\dfrac{dy}{dx}$.

1. $y = e^{(3x - x^2)}$

2. $y = e^{\pi x} + \pi x$

3. $y = x^2 e^x + x$

4. $y = e^{-\sqrt{x+1}}$

5. $y = (e^{2x} + 2e^x + 1)^3$

6. $y = e^{\cos x} + e^e$

7. $y = e^{-x} - x^{-e}$

8. $y = e^{(x - 7x^2)}$

Alternate Example 6 **Finding the Domain**

If $f(x) = \ln(6x - 3)$, find $f'(x)$. State its domain.

SOLUTION

The domain of f is $\left(\dfrac{1}{2}, \infty\right)$.

$$f'(x) = \frac{6}{6x - 3}$$

$$= \frac{2}{2x - 1}$$

The domain of f' appears to be all $x \neq \dfrac{1}{2}$. However, since f is not defined for $x \leq \dfrac{1}{2}$, neither is f'. Thus,

$$f'(x) = \frac{2}{2x - 1}, \qquad x > \frac{1}{2}.$$

That is, the domain of f' is $\left(\dfrac{1}{2}, \infty \right)$.

Exercises for Alternate Example 6

In Exercises 9–16, find $f'(x)$ and state the domain.

9. $y = \ln(8x - 1)$ **10.** $y = \ln\sqrt{x - 9}$ **11.** $y = \ln(1 + \cos x)$ **12.** $y = \ln(x^2 - 1)$ **13.** $y = \log_\pi(x^3)$

14. $y = \ln(x^2 e^x)$ **15.** $y = \log_3(4 \cdot 3^x)$ **16.** $y = \ln 4(x - 2)$

Alternate Example 7   Logarithmic Differentiation

Find $\dfrac{dy}{dx}$ if $y = x^{4x}$, $x > 0$.

SOLUTION

$$y = x^{4x}$$

$$\ln y = \ln x^{4x} \qquad\qquad \text{Logarithms of both sides are equal.}$$

$$\ln y = (4x) \ln x \qquad\qquad \text{Property of Exponents of Logarithms.}$$

$$\frac{d}{dx}(\ln y) = \frac{d}{dx}(4x \ln x) \qquad\qquad \text{Differentiate implicitly.}$$

$$\frac{1}{y}\left(\frac{dy}{dx} \right) = (4 \cdot \ln x) + 4x \cdot \frac{1}{x}$$

$$\frac{dy}{dx} = y(4 \ln x + 4)$$

$$= x^{4x}(4 \ln x + 4)$$

$$= 4x^{4x}(\ln x + 1).$$

Exercises for Alternate Example 7

In Exercises 23–28, find $\dfrac{dy}{dx}$.

17. $y = x^{\sin x}$ **18.** $y = (\ln x)^x$ **19.** $y = x^{-x}$, $x > 0$ **20.** $y = (\cos x)^{2x+1}$ **21.** $y = \sqrt[3]{\dfrac{(x-2)^3(2x^2+3)}{(x+1)^2}}$

22. $y = (x^2 + 1)^{\ln x}$

Chapter 4 Applications of Derivatives

4.1 Extreme Values of Functions

Alternate Example 1 Exploring Extreme Values

What are the extreme values of $f(x) = \sin 2x$ on $\left[-\dfrac{\pi}{2}, \dfrac{\pi}{2}\right]$?

SOLUTION

$f(x)$ takes on a maximum value of 1 at $x = \dfrac{\pi}{4}$ (once) and a minimum value of -1 (once)

at $x = -\dfrac{\pi}{4}$ (Figure 4.1)

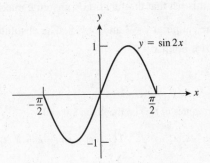

Figure 4.1 (Alternate Example 1)

Exercises for Alternate Example 1

In Exercises 1–4, what are the extreme values of $f(x)$ on $\left[-\dfrac{\pi}{2}, \dfrac{\pi}{2}\right]$?   In Exercises 5–8, what are the extreme values of $f(x)$ on $[-4, 4]$?

1. $f(x) = \cos 2x$

2. $f(x) = 3\cos 3x$

3. $f(x) = 1 - \cos 2x$

4. $f(x) = 1 - \sin 2x$

5. $f(x) = \dfrac{x^3}{2} + 1$

6. $f(x) = -e^{x+1}$

7. $f(x) = 2\ln(x + 5)$

8. $f(x) = \dfrac{3^x - 1}{2x}$

Alternate Example 3 **Finding Absolute Extrema**

Find the absolute maximum and minimum values of $f(x) = x^{4/5}$ on the interval $[-3, 3]$.

SOLUTION

Solve Graphically Figure 4.2 suggests that f has an absolute maximum value of about 2.5 at $x = 3$ and $x = -3$ and an absolute minimum value of 0 at $x = 0$.

Confirm Analytically We evaluate the function at the critical points and endpoints, and then take the largest and smallest of the resulting values.

The first derivative

$$f'(x) = \frac{4}{5}x^{-1/5} = \frac{4}{5\sqrt[5]{x}}$$

has no zero but is undefined at $x = 0$. The values of f at this one critical point and at the endpoints are

Critical point value: $f(0) = 0$

Endpoints: $f(-3) = \sqrt[5]{(-3)^4}$

$$f(3) = \sqrt[5]{(3)^4}$$

We can see from this list that the function's absolute maximum value is $\sqrt[5]{(-3)^4} \approx 2.41$, and occurs twice at the endpoint $x = 3$ and $x = -3$. The absolute minimum value is 0, and occurs at the interior point $x = 0$.

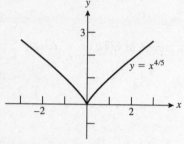

$y = x^{4/5}$

Figure 4.2 (Alternate Example 3)

Exercises for Alternate Example 3

In Exercises 9–14, find the absolute maximum and minimum values of $f(x)$ on the given interval.

9. $f(x) = 5x^{2/3}$ on $[-1, 1]$

10. $f(x) = -4x^{4/5}$ on $[-2, 2]$

11. $f(x) = \sin\frac{x}{2}$ on $[-\pi, \pi]$

12. $f(x) = \ln\sqrt{2x+1}$ on $[0, 10]$

13. $f(x) = x^{8/9}$ on $[-5, 5]$

14. $f(x) = xe^x$ on $[-2, 2]$

Alternate Example 4 **Finding Extreme Values**

Find the extreme values of $f(x) = \dfrac{1}{\sqrt{9 - x^2}}$.

SOLUTION

Solve Graphically Figure 4.3 suggests that f has an absolute minimum about 1/3 at $x = 0$. There also appear to be local maxima at $x = -3$ and $x = 3$. However, f is not defined at these points and there do not appear to be maxima anywhere else.

Confirm Analytically The function is defined only for $9 - x^2 > 0$, so its domain is the open interval $(-3, 3)$. The domain has no endpoints, so all the extreme values must occur at critical points. We rewrite the formula for f and $f'(x)$:

$$f(x) = \frac{1}{\sqrt{9 - x^2}}$$

$$= \left(9 - x^2\right)^{-\frac{1}{2}}$$

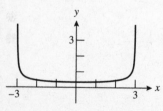

Figure 4.3 (Alternate Example 1)

Thus,

$$f'(x) = -\frac{1}{2}(-2x)\left(9 - x^2\right)^{3/2} \qquad \text{Use the chain rule to find the derivative.}$$

$$= \frac{x}{\sqrt{\left(9 - x^2\right)^3}}$$

To find critical points, set $f'(x) = 0$. (Note that $f'(x)$ has no undefined points in the open interval $(-3, 3)$.)

$$\frac{x}{\sqrt{\left(9 - x^2\right)^3}} = 0$$

$$x = 0$$

So, the only critical point in the domain $(-3, 3)$ is $x = 0$. The value

$$f(0) = \frac{1}{\sqrt{9 - 0^2}}$$

$$= \frac{1}{3}$$

is therefore, the sole candidate for an extreme value. To determine whether $\frac{1}{3}$ is an extreme value of f, we examine the formula

$$f(x) = \frac{1}{\sqrt{9 - x^2}}.$$

As x moves away from 0 on either side, the denominator gets smaller, the values of f increase, and the graph rises. We have a minimum value at $x = 0$, and the minimum is absolute.

The graph has no maxima, either local or absolute. This does not violate the Extreme Value Theorem because here f is defined on an open interval. To invoke the Extreme Value Theorem's guarantee of extreme points, the interval must be closed.

Exercises for Alternate Example 4

In Exercises 15–20, find the absolute maximum and minimum values of $f(x)$ on the function's domain.

15. $f(x) = \dfrac{-7}{\sqrt{1 - 4x^2}}$

16. $f(x) = \dfrac{5}{\sqrt{21 - x^2}}$

17. $f(x) = 2x^3 - 3x^2 - 12x + 8$

18. $f(x) = \dfrac{-2x}{x^2 - 1}$

19. $f(x) = \dfrac{11}{\sqrt{7 - 28x^2}}$

20. $f(x) = \sqrt{x^2 + 1}$

Alternate Example 5 **Finding Extreme Values**

Find the extreme values of

$$f(x) = \begin{cases} 2 - 3x^2 & x \le 1 \\ 2x - 3 & x > 1 \end{cases}$$

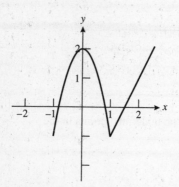

Figure 4.4 The function in Alternate Example 5.

SOLUTION

Solve Graphically The graph in Figure 4.4 suggests that $f'(0) = 0$ and that $f'(1)$ does not exist. There appears to be a local maximum value of 2 at $x = 0$ and a local minimum value of -1 at $x = 1$.

Confirm Analytically For $x \neq 1$, the derivative is

$$f'(x) = \begin{cases} \dfrac{d}{dx}(2 - 3x^2) & x < 1 \\[2mm] \dfrac{d}{dx}(2x - 3) & x > 1 \end{cases}$$

$$= \begin{cases} -6x & x < 1 \\ 2 & x > 1 \end{cases}$$

The only point where $f' = 0$ is $x = 0$. What happens at $x = 1$?

At $x = 1$, the right-hand and left-hand derivatives are respectively

$$\lim_{h \to 0^+} \frac{f(1 + h) - f(1)}{h} = \lim_{h \to 0^+} \frac{(2(1 + h) - 3) - (2(1) - 3)}{h}$$

$$= \lim_{h \to 0^+} \frac{2h}{h}$$

$$= 2$$

$$\lim_{h \to 0^-} \frac{f(1 + h) - f(1)}{h} = \lim_{h \to 0^+} \frac{2 - 3(1 + h)^2 - (2 - 3(1)^2)}{h}$$

$$= \lim_{h \to 0^+} \frac{2 - 3 - 6h - 3h^2 + 1}{h}$$

$$= \lim_{h \to 0^+} \frac{3h(-2 - h)}{h}$$

$$= \lim_{h \to 0^+} 3(-2 - h)$$

$$= -6$$

Since the derivatives differ, f has no derivative at $x = 1$, and 1 is a second critical point of f.

The domain $(-\infty, \infty)$ has no endpoints, so the only values of f that might be local extrema are those at the critical points:

$$f(0) = 2 \qquad \text{and} \quad f(1) = -1$$

From the formula for f, we see that the values of f immediately to either side of $x = 0$ is are less than 2, so 2 is a local maximum. Similarly, the values of f immediately to either side of $x = 1$ are greater than -1, so -1 is a local minimum.

Exercises for Alternate Example 5

In Exercises 21–26, find the extreme values of $f(x)$.

21. $f(x) = -x^{2/3}(x - 2)$

22. $f(x) = \begin{cases} 6 - x^2 & x \leq 2 \\ 3x - 4 & x > 2 \end{cases}$

23. $f(x) = \begin{cases} 5 - x^2 & x \leq 1 \\ 6x - 2 & x > 1 \end{cases}$

24. $f(x) = 2x\sqrt{16 - x^2}$

25. $f(x) = x^2\sqrt{x + 1}$

26. $f(x) = x^{1/3}(x^2 - 1)$

4.2 Mean Value Theorem

Alternate Example 1 Exploring the Mean Value Theorem

Show that $f(x) = 2x^2$ satisfies the hypotheses of the Mean Value Theorem on the interval $[-1, 2]$. Then find a solution c to the equation

$$f'(x) = \frac{f(b) - f(a)}{b - a}$$

on this interval.

SOLUTION

The function $f(x) = 2x^2$ is continuous on $[-1, 2]$ and differentiable on $(-1, 2)$. Since $f(-1) = 2$ and $f(2) = 8$, the Mean Value Theorem guarantees a point c in the interval $[1, 2]$ for which

$$\begin{aligned} f'(c) &= \frac{f(b) - f(a)}{b - a} \\ &= \frac{f(2) - f(-1)}{2 - (-1)} \\ &= \frac{8 - 2}{3} \\ &= 2 \end{aligned}$$

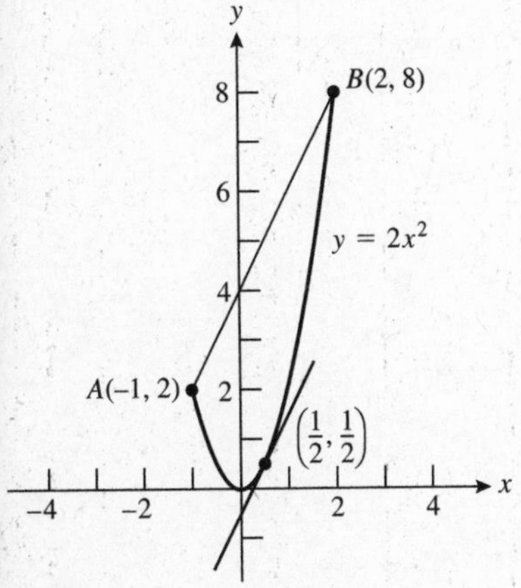

Figure 4.5 (Alternate Example 1)

Since $f'(x) = 4x$ and $f'(c) = 4c$, therefore,

$$\begin{aligned} 4c &= 2 \\ c &= \frac{2}{4} \\ &= \frac{1}{2} \end{aligned}$$

Interpret The tangent line to $f(x) = 2x^2$ at $x = \frac{1}{2}$ has a slope 2 and is parallel to the chord joining $A(-1, 2)$ and $B(2, 8)$ (Figure 4.5)

Exercises for Alternate Example 1

In Exercises 1–8, show that $f(x)$ satisfies the hypotheses of the Mean Value Theorem on the given interval. Then find a solution c to the equation $f'(x) = \dfrac{f(b) - f(a)}{b - a}$ on the given interval

1. $f(x) = x^2 - 3$ on $[1, 8]$

2. $f(x) = x^2 + 2x$ on $[3, 7]$

3. $f(x) = -3x^2 + 3$ on $[2, 5]$

4. $f(x) = x^2 + 4$ on $[2, 7]$

5. $f(x) = 2x^2 - 5x + 3$ on $[1, 5]$

6. $f(x) = \cos^{-1} x$ on $[-1, 1]$

7. $f(x) = 2\ln(x + 3)$ on $[-2, 0]$

8. $f(x) = -3x^2 + 8x - 2$ on $[2, 8]$

■

Alternate Example 6 Determining where Graphs Rise or Fall

Where is the function $f(x) = 3x^3 - 2x$ increasing and where is it decreasing ?

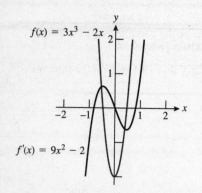

$f(x) = 3x^3 - 2x$

$f'(x) = 9x^2 - 2$

Figure 4.6 By comparing the graphs of $f(x) = 3x^3 - 2x$ and $f'(x) = 9x^2 - 2$, we can relate the increasing and decreasing behavior of f to the sign of f'.

SOLUTION

Solve Graphically The graph of $f(x)$ in Figure 4.6 suggests that f is increasing from $-\infty$ to the x-coordinate of the local maximum, decreasing between the two local extrema, and increasing again from the x-coordinate of the local minimum to ∞. This information is supported by the superimposed graph of

$$f'(x) = 9x^2 - 2.$$

Confirm Analytically The function is increasing where $f'(x) > 0$.

$$9x^2 - 2 > 0$$
$$9x^2 > 2$$
$$x^2 > \frac{2}{9}$$
$$x < -\sqrt{\frac{2}{9}} \text{ or } x > \sqrt{\frac{2}{9}}$$

The function is decreasing where $f'(x) < 0$.

$$9x^2 - 2 < 0$$
$$9x^2 < 2$$
$$x^2 < \frac{2}{9}$$
$$-\sqrt{\frac{2}{9}} < x < \sqrt{\frac{2}{9}}$$

In interval notation, $f(x)$ is increasing on $\left(-\infty, \dfrac{\sqrt{2}}{3}\right]$, decreasing on $\left[-\dfrac{\sqrt{2}}{3}, \dfrac{\sqrt{2}}{3}\right]$, and increasing on $\left[\dfrac{\sqrt{2}}{3}, \infty\right)$.

Exercises for Alternate Example 6

In Exercises 9–16, where is the function $f(x)$ increasing and where is it decreasing?

9. $f(x) = x^2 - 12x$

10. $f(x) = 2x^3 - 3x^2$

11. $f(x) = x\sqrt{16 - x^2}$

12. $f(x) = -2\cos(2x + \pi)$

13. $f(x) = -3x^2 - 5x$

14. $f(x) = xe^x$

15. $f(x) = 3x^3 - x$

16. $f(x) = \dfrac{(x-1)(x+2)}{x^2 + 4}$

Alternate Example 7 **Applying Corollary 3**

Find the function $f(x)$ whose derivative is $\cos x$ and whose graph passes through the point $\left(\dfrac{\pi}{2}, 7\right)$.

SOLUTION

Since f has the same derivative as $g(x) = \sin x$, by Corollary 3, we know that $f(x) = \sin x + C$ for some constant C. To identify C, we use the condition that the graph must pass through $\left(\dfrac{\pi}{2}, 7\right)$. This is equivalent to saying that

$$f\left(\frac{\pi}{2}\right) = 7$$

$$\sin\frac{\pi}{2} + C = 7$$

$$1 + C = 7$$

$$C = 6$$

The formula for f is $f(x) = \sin x + 6$.

Exercises for Alternate Example 7

In Exercises 17–22, find the function $f(x)$ whose derivative is $f'(x)$ and whose graph includes the given point A.

17. $f'(x) = 2x - 3; A(1, 2)$

18. $f'(x) = 6x^2 - 3; A(1, 0)$

19. $f'(x) = -\dfrac{2}{x^3};\ A(1, 4)$

20. $f'(x) = -2\cos x; A\left(\dfrac{\pi}{4}, -1\right)$

21. $f'(x) = -\dfrac{3}{2x+1};\ A(0,0)$

22. $f'(x) = \sin x - \cos x; A\left(\dfrac{\pi}{2}, 1\right)$

■

| **Alternate Example 8** | **Finding Velocity and Position** |

Find the velocity and position functions of a freely falling body on the Moon from a height of 0 meters under each of the following sets of conditions:

(a) The acceleration is 1.6 m/sec^2 and the body falls from rest.

(b) The acceleration is 1.6 m/sec^2 and the body is propelled downward with an initial velocity of 2 m/sec.

SOLUTION

(a) *Falling from Rest.* We measure distance fallen in meters and time in seconds, and assume that the body is released from rest at time $t = 0$.

Velocity: We know that the velocity $v(t)$ is an antiderivative of the constant function 1.6. We also know that $g(t) = 1.6t$ is an antiderivative of 1.6. Because functions with the same derivative differ by a constant (Corollary 3), we know that

$$v(t) = 1.6t + C$$

for some constant C. Since the body falls from rest, $v(0)$. Thus,

$$1.6(0) + C = 0 \text{ and } C = 0$$

The body's velocity function is $v(t) = 1.6t$.

Position: We know that the position $s(t)$ is an antiderivative of $v(t) = 1.6t$. We also know that $h(t) = 0.8t^2$ is an antiderivative of $v(t) = 1.6t$. Because functions with the same derivative differ by a constant,

$$s(t) = 0.8t^2 + C$$

for some constant C. Since $s(0) = 0$,

$$0.8(0)^2 + C = 0 \text{ and } C = 0$$

The body's position function is $s(t) = 0.8t^2$.

(b) *Propelled downward*. We measure distance fallen in meters and time in seconds, and assume that the body is propelled downward with velocity of 2 m/sec at time $t = 0$.

Velocity: The velocity function still has the form $1.6t + C$, but instead of being zero, the initial velocity (velocity at $t = 0$) is now 2 m/sec. thus,

$$1.6(0) + C = 2$$

$$C = 2$$

The body's velocity function is $v(t) = 1.6t + 2$

Position: We know that the position $s(t)$ is an antiderivative of $1.6t + 2$. We also know that $k(t) = 0.8t^2 + 2t$ is an antiderivative of $1.6t + 2$.

By Corollary 3,

$$s(t) = 0.8t^2 + 2t + C$$

for some constant C. Since $s(0) = 0$,

$$0.8(0^2) + 2(0) + C = 0$$

$$C = 0$$

The body's position function is $s(t) = 0.8t^2 + 2t$

Exercises for Alternate Example 8

Exercise 23–30 refer to the motion of a particle which travels with acceleration at time t given by $a(t)$, measured in m/sec^2, and whose velocity at time $t = 0$ is given by v_0, measured in m/sec. Find the velocity function of a particle with the following accelerations and initial velocities.

23. $a(t) = 9.8$ and $v_0 = 4$ **24.** $a(t) = 9.8$ and $v_0 = 9$ **25.** $a(t) = t$ and $v_0 = 4$ **26.** $a(t) = \sin t$ and $v_0 = 3$

27. $a(t) = -e^t$ and $v_0 = 7$ **28.** $a(t) = \dfrac{1}{t+1}$ and $v_0 = 0$ **29.** $a(t) = \sec t \tan t$ and $v_0 = 3$

30. $a(t) = \sec^2(t)$ and $v_0 = 6$

4.3 Connecting f' and f'' with the Graph of f

Alternate Example 2 **Determining Concavity**

Use the Concavity Test to determine the concavity of the given functions on the given intervals:

(a) $y = -6x^2$ on (4, 12)   **(b)** $y = 2 - 3\sin x$ on $(0, 2\pi)$

SOLUTION

(a) Since $y'' = -12$ is always negative, the graph of $y = -6x^2$ is concave down on any interval. In particular, it is concave down on (4, 12).

(b) Since $y'' = 3 \sin x$, the graph of y is concave up on $(0, \pi)$ where $y'' > 0$ and concave down on $(\pi, 2\pi)$ where $y'' < 0$.

Exercises for Alternate Example 2

In Exercises 1–6, use the Concavity Test to determine the concavity of the given functions on the given intervals.

1. (a) $y = -3x^2$ on $(-4, -12)$

   (b) $y = 3 - \sin x$ on $(0, 2\pi)$

2. (a) $y = 5x^2 + x$ on $(4, 12)$

   (b) $y = 5x - \cos x$ on $(\pi, 2\pi)$

3. (a) $y = -x^4 + 12x^3 - 12x + 24$ on $(0, 10)$

   (b) $y = 2 - 3\sin x$ on $(0, 2\pi)$

4. (a) $y = (-1/2)e^{-x^2}$ on $(0, 1)$

   (b) $y = (1/2)x^2 + \cos x$ on $(0, 2\pi)$

5. (a) $y = 2 + x^{1/5}$ on $(1, 4)$

   (b) $y = \sin x - \cos x$ on $(0, \pi)$

6. (a) $y = -x^{2/5}$ on $(-5, 0)$

   (b) $y = -4 - 3\cos x$ on $(0, 2\pi)$

Alternate Example 3   Finding Points of Inflection

Find all points of inflection of the graph of $y = -e^{-x^2}$.

SOLUTION

First we find the second derivative, recalling the Chain and Product Rules:

$$y = -e^{-x^2}$$

$$y' = -e^{-x^2}(-2x) \qquad \text{Chain rule}$$

$$= e^{-x^2}(2x)$$

$$y'' = e^{-x^2}(-2x)(2x) + (2)e^{-x^2} \qquad \text{Product rule}$$

$$= 2e^{-x^2}\left[(-2x)(x) + 1\right]$$

$$= 2e^{-x^2}\left(-2x^2 + 1\right)$$

The factor $2e^{-x^2}$ is always positive, while the factor $\left(-2x^2 + 1\right)$ changes sign at $-\dfrac{\sqrt{2}}{2}$ and at $\dfrac{\sqrt{2}}{2}$. (We obtain these values of x by letting $y'' = 0$.) Since y'' must also change sign at these two points, the points of inflection are $\left(-\dfrac{\sqrt{2}}{2}, -\dfrac{\sqrt{e}}{e}\right)$ and $\left(\dfrac{\sqrt{2}}{2}, -\dfrac{\sqrt{e}}{e}\right)$.

We confirm our solution graphically by observing the changes of curvature in Figure 4.7.

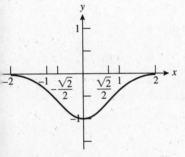

Figure 4.7 Graphical confirmation that the graph of $y = -e^{-x^2}$ has points of inflection at $x = -\dfrac{\sqrt{2}}{2}$ and at $x = \dfrac{\sqrt{2}}{2}$.

Exercises for Alternate Example 3

In Exercises 7–12, find all points of inflections of the graph of y.

7. $y = 4 + e^{-x^2}$

8. $y = 3 - 2e^{-x^2}$

9. $y = x\sqrt{16 - x^2}$

10. $y = \dfrac{x^2 - 1}{x^2 + 3x + 2}$

11. $y = \sin\left(2x + \dfrac{\pi}{2}\right)$ on $(-\pi, \pi)$

12. $y = -\tan^{-1}(2x)$

Alternate Example 7   Using the Second Derivative Test

Find the local extreme values of $f(x) = -x^3 + 48x - 11$.

SOLUTION

We have

$$f'(x) = -3x^2 + 48$$

$$= -3(x^2 - 16)$$

Letting $f'(x) = 0$, the critical points are

$$x = -4 \text{ and } x = 4$$

The second derivative is

$$f''(x) = -6x$$

Testing the critical points $x = \pm 4$ (there are no endpoints), we find

$$f''(-4) = +24 > 0$$

Thus f has a local minimum at $x = -4$

$$f''(-4) = -24 < 0$$

Therefore, f has a local maximum at $x = 4$.

Exercises for Alternate Example 7

In Exercises 13–18, find the local extreme values of y.

13. $f(x) = -2x^3 + 8x - 6$ **14.** $f(x) = x^3 - 3x - 7$ **15.** $f(x) = -x^3 + 3x + 4$ **16.** $f(x) = 2x^3 - 3x - 5$

17. $f(x) = x^2 e^{-x}$ **18.** $f(x) = -xe^{x^2}$

Alternate Example 8   **Using f' and f'' to Graph f**

Let $f'(x) = 4x^3 - 8x^2$.

(a) Identify where the extrema of f occur.

(b) Find the intervals on which f is increasing and the intervals on which f is decreasing.

(c) Find where the graph of f is concave up and where it is concave down.

(d) Sketch a possible graph of f.

SOLUTION

f is continuous since f' exists. The domain of f' is $(-\infty, \infty)$, so the domain of f is also $(-\infty, \infty)$. Thus, the critical points of f occur only at the zeros of f'. Since

$$f'(x) = 4x^3 - 8x^2$$
$$= 4x^2(x - 2),$$

the first derivative is zero at $x = 0$ and $x = 2$.

Intervals	$x < 0$	$0 < x < 2$	$2 < x$
Sign of f'	−	−	+
Behavior of f	Decreasing	Decreasing	Increasing

(a) Using the first derivative test and the table above, we see that there is no extremum at $x = 0$ and a local minimum at $x = 2$.

(b) Using the table above, we see that f is decreasing on $(-\infty, 2]$ and $[0, 2]$, and increasing on $[2, \infty)$.

(c) $f''(x) = 12x^2 - 16x = 4x(3x - 4)$ is zero at $x = 0$ and $x = \dfrac{4}{3}$.

Intervals	$x < 0$	$0 < x < \dfrac{4}{3}$	$\dfrac{4}{3} < x$
Sign of f''	+	−	+
Behavior of f	Concave up	Concave down	Concave up

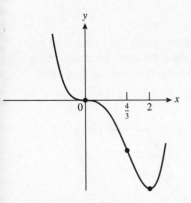

Figure 4.8 The graph for f has no extremum but has points of inflection where $x = 0$ and $x = 4/3$, and a local minimum where $x = 2$.

We see that f is concave up on the interval $(-\infty, 0)$ and $\left[4/3, \infty\right)$ and is concave down on $\left(0, 4/3\right)$.

(d) Summarizing the information in the tables above, we obtain

$x < 0$	$0 < x < \dfrac{4}{3}$	$\dfrac{4}{3} < x < 2$	$2 < x < \infty$
Decreasing	Decreasing	Decreasing	Increasing
Concave up	Concave down	Concave up	Concave up

Figure 4.8 shows possibility of the graph of f.

Exercises for Alternate Example 8

In Exercises 19–24, given $f'(x)$, **(a)** Identify where the extrema of f occur. **(b)** Find the intervals on which f is increasing and the intervals on which f is decreasing. **(c)** Find where the graph of f is concave up and where it is concave down. **(d)** Sketch a possible graph of f

19. $f'(x) = x^3 - 2x^2$ **20.** $f'(x) = -4x^3 - x^2$ **21.** $f'(x) = 5x^3 + x^2$ **22.** $f'(x) = (x+2)(x+3)^2$

23. $f'(x) = (x-1)(x+2)(x+3)$ **24.** $f'(x) = (x+1)(x+2)(x+3)^2$

4.4 Modeling and Optimization

Alternate Example 1   Using the Strategy

Find two numbers whose sum is 16 and their product is as large as possible.

SOLUTION

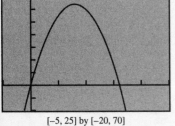

[−5, 25] by [−20, 70]

Figure 4.9 The graph of $f(x) = x(16 - x)$.

Model If one of the numbers is x, then the other is $(16 - x)$, and their product is $f(x) = x(16 - x)$.

Solve Graphically We can see from the graph of f in Figure 4.9 that there is a maximum. From what we know about parabolas, the maximum occurs at $x = 8$.

Interpret The two numbers we seek are $x = 8$ and $16 - x = 8$.

Exercises for Alternate Example 1

In Exercises 1–4, find two numbers whose sum is S and their product is as large as possible.

1. $S = 24$ **2.** $S = 28$ **3.** $S = 32$ **4.** $S = 36$

In Exercises 5–8, solve the problem analytically. Support your answer graphically.

5. Find the number in the interval $(0, 2)$ such that the sum of the number and its reciprocal is as small as possible.

6. Find the dimensions of the rectangle with the smallest perimeter whose area is 36 sq. in.

7. A rectangular plot of land is bounded on one side by a river and is fenced on the other three sides. If the total length of fencing is 400 ft, what is the maximum area enclosed, and what are the dimensions of the plot of land?

8. What is the area of the largest right triangle whose hypotenuse is 10, and what are the lengths of its legs?

Alternate Example 3 **Fabricating a Box**

An open-top box is to be made by cutting squares of sides length x from corners of a 14-by-18 inches sheet of tin and bending up the sides (Figure 4.10). How large should the square be to make the box hold as much as possible? What is the resulting maximum volume?

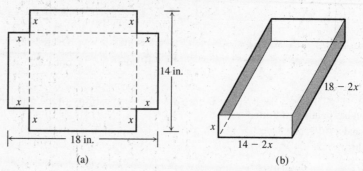

Figure 4.10 An open box made by cutting the corners from a piece of tin.

SOLUTION

Model The height of the box is x, and the other two dimensions are $(14 - 2x)$ and $(18 - 2x)$. Thus, the volume of the box is

$$V(x) = x(14 - 2x)(18 - 2x).$$

Solve Graphically Because $2x$ cannot exceed 14, we have $0 \le x \le 7$. Figure 4.11 suggests that the maximum value of V is about 300 and occurs at $x \approx 2.5$.

Confirm Analytically Expanding, we obtain $V(x) = 4x^3 - 64x^2 + 252x$. The first derivative of V is

$$V'(x) = 12x^2 - 128x + 252$$

Letting $V'(x) = 0$, we obtain the quadratic equation

$$12x^2 - 128x + 252 = 0 \quad \Rightarrow \quad 6x^2 - 64x + 126 = 0$$

The solutions of this equations are

$$c_1 = \frac{64 - \sqrt{4096 - 3024}}{12}$$

$$= 2.60$$

$$c_2 = \frac{64 + \sqrt{4096 - 3024}}{12}$$

$$= 8.06$$

Only $c_1 = 2.60$ is in the domain $[0, 7]$ of $V(x)$. The values of V at this one critical point and the two endpoints are

Critical point value: $V(c_1) = 292.86$

Endpoints: $V(0) = 0$ and $V(7) = 0$

Interpret Cut out squares that are about 2.60 inches on a side give the maximum volume of about 292.86 in^3.

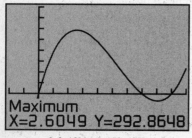

Maximum
X=2.6049 Y=292.8648

[-2, 10] by [-150, 400]

Figure 4.11 We chose the –150 in $-150 \le y \le 400$ so that the coordinates of the local maximum at the bottom of the screen would not interfere with the graph.

Exercises for Alternate Example 3

In each of Exercises 9–14, an open-top box is to be made by cutting squares of sides length x from corners of an m- by -n inch sheet of tin and bending up the sides. How large should the square be to make the box hold as much as possible? What is the resulting maximum volume?

9. $m = 5$ and $n = 8$ **10.** $m = 10$ and $n = 12.5$ **11.** $m = 15$ and $n = 24$ **12.** $m = 12$ and $n = 12$

13. $m = 4$ and $n = 5$ **14.** $m = 12$ and $n = 15$ ■

Alternate Example 5 **Maximizing Profit**

The function that represents the revenue for selling x thousand units is $r(x)$, and the function that represents the cost of producing the x thousand units is $c(x)$.
Suppose that $r(x) = 12x$ and $c(x) = x^3 - 8x^2 + 16x$, where x represents thousands of units. Is there a production level that maximizes profit? If so, what is it?

SOLUTION

If $p(x)$ represents the profit function, then $p(x) = r(x) - c(x)$. It has a maximum value at $p'(x) = 0$. Since $p'(x) = r'(x) - c'(x)$, $p'(x) = 0$ when $r'(x) = c'(x)$.

Notice that $r'(x) = 12$ and $c'(x) = 3x^2 - 16x + 16$.

$3x^2 - 16x + 16 = 12$ Set $r'(x) = c'(x)$ to find where the profit is maximum.

$3x^2 - 16x + 4 = 0$

The two solutions to the quadratic equation are

$$x_1 = \frac{16 - \sqrt{208}}{6}$$

$$\approx 0.26$$

$$x_2 = \frac{16 + \sqrt{208}}{6}$$

$$\approx 5.07$$

The production level for maximum profits is $x \approx 5.07$ thousand units. The graph in figure 4.12 verifies this.

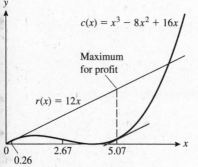

Figure 4.12 The cost and revenue curves for Alternate Example 5.

Exercises for Alternate Example 5

In each of Exercises 15–20, suppose that $r(x)$ and $c(x)$ are revenue and cost functions, respectively, where x represents thousands of units. Is there a production level that maximizes profit? If so, what is that number?

15. $r(x) = 11x$ and $c(x) = x^3 - 7x^2 + 14x$ **16.** $r(x) = 14x$ and $c(x) = x^3 - 6x^2 + 17x$ **17.** $r(x) = 12x$ and $c(x) = x^3 - 8x^2 + 15x$

18. $r(x) = 4\sqrt{6x + 2}$ and $c(x) = 2x - 8$ **19.** $r(x) = 5 - \frac{1}{x^2}$ and $c(x) = 2x - 1$ **20.** $r(x) = x^2 \ln x$ and $c(x) = \sqrt{x}$ ■

Alternate Example 6 **Minimizing Average Cost**

Suppose a cost function $c(x) = x^3 - 9x^2 + 15x$, where x represents thousands of units. Is there a production level that minimizes average cost? If so, what is it?

SOLUTION

We look for levels at which average cost equals marginal cost.

Marginal cost: $c'(x) = 3x^2 - 18x + 15$

Average cost: $\dfrac{c(x)}{x} = x^2 - 9x + 15$

$$3x^2 - 18x + 15 = x^2 - 9x + 15 \qquad \text{Marginal cost = Average cost}$$

$$2x^2 - 9x = 0$$

$$x(2x - 9) = 0$$

$$x = 0 \text{ or } x = 4.5$$

Since $x > 0$, the only production level that might minimize average cost is $x = 4.5$ thousand units.

We use second derivative test.

$$\frac{d}{dx}\left(\frac{c(x)}{x}\right) = 2x - 9$$

$$\frac{d^2}{dx^2}\left(\frac{c(x)}{x}\right) = 2 > 0$$

The second derivative is positive for all $x > 0$, so $x = 4.5$ gives an absolute minimum.

Exercises for Alternate Example 6

In Exercises 21–26, a cost function $c(x)$ is given, where x represents thousands of units. Is there a production level that minimizes average cost?

21. $c(x) = x^3 - 5x^2 + 9x$ **22.** $c(x) = x^3 - 7x^2 + 11x$ **23.** $c(x) = x^3 - 8x^2 + 12x$ **24.** $c(x) = x\sqrt{x^2 + 1}$

25. $c(x) = x^2 e^{-x}$ **26.** $c(x) = xe^{\sin x}$

4.5 Linearization and Newton's Method

Alternate Example 2   **Finding a Linearization**

Find the linearization of $f(x) = \sin x$ at $x = \dfrac{\pi}{3}$ and use it to approximate $\sin 1.25$ without a calculator. Then use a calculator to determine the accuracy of the approximation.

SOLUTION

Since $f\left(\dfrac{\pi}{3}\right) = \sin \dfrac{\pi}{3} = \dfrac{\sqrt{3}}{2}$, the point of tangency is $\left(\dfrac{\pi}{3}, \dfrac{\sqrt{3}}{2}\right)$. The slope of tangent

line is $f'\left(\dfrac{\pi}{3}\right) = \cos \dfrac{\pi}{3} = \dfrac{1}{2}$. Thus

$$L(x) = \frac{\sqrt{3}}{2} + \left(\frac{1}{2}\right)\left(x - \frac{\pi}{3}\right)$$

$$= \frac{\sqrt{3}}{2} + \frac{1}{2}x - \frac{\pi}{6}$$

To approximate sin (1.25), we use $x = 1.25$:

$$\sin 1.25 = f(1.25)$$
$$\approx L(1.25)$$
$$= \frac{\sqrt{3}}{2} + \frac{1}{2}(1.25) - \frac{\pi}{6}$$
$$= 0.866 + 0.625 - 0.524$$
$$= 0.967$$

The calculator gives sin $1.25 = 0.9489846194$, so the approximation error is

$$\left| 0.9489846194 - \left(\frac{\sqrt{3}}{2} + \frac{1.25}{2} - \frac{\pi}{6} \right) \right| = 0.0184 = 1.84 \times 10^{-2}.$$ We report that the error is

less than 10^{-1}.

Exercises for Alternate Example 2

In Exercises 1–6, find the linearization of $f(x)$ at $x = a$ and use it to approximate the value of the function at a specified point near a without a calculator. Compare your approximation with the true value of the function using a calculator.

1. $f(x) = \sin x$ at $x = \pi/6$, sin (0.5)   **2.** $f(x) = \sin x$ at, $x = \pi/3$, sin (1)   **3.** $f(x) = \sin x$ at $x = \pi/4$, sin (0.8)

4. $f(x) = \cos x$ at $x = \frac{\pi}{2}$, cos (1.6)   **5.** $f(x) = \cos x$ at $x = 0$, cos (0.1)   **6.** $f(x) = \cos x$ at $x = -\frac{2\pi}{3}$, cos (–2)

Alternate Example 5   Using Newton's Method

Use Newton's Method to solve $x^3 + 7x + 3 = 0$

SOLUTION

Let $f(x) = x^3 + 7x + 3$, then $f'(x) = 3x^2 + 7$ and

$$x_{n+1} = x_n - \frac{f(x_n)}{f'(x_n)}$$

$$= x_n - \frac{x_n^3 + 7x_n + 3}{3x_n^2 + 7}$$

The graph of f in Figure 4.13 suggests that $x_1 = -0.4$ is a good first approximation to the zero of f in the interval $-1 \leq x \leq 1$. Then,

$$x_1 = -0.4$$

$$x_2 = -0.4 - \frac{(-0.4)^3 + 7(-0.4) + 3}{3(-0.4)^2 + 7}$$

$$= -0.4181818182$$

$$x_3 = -0.4181283$$

$$x_4 = -0.4181282995$$

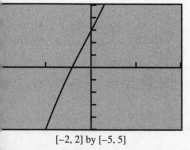

[–2, 2] by [–5, 5]

Figure 4.13 A calculator graph of $y = x^3 + 7x + 3$ suggests that –0.4 is a first good guess at the zero to begin Newton's Method.

The x_n for $n \geq 5$ all appear to equal to x_4 on the calculator we used for our computations. We conclude that the solution to the equation $x^3 + 7x + 3 = 0$ is about -0.4181282995.

Exercises for Alternate Example 5

In Exercises 7–12, use Newton's Method to give an estimate for a zero, which lies in the given interval, for the given equation. Make sure that your estimate agrees with the true zero through the first four decimal places.

7. $x^3 + 5x + 3 = 0$, [–2, 0]   **8.** $x^3 + 11x + 1 = 0$, [–1, 1]   **9.** $x^3 - 9x + 2 = 0$, [0, 2]

10. $x^3 - 3x - 1 = 0$, [1, 3]   **11.** $x^4 - 2x - 8 = 0$, [–2, 0]   **12.** $x^4 - 6 = 0$, [0, 2]

Alternate Example 6 **Finding the Differential *dy***

Find the differential dy and evaluate dy for the given values of x and dx.

(a) $y = x^3 + 29x$, $x = 2$, $dx = 0.02$

(b) $y = \cos 2x$, $x = 2\pi$, $dx = -0.01$

(c) $x - 2y = 3xy$, $x = 4$, $dx = 0.03$

SOLUTION

(a) $dy = (3x^2 + 29)dx$. When $x = 2$ and $dx = 0.02$, $dy = (3(2)^2 + 29)(0.02) = 0.82$

(b) $dy = (-2\sin 2x)dx$. When $x = 2\pi$ and $dx = -0.01$, $dy = (-2\sin 4\pi)(-0.01) = 0$

(c) We could solve explicitly for y before differentiating, but it is easier to use implicit differentiation:

$$d(x - 2y) = d(3xy)$$
$$dx - 2dy = 3ydx + 3xdy \qquad \text{Sum and Product Rules in differential form}$$
$$dx - 3ydx = 2dy + 3xdy$$
$$(1 - 3y)dx = (2 + 3x)dy$$
$$dy = \left(\frac{1 - 3y}{2 + 3x}\right)dx$$

When $x = 4$ in the original equation, $y = \dfrac{2}{7}$. Therefore,

$$dy = \left(\frac{1 - 3\left(\dfrac{2}{7}\right)}{2 + 3(4)}\right)(0.03)$$

$$= \frac{1}{98}(0.03)$$

$$\approx 0.0003$$

Exercises for Alternate Example 6

In Exercises 13–20, find the value of the differential dy for the given values of x and dx.

13. $y = x^2 + 2x$, $x = 2$, $dx = .01$ **14.** $y = 3x^3 + x$, $x = -1$, $dx = .02$ **15.** $y = 5\cos 3x$, $x = 5\pi$, $dx = 0.01$

16. $y = -\sin 6x$, $x = \pi$, $dx = 0.04$ **17.** $3x + y = xy$, $x = 2$, $dx = 0.01$ **18.** $-x + 2y = -xy$, $x = 3$, $dx = 0.02$

19. $y = x^2 e^{2x}$, $x = \ln 3$, $dx = 0.01$ **20.** $y = 2x\tan x$, $x = \pi/4$, $dx = 0.02$

Alternate Example 8 **Estimating Change with Differentials**

The length s of a side of a cube increases from $a = 5$ inches to $a = 5.01$ inches. Use dV to estimate the increase in the cube's volume, V. Compare this estimate with the true change ΔV and find the approximation error.

SOLUTION

Since $V = s^3$, the estimated increase is

$$dV = V'(a)\,ds = 3a^2 ds = 3(5)^2(0.01) = 0.75\ \text{in}^2$$

The true change is

$$\Delta V = (5.01)^3 - 5^3 = 0.751501.$$

The approximation error is

$$\Delta V - dV = 0.751501 - 0.75 = 0.001501.$$

Exercises for Alternate Example 8

In Exercises 21–24, the function f changes in value as x changes from a to $a + dx$. In each case, find **(a)** the true change Δf, **(b)** the estimated change df, and **(c)** the approximation error $|\Delta f - df|$.

21. $f(x) = 2x^3 - 3x^2 + 1$, $a = 2$, $dx = 0.1$

22. $f(x) = 2\cos(3x) + 2x$, $a = \dfrac{\pi}{3}$, $dx = 0.05$

23. $f(x) = \dfrac{e^x}{(1+x)^2}$, $a = 0$, $dx = 0.02$

24. $f(x) = x\sqrt{\ln(x) + 4}$, $a = 1$, $dx = 1$

Exercises 25 and 26 refer to the surface area S of a right circular cylinder of radius r and height h, which is given by $S = 2\pi r^2 + 2\pi rh$

25. Write a differential formula that estimates the change in surface area when the height changes from a to $a + dh$ and the radius is not changing.

26. Write a differential formula that estimates the change in surface area when the radius changes from b to $b + dh$ and the height is not changing. ∎

4.6   Related Rates

Alternate Example 1   **Finding Related Rate Equations**

Assume that the width a and the length b of a rectangle are functions of t and let A be the area of the rectangle. Find an equation that relates $\dfrac{dA}{dt}$, $\dfrac{da}{dt}$, and $\dfrac{db}{dt}$.

SOLUTION

We have the area of the rectangle as follows:

$A = ab$

Take derivative of both sides with respect to t.

$$\frac{dA}{dt} = \left(\frac{da}{dt}\right)b + \left(\frac{db}{dt}\right)a.$$

Exercises for Alternate Example 1

1. Assume that a height h and the base b of a triangle are functions of t, and let A be the area of the triangle.

Find an equation that relates $\dfrac{dA}{dt}$, $\dfrac{dh}{dt}$, and $\dfrac{db}{dt}$.

2. Assume that a height h and the sum of the bases m of a trapezoid are functions of t, and let A be the area of a trapezoid.

Find an equation that relates $\dfrac{dA}{dt}$, $\dfrac{dm}{dt}$, and $\dfrac{dh}{dt}$.

3. Assume that the height h and the base area A of a rectangular prism are functions of t, and let V be the volume of the prism.

Find an equation that relates $\dfrac{dA}{dt}$, $\dfrac{dh}{dt}$, and $\dfrac{dV}{dt}$.

4. Assume that the central angle θ and the radius r of a sector of a circle are functions of t, and let A be the area of the sector.

Find an equation that relates $\dfrac{dA}{dt}$, $\dfrac{d\theta}{dt}$, and $\dfrac{dr}{dt}$.

5. Assume that the semimajor and semiminor axes a and b of an ellipse are functions of t, and let K be the area of ellipse. If $K = \pi ab$,

find an equation that relates $\dfrac{dK}{dt}$, $\dfrac{da}{dt}$, and $\dfrac{db}{dt}$.

6. Assume that a height h and the base b of a parallelogram are functions of t, and let A be the area of the parallelogram.

Find an equation that relates $\dfrac{dA}{dt}$, $\dfrac{dh}{dt}$, and $\dfrac{db}{dt}$. ∎

Alternate Example 2   **A Rising Balloon**

A hot-air balloon rising straight up from a level field is tracked by a range finder 700 feet from the lift-off point. At the moment the range finder's elevation angle is $\pi/6$, the angle is increasing at the rate of 0.16 radian per minute. How fast is the balloon rising at that moment?

SOLUTION

We will carefully identify the six steps of the strategy in this first example.

Step 1: Let h be the height of the balloon and let θ be the elevation angle.

We seek: $\dfrac{dh}{dt}$

We know: $\dfrac{d\theta}{dt} = 0.16$ rad/min when $\theta = \dfrac{\pi}{6}$.

Step 2: We draw a picture (Figure 4.14). We label the horizontal distance "700 ft" because it does not change over time. We label the height "h" and the angle of elevation

"θ." Notice that we do not label the angle "$\dfrac{\pi}{6}$," as that would freeze the picture.

Step 3: We need a formula that relates h and θ. From trigonometry, we know that

$\dfrac{h}{700} = \tan\theta$, or simply $h = 700\tan\theta$.

Step 4: Differentiate implicitly:

$$\frac{d}{dt}(h) = \frac{d}{dt}(700\tan\theta)$$

$$\frac{dh}{dt} = 700\sec^2\theta\,\frac{d\theta}{dt}$$

Step 5: Let $\dfrac{d\theta}{dt} = 0.16$ and let $\theta = \dfrac{\pi}{6}$. (Note that it is now safe to specify our moment in time.)

$$\frac{dh}{dt} = 700\sec^2\left(\frac{\pi}{6}\right)(0.16)$$

$$= 700\left(\frac{2}{\sqrt{3}}\right)^2(0.16)$$

$$= 700\left(\frac{4}{3}\right)(0.16)$$

$$= 149.33$$

Step 6: At the moment in question, the balloon is rising at the rate of 149.33 ft/min.

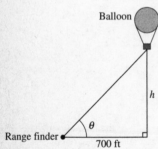

Figure 4.14 The picture shows how h and θ are related geometrically. We seek $\dfrac{dh}{dt}$ when $\theta = \dfrac{\pi}{6}$ and $\dfrac{d\theta}{dt} = 0.16$ rad/min.

Exercises for Alternate Example 2

In Exercises 7–12, a hot-air balloon rising straight up from a level field is tracked by a range finder x feet from the lift-off point. At the moment the range finder's elevation angle is θ, the rate of increase in angle θ is r radians per minute. How fast is the balloon rising at that moment?

7. $x = 550$, $\theta = \dfrac{3\pi}{10}$, $r = 0.14$ radian per minute

8. $x = 650$, $\theta = \dfrac{2\pi}{7}$, $r = 0.11$ radian per minute

9. $x = 750$, $\theta = \dfrac{\pi}{7}$, $r = 0.10$ radian per minute

10. $x = 800$, $\theta = \dfrac{\pi}{5}$, $r = 0.15$ radian per minute

11. $x = 700$, $\theta = \dfrac{4\pi}{9}$, $r = 0.14$ radian per minute

12. $x = 400$, $\theta = \dfrac{5\pi}{14}$, $r = 0.16$ radian per minute

Alternate Example 3   **A Highway Chase**

A police cruiser approaching a right-angled intersection from the north is chasing a speeding car that has turned the corner and is now moving straight east. When the cruiser is 0.70 mile north of the intersection and the car is 0.80 mile to the east, the police determine with radar that the distance between them and the car is increasing at 15 mph. If the cruiser is moving at 45 mph at the instant of measurement, what is the speed of the car?

SOLUTION

Let x be the distance of the speeding car from the intersection, let y be distance of the police cruiser from the intersection, and let z be the distance between the car and the

cruiser. Distances x and z are increasing, but distance y is decreasing; so $\dfrac{dy}{dt}$ is negative.

We seek: $\dfrac{dx}{dt}$

We know: $\dfrac{dz}{dt} = 15$ mph and $\dfrac{dy}{dt} = -45$ mph.

A sketch (Figure 4.15) shows that x, y, and z form three sides of a right triangle. We need to relate those three variables, so we use the Pythagorean Theorem:

$$x^2 + y^2 = z^2$$

Differentiating implicitly with respect to t, we get

$$2x\frac{dx}{dt} + 2y\frac{dy}{dt} = 2z\frac{dz}{dt},$$

which reduces to

$$x\frac{dx}{dt} + y\frac{dy}{dt} = z\frac{dz}{dt}.$$

Since $z^2 = x^2 + y^2$, we know that $z = \sqrt{x^2 + y^2}$.

We now substitute the numerical values for x, y, $\dfrac{dy}{dt}$, $\dfrac{dy}{dt}$, and z:

$$(0.80)\frac{dx}{dt} + (0.70)(-45) = \left(\sqrt{(0.80)^2 + (0.70)^2}\right)(15)$$

$$0.80\frac{dx}{dt} - 31.5 = 15.95$$

$$(0.80)\frac{dx}{dt} = 47.45$$

$$\frac{dx}{dt} = 59.31.$$

At the moment in question, the car's speed is about 59.31 mph.

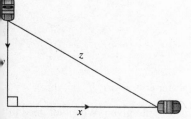

Figure 4.15 A sketch showing the variables in Alternate Example 3. We know $\dfrac{dy}{dt}$ and $\dfrac{dz}{dt}$. The variables x, y, and z are related by the Pythagorean Theorem $x^2 + y^2 = z^2$.

Exercises for Alternate Example 3

In each of Exercises 13–15, a police cruiser approaching a right-angled intersection from the north is chasing a speeding car that has turned the corner and is now moving straight east. When the cruiser is the given distance y miles north of the intersection and the car is the given distance x miles to the east, the police determine with radar that the distance between them and the car is increasing at the given speed s mph. If the cruiser is moving at the given speed v mph at the instant of measurement, what is the speed of the car?

13. $y = 1$ mi, $x = 0.7$ mi, $s = 16$ mph, $v = 58$ mph   **14.** $y = 0.9$ mi, $x = 0.8$ mi, $s = 15$ mph, $v = 54$ mph

15. $y = 0.9$ mi, $x = 0.6$ mi, $s = 16$ mph, $v = 55$ mph

In each of exercises 16–18, an airplane is flying at an altitude of 7 miles and passes directly over a radar antenna. Let s represent the distance between the radar antenna and the plane as a function of time t. When the plane is s_0 miles from the antenna, the radar detects that the distance s is changing at a rate of ds/dt miles per hour. Find the speed of the airplane when $s = s_0$ and ds/dt is the given value.

16. $s_0 = 15, \dfrac{ds}{dt} = 300$ **17.** $s_0 = 10, \dfrac{ds}{dt} = 250$ **18.** $s_0 = 12, \dfrac{ds}{dt} = 200$

Alternate Example 4   Filling a Conical Tank

Water runs into a conical tank at the rate of 12 ft³/min. The tank stands point down and has a height of 12 ft and a base radius of 9 ft. How fast is the water level rising when the water is 8 ft deep?

SOLUTION

Figure 4.16 shows a partially filled conical tank. The tank itself does not change over time; what we are interested in is the changing cone water inside the tank. Let V be the volume, r the radius, and h the height of the cone of water.

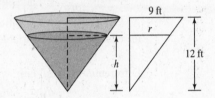

Figure 4.16 In Alternate Example 4, the cone of water is increasing in volume inside the reservoir. We know dV/dt and we seek dh/dt. Similar triangles enable us to relate V directly to h.

We seek: $\dfrac{dh}{dt}$

We know: $\dfrac{dV}{dt} = 12$ ft³/ min

We need to relate V and h. The volume of the cone of water is $V = \dfrac{1}{3}\pi r^2 h$, but this formula also involves the variable r, whose rate of change is not given. We either need to find $\dfrac{dr}{dt}$ or eliminate r from the equation, which we can do by using the similar triangles in Figure 4.15 to relate r and h:

$$\frac{r}{h} = \frac{9}{12}$$

or simplify

$$\frac{r}{h} = \frac{3}{4}$$

$$r = \left(\frac{3}{4}\right)h$$

Therefore,

$$V = \frac{1}{3}\pi\left(\frac{3h}{4}\right)^2 h$$

$$= \frac{3}{16}\pi h^3$$

Differentiate with respect to t:

$$\frac{dV}{dt} = \frac{9}{16}\pi h^2 \left(\frac{dh}{dt}\right)$$

Let $h = 8$ and $\frac{dV}{dt} = 12$; then solve for $\frac{dh}{dt}$:

$$12 = \frac{9}{16}\pi(8^2)\left(\frac{dh}{dt}\right)$$

$$9\pi(64)\left(\frac{dh}{dt}\right) = 192$$

$$\frac{dh}{dt} \approx 0.106$$

At the moment in question, the water level is rising at about 0.11 ft/min.

Exercises for Alternate Example 4

In each of Exercises 19–21, water runs into a conical tank at a rate of $\frac{dV}{dt}$. The tank stands point down and has a given height h ft and a given base radius r. How fast is the water level rising when the water is at the given depth d?

19. $\frac{dV}{dt} = 15$ ft³/min, $h = 14$ ft, $r = 12$ ft, $d = 8$ ft

20. $\frac{dV}{dt} = 16$ ft³/min, $h = 18$ ft, $r = 16$ ft, $d = 10$ ft

21. $\frac{dV}{dt} = 16$ ft³/min, $h = 20$ ft, $r = 16$ ft, $d = 12$ ft

In each of exercises 22–24, water flows out of a conical tank at a rate of $\frac{dV}{dt}$ ft³/min. The tank stands point down and has a given height h ft and a given base radius r. How fast is the radius of the surface of the water decreasing when the water is at the given depth d?

22. $\frac{dr}{dt} = 18$ ft³/min, $h = 22$ ft, $r = 18$ ft, $d = 14$ ft

23. $\frac{dr}{dt} = 22$ ft³/min, $h = 24$ ft, $r = 18$ ft, $d = 16$ ft

24. $\frac{dr}{dt} = 25$ ft³/min, $h = 28$ ft, $r = 20$ ft, $d = 20$ ft

Chapter 5

The Definite Integral

5.1 Estimating with Finite Sums

A particle starts at $x = 0$ and moves along the x-axis with velocity $v(t) = 3t^2$ for time $t \geq 0$. Where is the particle at $t = 6$?

SOLUTION

We graph v and partition the time interval [0, 6] into subintervals of length Δt. (Figure 5.1 shows twelve subintervals of length $\dfrac{6}{12} = \dfrac{1}{2}$ each.)

Notice that the region under the curve is partitioned into thin strips with bases of length 1/2 and curved tops that slope upward from left to right. You might not know how to find the area of such a strip, but you can get a good approximation of it by finding the area of a suitable rectangle. In Figure 5.2, we use the rectangle whose height is the y-coordinate of the function at the midpoint of its base. The area of this narrow rectangle approximates the distance traveled over the time subinterval. Adding all the areas (distances) gives an approximation of the total area under the curve (total distance traveled) from $t = 0$ to $t = 6$ (Figure 5.3).

Computing this sum of areas is straightforward. Each rectangle has a base of length = 1/2, while the height of each rectangle can be found by evaluating the function at the midpoint of the subinterval. Table 5.1 shows the computations for the first four rectangles.

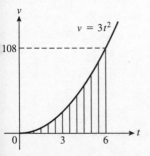

Figure 5.1 The region under the parabola $v = 3t^2$ from $t = 0$ to $t = 6$ partitioned into 12 thin strips, each with the base $\Delta t = 1/2$. The strips have curved top.

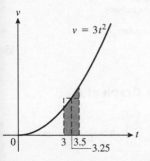

Figure 5.2 The area of the shaded region is approximated by the areas of the rectangle whose height is the function value at the midpoint of the interval.

Table 5.1

Subinterval	$\left[0, \dfrac{1}{2}\right]$	$\left[\dfrac{1}{2}, 1\right]$	$\left[1, \dfrac{3}{2}\right]$	$\left[\dfrac{3}{2}, 2\right]$
Midpoint m_i	$\dfrac{1}{4}$	$\dfrac{3}{4}$	$\dfrac{5}{4}$	$\dfrac{7}{4}$
Height = $3(m_i)^2$	$\dfrac{3}{16}$	$\dfrac{27}{16}$	$\dfrac{75}{16}$	$\dfrac{147}{16}$
Area = $\dfrac{3}{2}(m_i)^2$	$\dfrac{3}{32}$	$\dfrac{27}{32}$	$\dfrac{75}{32}$	$\dfrac{147}{32}$

Continuing in this manner, we derive the area $\frac{3}{2}(m_i)^2$ for each of the twelve subintervals and add them:

$$\frac{3}{32}+\frac{27}{32}+\frac{75}{32}+\frac{147}{32}+\frac{243}{32}+\frac{363}{32}+\frac{507}{32}$$

$$+\frac{675}{32}+\frac{867}{32}+\frac{1083}{32}+\frac{1323}{32}+\frac{1587}{32}=215.63$$

Since this number approximates the area and hence the total distance traveled by the particle, we conclude that the particle has moved approximately 216 units in 6 seconds. If it starts at $x = 0$, then it is very close to $x = 216$ when $t = 6$.

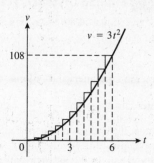

Figure 5.3 These rectangles have approximately the same areas as the strips in Figure 5.1. Each rectangle has height $3m_i^2$, where m_i is the midpoint of its base.

Exercises for Alternate Example 1

In each of Exercises 1–8, a particle starts at $x = 0$ and moves along the x-axis with velocity $v(t)$ for time $t \geq 0$. Where is the particle at t? Approximate the area under the curve using the given number of rectangles of equal width and heights determined by the midpoints of the intervals.

1. $v(t) = 2$, $t = 6$; 3 rectangles

2. $v(t) = -3$, $t = 15$; 5 rectangles

3. $v(t) = 3t$, $t = 5$; 10 rectangles

4. $v(t) = 3 + t$, $t = 6$; 12 rectangles

5. $v(t) = 4t^2$, $t = 9$; 6 rectangles

6. $v(t) = 5t^2$, $t = 6$; 12 rectangles

7. $v(t) = 6t^2 + 1$, $t = 3$; 12 rectangles

8. $v(t) = 4t^2 + t + 2$, $t = 4$; 8 rectangles

| **Alternate Example 2** | **Estimating Area Under the Graph of a Nonnegative Function** |

Figure 5.4 shows the graph of $f(x) = x \sin x$ on the interval $[0, 3]$. Estimate the area under the curve from $x = 0$ to $x = 3$.

SOLUTION

We use the Rectangular Approximation Method (RAM) program on a graphing calculator to get the numbers in this table.

n	LRAM$_n$	MRAM$_n$	RRAM$_n$
5	2.89876	3.15393	3.15278
10	3.02635	3.12173	3.15336
25	3.08230	3.11280	3.13310
50	3.09755	3.11152	3.12295
100	3.10453	3.11120	3.11724
1000	3.11046	3.11110	3.11173

[0, 5] by [0, 3]

Figure 5.4 The graph of $y = x \sin x$ over the interval $[0, 5]$.

It is not necessary to compute all three sums each time just to approximate the area, but we wanted to show again how all three sums approach the same number. With 1000 subintervals, all three agree in the first three digits. (The exact area is $-3\cos 3 + \sin 3$ which is 3.111097498 to ten digits.)

Exercises for Alternate Example 2

In Exercises 9–14, use RAM to estimate the area of the region enclosed between the graph of $f(x)$ and the x-axis for $a \le x \le b$.

9. $f(x) = -x^2 + 3x + 1$, $a = 0$ and $b = 1$

10. $f(x) = \dfrac{2}{2x+3}$, $a = 1$ and $b = 7$

11. $f(x) = x\cos^2 x$, $a = 0$ and $b = 1$

12. $f(x) = xe^{2x^2+1}$, $a = 0$ and $b = 2$

13. $f(x) = 1 + x\sin x$, $a = 0$ and $b = 3$

14. $f(x) = \ln(x)$, $a = 1$ and $b = 1000$

Alternate Example 4	**Computing Cardiac Output from Dye Concentration**

The data in Table 5.2 and Figure 5.5(a) show the response of a patient to an injection of 5 mg of dye. Estimate the cardiac output of the patient whose data appear below.

SOLUTION

The graph shows dye concentration (measured in milligrams of dye per liter of blood) as a function of time (in seconds). To find the cardiac output (measured in liters of blood per second), we divide the number of milligrams of dye by the area under the dye concentration curve.

We cannot use the RAM program because there is no formula for the function. We can draw the MRAM rectangles and estimate their heights from the graph. In Figure 5.5b, each rectangle has a base 2 units long and a height $f(m_i)$ equal to the height of the curve above the midpoint of the base.

The area of each rectangle, then, is $f(m_i)$ times 2, and the sum of the rectangular areas is the MRAM estimate for the area under the curve:

$$\text{Area} \approx f(1) \cdot 2 + f(3) \cdot 2 + f(5) \cdot 2 + \cdots f(19) \cdot 2$$
$$\approx 2 \cdot (0.1 + 1.4 + 4.5 + 8.6 + 9.5 + 7.6 + 4.9 + 3.1 + 1.7 + 0.5)$$
$$= 83.8$$

Dividing 5 mg by this figure gives an estimate for cardiac output in liters per second. Multiplying by 60 converts the estimate to liters per minute:

$$\frac{5 \text{ mg}}{83.8 \text{ mg} \cdot \text{sec/L}} \cdot \frac{60 \text{ sec}}{1 \text{ min}} \approx 3.58 \text{ L/min}$$

So the heart is pumping at approximately 3.58 liters per minute.

Table 5.2

Seconds after injection	Dye Concentration (adjusted for recirculation)
t	c
0	0.0
2	0.4
4	2.8
6	6.5
8	9.8
10	8.9
12	6.1
14	4.0
16	2.3
18	1.1
20	0.0

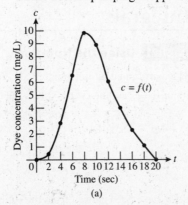
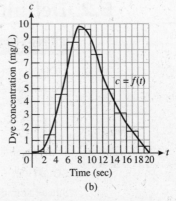

Figure 5.5 (a) The dye concentration in Alternate Example 4, plotted and fitted with a smooth curve. (b) The region under the curve is approximated with rectangles.

Exercises for Alternate Example 4

For Exercises 15 and 16, the tables give time after injection (t) and dye concentration $c(t)$ for a dye-concentration cardiac-output determination like the one in Alternate Example 4. Use rectangles to estimate the area under the dye concentration curve, and then estimate the patient's cardiac output.

15. The amount of dye injected in this patient was 4.8 mg.

t	$c(t)$
0	0
2	0.77
4	2.69
6	4.84
8	6.19
10	6.13
12	4.47
14	2.75
16	1.15
18	0.3
20	0

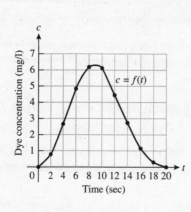

16. The amount of dye injected in this patient was 5.2 mg.

t	$c(t)$
0	0
2	0.82
4	2.73
6	4.96
8	6.54
10	6.22
12	5.26
14	2.75
16	1.3
18	0.4
20	0

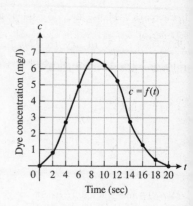

For Exercises 17–20, refer to the data in the table below. Use the information to estimate how far an object, whose velocity is given at various times, has traveled over the one hour interval, using n subintervals and the left-hand endpoint or right-hand endpoint as specified.

Time (min)	Velocity (ft/min)	Time (min)	Velocity (ft/min)
0	0	35	8.9
5	5.3	40	9.9
10	9.4	45	11.4
15	11.9	50	14.0
20	13.2	55	16.8
25	9.3	60	20.2
30	6.2		

17. $n = 12$, left-hand endpoints

18. $n = 12$, right-hand endpoints

19. $n = 6$, left-hand endpoints

20. $n = 6$, right-hand endpoints

5.2 Definite Integrals

Alternate Example 1 Using the Notation

The interval $[-2, 4]$ is partitioned into n subintervals of equal length $\Delta x = 6/n$. Let m_k denote the midpoint of the kth subinterval. Express the limit

$$\lim_{n \to \infty} \sum_{k=1}^{n} (6(m_k)^2 - 4m_k + 7)\Delta x$$

as an integral.

SOLUTION

Since the midpoints m_i have been chosen from the subintervals of the partition, this expression is indeed a limit of Riemann sums. (The points chosen did not have to be midpoints; they could have been chosen from the subintervals in any arbitrary fashion.)

The function being integrated is $f(x) = 6x^2 - 4x + 7$ over the interval $[-2, 4]$. Therefore,

$$\lim_{n \to \infty} \sum_{k=1}^{n} (6(m_k)^2 - 4m_k + 7)\Delta x = \int_{-2}^{4} (6x^2 - 4x + 7)dx$$

Exercises for Alternate Example 1

In Exercises 1–8, the interval $[-3, 3]$ is partitioned into n subintervals of equal length $\Delta x = 6/n$. Let m_k denote the midpoint of the kth subinterval. Express the limit $g(x)$ as an integral.

1. $g(x) = \lim\limits_{n \to \infty} \sum\limits_{k=1}^{n} ((m_k)^4 - (m_k)^3 + 4m_k)\Delta x$

2. $g(x) = \lim\limits_{n \to \infty} \sum\limits_{k=1}^{n} (-4(m_k)^2 + 3m_k - 8)\Delta x$

3. $g(x) = \lim\limits_{n \to \infty} \sum\limits_{k=1}^{n} \dfrac{4(m_k)^2 - m_k + 24}{(m_k)^2 + 1}\Delta x$

4. $g(x) = \lim\limits_{n \to \infty} \sum\limits_{k=1}^{n} (\sin^2(2m_k) + m_k)\Delta x$

5. $g(x) = \lim\limits_{n \to \infty} \sum\limits_{k=1}^{n} \sqrt{2m_k - 10}\,\Delta x$

6. $g(x) = \lim\limits_{n \to \infty} \sum\limits_{k=1}^{n} (m_k)^2 e^{2m_k}\Delta x$

7. $g(x) = \lim\limits_{n \to \infty} \sum\limits_{k=1}^{n} \ln(2m_k + 10)\Delta x$

8. $g(x) = \lim\limits_{n \to \infty} \sum\limits_{k=1}^{n} 2^{-m_k}\Delta x$

Alternate Example 2 Revisiting Area Under a Curve

Evaluate the integral $\displaystyle\int_{-4}^{4} \sqrt{16 - x^2}\,dx$.

SOLUTION

We recognize $f(x) = \sqrt{16 - x^2}$ as a function whose graph is a semicircle of radius 4 centered at the origin (Figure 5.6). The area between the semicircle and the x-axis from -4 to 4 can be computed using the geometry formula

$$\text{Area} = \frac{1}{2}\pi\,^2$$

$$= \frac{1}{2}\pi(4)^2$$

$$= 8\pi$$

Because the area is also the value of the integral of f from -4 to 4,

$$\int_{-4}^{4} \sqrt{16 - x^2}\,dx = 8\pi.$$

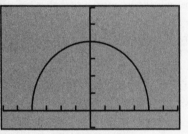

[−6, 6] by [−1, 6]

Figure 5.6 A square viewing window on $y = \sqrt{16 - x^2}$. The graph is a semicircle because $y = \sqrt{16 - x^2}$ is the same as $y^2 = 16 - x^2$ or $x^2 + y^2 = 16$, where $y \geq 0$.

Exercises for Alternate Example 2

In Exercises 9–16, use the graph of the integrand and areas to evaluate each integral.

9. $\displaystyle\int_{-1}^{1} \sqrt{1 - x^2}\,dx$

10. $\displaystyle\int_{2}^{10} \pi\,dx$

11. $\displaystyle\int_{1}^{4} |x - 3|\,dx$

12. $\displaystyle\int_{-2}^{3} |x + 1|\,dx$

13. $\displaystyle\int_{-3}^{0} (-2x + 3)\,dx$

14. $\displaystyle\int_{-2}^{2} (-|x| + 4)\,dx$

15. $\displaystyle\int_{-12}^{12} (\sqrt{144 - x^2} + 1)\,dx$

16. $\displaystyle\int_{-4}^{4} (|x| + 10)\,dx$

Alternate Example 3 **Revisiting The Train Problem**

A train moves along a track at a steady 60 miles per hour from 6:00 A.M. to 11:00 A.M. Express its total distance as an integral. Evaluate the integral using Theorem 2 (Integral of a Constant).

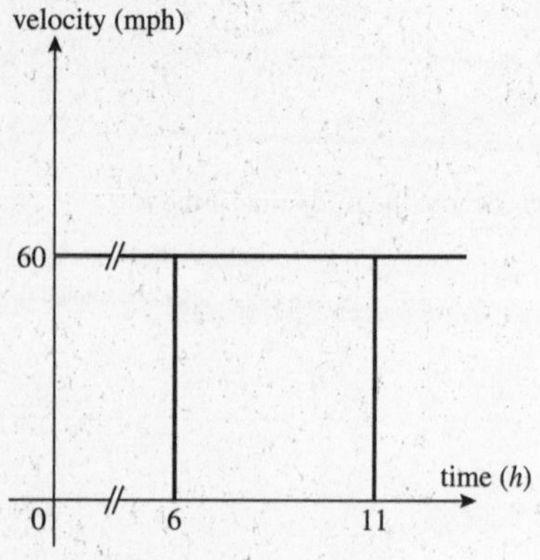

SOLUTION

If $f(x) = c$ (c a constant) on the interval $[a, b]$, then $\displaystyle\int_a^b f(x)\,dx = \int_a^b c\,dx = c(b - a)$

$$\text{Distance traveled} = \int_6^{11} 60\,dt$$
$$= 60(11 - 6)$$
$$= 300$$

velocity (mph)

60

time (h)

0   6   11

Figure 5.7 The area of the rectangle is a special case of Theorem 2.

Since 60 is measured in miles/hour and $(11 - 6)$ is measured in hours, the 300 is measured in miles. The train traveled 300 miles. Figure 5.7 demonstrates this result.

Exercises for Alternate Example 3

In Exercises 17–24, express the desired quantity as a definite integral and evaluate the integral using Theorem 2 (The Integral of a Constant).

17. Find the distance traveled by an ant crawling at 12 inches per hour from 10:00 am to 11:20 am.

18. A bank account has a daily withdrawal limit of $200. Find the total amount withdrawn in the month of May if the maximum is taken out daily.

19. Water flows through a drainpipe at a rate of 6 gallons every fifteen minutes. Find how much water goes through the pipe in 2 hours.

20. An internet connection operates at 3 megabytes of information per second. How many megabytes are communicated after 15 minutes?

21. A waste water treatment plant produces 10,000 gallons of effluent on a daily basis. How many gallons of effluent are produced in a week?

22. A keg dispenses beer at a rate of one pint every minute. Find how many quarts are dispensed in one-half hour.

23. If the snow is falling one morning at a rate of 1.2 inches every hour, how much snow falls between 8:12 am and 10:27 am?

24. A dishwasher can wash 20 plates in five minutes. How many plates does he wash between 5:00 pm and 6:20 pm?

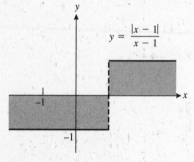

Figure 5.8 A discontinuous integrable function:
$$\int_0^5 \frac{|x - 1|}{x - 1}\,dx =$$
$-(\text{area below } x\text{-axis}) + (\text{area above } x\text{-axis}).$

Alternate Example 5 **Integrating a Discontinuous Function**

Find $\displaystyle\int_0^5 \frac{|x - 1|}{x - 1}\,dx$.

SOLUTION

This function has a discontinuity at $x = 1$, where the graph jumps from $y = -1$ to $y = 1$. The graph, however, determines two rectangles, one below the x-axis and one above the x-axis (Figure 5.8).

Using the idea of net area, we have

$$\int_0^5 \frac{|x - 1|}{x - 1}\,dx = -1 + 4$$

$$= 3$$

Exercises for Alternate Example 5

In Exercises 25–30, (a) find the points of discontinuity of the integrand on the interval of integration, and (b) use area to evaluate the integral.

25. $\displaystyle\int_{-2}^{3} \frac{|x+1|}{x+1}\, dx$
  26. $\displaystyle\int_{-3}^{2} \frac{4x^2-9}{2x-3}\, dx$
  27. $\displaystyle\int_{-2}^{2} \frac{\sqrt{4x^2-x^4}}{|x|}\, dx$
  28. $\displaystyle\int_{-1}^{5} \frac{|3x+1|}{3x+1}\, dx$
  29. $\displaystyle\int_{-2}^{3} \left(\frac{16-x^2}{x+4}\right) dx$

30. $\displaystyle\int_{-1}^{3} \left(\frac{2-2x}{|x-1|}+1\right) dx$

■

5.3 Definite Integrals and Antiderivatives

Alternate Example 1 Using the Rules for Definite Integrals

Suppose

$$\int_{-4}^{3} f(x)\, dx = 9, \quad \int_{3}^{5} f(x)\, dx = -11, \quad \text{and} \quad \int_{-4}^{3} h(x)\, dx = 14.$$

Find each of the following integrals, if possible:

(a) $\displaystyle\int_{5}^{3} f(x)\, dx$
  (b) $\displaystyle\int_{-4}^{5} f(x)\, dx$
  (c) $\displaystyle\int_{-4}^{3} \left[3f(x)-4h(x)\right] dx$

(d) $\displaystyle\int_{3}^{4} f(x)\, dx$
  (e) $\displaystyle\int_{-8}^{6} h(x)\, dx$
  (f) $\displaystyle\int_{-3}^{5} \left[f(x)+h(x)\right] dx$

SOLUTION

(a) $\displaystyle\int_{5}^{3} f(x)\, dx = -\int_{3}^{5} f(x)\, dx$

$$= -(-11)$$
$$= 11$$

(b) $\displaystyle\int_{-4}^{5} f(x)\, dx = \int_{3}^{5} f(x)\, dx + \int_{-4}^{3} f(x)\, dx$

$$= -11 + 9$$
$$= -2$$

(c) $\displaystyle\int_{-4}^{3} \left[3f(x)-4h(x)\right] dx = \int_{-4}^{3} 3f(x)\, dx + \int_{-4}^{3} -4h(x)\, dx$

$$= 3\int_{-4}^{3} f(x)\, dx - 4\int_{-4}^{3} h(x)\, dx$$

$$= 3(9) - 4(14)$$
$$= 27 - 56$$
$$= -29$$

(d) Not enough information is given. (We cannot assume, for example, that integrating over half the interval would give half the integral.)

(e) Not enough information given. (We have no information about the function h outside the interval $[-4, 3]$.)

(f) Not enough information given (same reason as in (e)).

Exercises for Alternate Example 1

In Exercises 1–6, given $\displaystyle\int_{-5}^{5} f(x)\,dx = 14$, $\displaystyle\int_{5}^{8} f(x)\,dx = -17$, and $\displaystyle\int_{-5}^{5} h(x)\,dx = 24$, find each integral if possible.

1. $\displaystyle\int_{5}^{-5} f(x)\,dx$

2. $\displaystyle\int_{5}^{-5} h(x)\,dx$

3. $\displaystyle\int_{8}^{5} -f(x)\,dx$

4. $\displaystyle\int_{0}^{5} h(x)\,dx$

5. $\displaystyle\int_{-5}^{5} \left[3f(x) - 7h(x)\right] dx$

6. $\displaystyle\int_{5}^{8} \left[4f(x) + 7h(x)\right] dx$

Alternate Example 2 **Finding Bounds for an Integral**

Show that the value of $\displaystyle\int_{0}^{3} \sqrt{1 + 2\sin x}\ dx$ is less than $\dfrac{11}{2}$.

SOLUTION

The Max-Min Inequality for definite integrals (Rule 6) says

that $\min f \cdot (b - a)$ is a lower bound for the value of $\displaystyle\int_{a}^{b} f(x)\,dx$ and that $\max f \cdot (b - a)$ is

an upper bound. The maximum value of $\sqrt{1 + 2\sin x}$ on $[0, 3]$ is $\sqrt{3}$, so

$$\int_{0}^{3} \sqrt{1 + 2\sin x}\ dx \le \sqrt{3}(3 - 0) = 3\sqrt{3}$$

Since $\displaystyle\int_{0}^{3} \sqrt{1 + 2\sin x}\ dx$ is bounded above by $3\sqrt{3}$ (which is 5.196152 ...), it is less than 11/2.

Exercises for Alternate Example 2

In Exercises 7–12, show that the value of each integral is less than the indicated value m.

7. $\displaystyle\int_{\pi/4}^{\pi/2} (\sin x - \cos x)\,dx$, $m = \dfrac{\pi}{4}$

8. $\displaystyle\int_{-2}^{2} e^{-x}\,dx$, $m = 4\pi^2$

9. $\displaystyle\int_{2}^{6} \sqrt{4 + \cos x}\,dx$, $m = 32$

10. $\displaystyle\int_{1}^{4} \ln x\,dx$, $m = 6$

11. $\displaystyle\int_{0}^{6} \sqrt{6 - 5\sin x}\ dx$, $m = 20$

12. $\displaystyle\int_{0.01}^{0.02} \dfrac{1}{x^2}\,dx$, $m = 100$

Alternate Example 3 **Applying the Definition**

Find the average value of $f(x) = 6 - x^2$ on $[0, 5]$. Where does f take on this value in the given interval?

SOLUTION

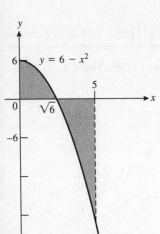

Figure 5.9   The rectangle with base [0, 5] and with height equal to –2.33 (the average value of the function $f(x) = 6 - x^2$) has area equal to the net area between f and the x-axis from 0 to 5.

$$av(f) = \frac{1}{b-a} \int_a^b f(x)\,dx$$

$$= \frac{1}{5-0} \int_0^5 \left(6 - x^2\right) dx$$

$$= \frac{1}{5-0}(-11.667) \qquad \text{Using NINT}$$

$$= -2.33$$

The average value of $f(x) = 6 - x^2$ over the interval [0, 5] is –2.33. The function assumes this value when $6 - x^2 = -2.33$ or $x = \pm 2.89$. Since 2.89 lies in the interval [0, 5], the function does assume its average value in the given interval (see Figure 5.9).

Exercises for Alternate Example 3

In Exercises 13–18, find the average value of $f(x)$ on $[a, b]$. Find the point c on the interval where $f(x)$ assumes its average value.

13. $f(x) = 3$ on [0, 3]   **14.** $f(x) = 2 - 3x$ on [0, 4]   **15.** $f(x) = 11 + 5x$ on [0, 5]

16. $f(x) = \cos x$ on $[0, \pi]$ **17.** $f(x) = 4 + 5x^2$ on [0, 6]   **18.** $f(x) = -3 + 4x^2$ on [0, 5]

Alternate Example 4   **Finding an Integral Using Antiderivatives**

Find $\displaystyle\int_{\pi/2}^{3\pi/2} \cos x\,dx$ using the formula $\displaystyle\int_a^x f(t)\,dt = F(x) - F(a)$.

SOLUTION

Since $F(x) = \sin x$ is an antiderivative of $\cos x$, we have

$$\int_{\pi/2}^{3\pi/2} \cos x\,dx = \sin\left(\frac{3\pi}{2}\right) - \sin\left(\frac{\pi}{2}\right)$$

$$= -1 - 1$$

$$= -2$$

Exercises for Alternate Example 4

In Exercises 19–26, find each integral using the formula $\displaystyle\int_a^x f(t)\,dt = F(x) - F(a)$

19. $\displaystyle\int_{-\pi}^{\pi} -\cos x\,dx$ **20.** $\displaystyle\int_{-\pi/2}^{\pi/2} \sin x\,dx$ **21.** $\displaystyle\int_1^3 3x^2\,dx$ **22.** $\displaystyle\int_0^{\pi/4} \sec x \tan x\,dx$

23. $\displaystyle\int_{-1}^{1} e^x\,dx$ **24.** $\displaystyle\int_3^4 10\,dx$ **25.** $\displaystyle\int_1^5 -4x^3\,dx$ **26.** $\displaystyle\int_2^e \frac{1}{x}\,dx$

5.4 Fundamental Theorem of Calculus

Alternate Example 2   **The Fundamental Theorem With The Chain Rule**

Find $\dfrac{dy}{dx}$ if $y = \displaystyle\int_{1}^{2x} \sin t \, dt$.

SOLUTION

The upper limit of integration is not x but $2x$. This makes y a composite of

$$y = \int_{1}^{u} \sin t \, dt \quad \text{and} \quad u = 2x$$

We must therefore apply the Chain Rule when finding dy/dx.

$$\frac{dy}{dx} = \frac{dy}{du} \cdot \frac{du}{dx}$$

$$= \left(\frac{d}{du} \int_{1}^{u} \sin t \, dt \right) \cdot \frac{du}{dx}$$

$$= \sin u \cdot \frac{du}{dx}$$

$$= (\sin 2x)(2)$$

$$= 2\sin 2x$$

Exercises for Alternate Example 2

In Exercises 1–6, find dy/dx given y.

1. $y = \displaystyle\int_{1}^{3x} \sin t \, dt$

2. $y = \displaystyle\int_{\pi}^{x^3+x} te^{t} \, dt$

3. $y = \displaystyle\int_{4}^{x^2} \frac{u^2 + u + 1}{u - 1} \, du$

4. $y = \displaystyle\int_{3}^{x^2+3x} \frac{\ln(2w)}{w} \, dw$

5. $y = \displaystyle\int_{1}^{1/x} \frac{1}{2} \cos t \, dt$

6. $y = \displaystyle\int_{-2}^{5x-1} \tan(t^2) \, dt$

Alternate Example 3   **Variable Lower Limits of Integration**

Find $\dfrac{dy}{dx}$.

(a) $y = \displaystyle\int_{x}^{6} 5t \cos t \, dt$

(b) $y = \displaystyle\int_{3x}^{x^3} \frac{dt}{3 - 2e^t}$

SOLUTION

The rules for integrals set these up for the Fundamental Theorem.

$$\textbf{(a)}\ \frac{d}{dx} \int_{x}^{6} 5t \cos t \, dt = \frac{d}{dx} \left(-\int_{6}^{x} 5t \cos t \, dt \right)$$

$$= -\frac{d}{dx} \left(\int_{6}^{x} 5t \cos t \, dt \right)$$

$$= -5 \frac{d}{dx}\left(\int_6^x t\cos t\, dt \right)$$

$$= -5x \cos x$$

$$\textbf{(b)}\ \frac{d}{dx}\int_{3x}^{x^3} \frac{dt}{3-2e^t} = \frac{d}{dx}\left(\int_0^{x^3} \frac{dt}{3-2e^t} - \int_0^{3x} \frac{dt}{3-2e^t} \right)$$

$$= \frac{1}{3-2e^{x^2}}\left(\frac{d}{dx}\left(x^3\right) \right) - \frac{1}{3-2e^{3x}}\left(\frac{d}{dx}\left(3x\right) \right)$$

$$= \frac{3x^2}{3-2e^{x^2}} - \frac{3}{3-2e^{3x}}$$

Exercises for Alternate Example 3

In Exercise 7–12, find dy/dx.

7. $y = \displaystyle\int_{-3x}^{-1} -4t\sin t\ dt$

8. $y = \displaystyle\int_{x^2}^{x^4} \ln\sqrt{2t+3}\, dt$

9. $y = \displaystyle\int_{3x}^{-3} 11t^2 \cos t\, dt$

10. $y = \displaystyle\int_{-2x}^{2} \frac{dt}{5-e^t}$

11. $y = \displaystyle\int_{-4x}^{3} \frac{2t+7}{t-4}\, dt$

12. $y = \displaystyle\int_{\tan x}^{x^3} t^{-2/3}\, dt$

Alternate Example 5 Evaluating an Integral

Evaluate $\displaystyle\int_{-3}^{5}\left(4x^3 - 6x + 5\right) dx$ using an antiderivative.

SOLUTION

Solve Analytically A simple antiderivative of $4x^3 - 6x + 5$ is $x^4 - 3x^2 + 5x$. Therefore,

$$\int_{-3}^{5}\left(4x^3 - 6x + 5\right) dx = \left[x^4 - 3x^2 + 5x \right]_{-3}^{5}$$

$$= (625 - 75 + 25) - (81 - 27 - 15)$$

$$= 536$$

Support Numerically $\text{NINT}\left(4x^3 - 6x + 5, x, -3, 5\right) = 536$

Exercises for Alternate Example 5

In Exercises 13–20, evaluate each integral using an antiderivative.

13. $\displaystyle\int_{-3}^{-1}(x^3 + x + 6)\, dx$

14. $\displaystyle\int_{1}^{4}\left(3\sqrt{x} - \frac{1}{x}\right) dx$

15. $\displaystyle\int_{-\pi/4}^{0}(2\sec x \tan x - 3\sin x)\, dx$

16. $\displaystyle\int_{-2}^{2}(-6x^3 - 3x^2 + 2x)\, dx$

17. $\displaystyle\int_{-2}^{0} \frac{e^{x+2}}{3}\, dx$

18. $\displaystyle\int_{-1}^{2}(x+1)^3\, dx$

19. $\displaystyle\int_{1}^{9} \frac{\sqrt{x}-1}{\sqrt{x}}\, dx$

20. $\displaystyle\int_{\pi/6}^{5\pi/6} 3\csc^2 x\, dx$

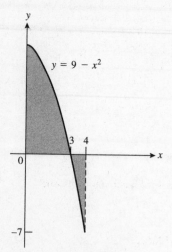

Figure 5.10 The function $f(x) = 9 - x^2$ changes sign only at $x = 3$ on the interval $[0, 4]$.

Finding Area Using Antiderivatives

Find the area of the region between the curve $y = 9 - x^2$, $0 \leq x \leq 4$, and the x-axis.

SOLUTION

The curve crosses the x-axis at $x = 3$, partitioning the interval $[0, 5]$ into two subintervals, on each of which $f(x) = 9 - x^2$ will not change sign.

We can see from the graph (Figure 5.10) that $f(x) > 0$ on $[0, 3]$ and $f(x) < 0$ on $[3, 5]$.

Over $[0, 3]$: $\displaystyle\int_0^3 (9 - x^2)\,dx = \left[9x - \frac{1}{3}x^3\right]_0^3$

$$= 18$$

Over $[3, 5]$: $\displaystyle\int_3^5 (9 - x^2)\,dx = \left[9x - \frac{1}{3}x^3\right]_3^5$

$$= -14\frac{2}{3}$$

The area of the region is $|18| + \left|-14\frac{2}{3}\right| = 32\frac{2}{3}$.

Exercises for Alternate Example 6

In Exercises 21–26, find the area of the region between the curve y, $a \leq x \leq b$, and the x-axis.

21. $y = 1 - x^2$, $0 \leq x \leq 4$

22. $y = 3x^2 - 3$, $0 \leq x \leq 4$

23. $y = 8 - 4x$, $1 \leq x \leq 6$

24. $y = \sin x$, $0 \leq x \leq 2\pi$

25. $y = \dfrac{1}{x} - 1$, $0.5 \leq x \leq 2$

26. $y = (x-1)(x-2)$, $-3 \leq x \leq 2$

5.5 Trapezoidal Rule

Applying the Trapezoidal Rule

Use the Trapezoidal Rule with $n = 4$ to estimate $\displaystyle\int_2^4 2x^2\,dx$. Compare the estimate with the value of NINT $\left(2x^2, x, 2, 4\right)$ and with the exact value.

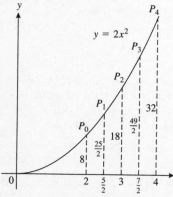

Figure 5.11 The trapezoidal approximation of the area under the graph of $y = 2x^2$ from $x = 2$ to $x = 4$ is a slight overestimate.

SOLUTION

Partition $[2, 4]$ into four subintervals of equal length (Figure 5.11). Then evaluate $y = 2x^2$ at each partition point (Table 5.3).

Using these y values, $n = 4$, $h = \dfrac{4 - 2}{4} = \dfrac{1}{2}$ in the Trapezoidal Rule, we have

$$T = \frac{h}{2}\left(y_0 + 2y_1 + 2y_2 + 2y_3 + y_4\right)$$

$$= \frac{1}{4}\left(8 + 2\left(\frac{25}{2}\right) + 2(18) + 2\left(\frac{49}{2}\right) + 32\right)$$

$$= \frac{1}{4}\left(8 + 25 + 36 + 49 + 32\right)$$

$$= \frac{150}{4}$$

$$= 37.50$$

Table 5.3

x	$y = 2x^2$
2	8
5/2	25/2
3	18
7/2	49/2
4	32

The value of NINT $\left(2x^2, x, 2, 4\right)$ is 37.3333.

The exact value of the integral is

$$\int_2^4 2x^2\,dx = \frac{2}{3}x^3 \bigg]_2^4$$

$$= \frac{128}{3} - \frac{16}{3}$$

$$= \frac{112}{3}$$

$$= 37.33$$

The T approximation overestimates the integral by about half of a percent of its true value

of $\dfrac{112}{3}$. The percentage error is $\dfrac{37.50 - \dfrac{112}{3}}{\dfrac{112}{3}} = 0.0044642857$.

Exercises for Alternate Example 1

In Exercises 1–6, (a) evaluate each integral using the Trapezoidal Rule with $n = 4$ and (b) find the true value of the integral.

1. $\displaystyle\int_2^4 x\,dx$ 2. $\displaystyle\int_{-1}^2 (x^3 + x)\,dx$ 3. $\displaystyle\int_1^5 \frac{1+x}{\sqrt{x}}\,dx$ 4. $\displaystyle\int_0^{\pi/2} \cos x\,dx$ 5. $\displaystyle\int_0^3 -x^2\,dx$ 6. $\displaystyle\int_0^4 e^x\,dx$ ∎

Alternate Example 2 Averaging Temperatures

An observer measures the outside temperature every hour from noon until midnight, recording the temperatures in the following table.

Time	N	1	2	3	4	5	6	7	8	9	10	11	M
Temp	58	62	64	67	58	76	72	80	59	72	68	56	66

What was the average temperature for the 12-hour period?

SOLUTION

We are looking for the average value of a continuous function (temperature) for which we know values at discrete times that are one unit apart. We need to find

$$av(f) = \frac{1}{b-a}\int_a^b f(x)\,dx,$$

without having a formula for $f(x)$. The integral, however, can be approximated by the Trapezoidal Rule, using the temperatures in the table as function values at the points of a 12-subinterval partition of the 12-hour interval (making $h = 1$).

$$T = \frac{h}{2}\left(y_0 + 2y_1 + 2y_2 + \cdots + 2y_{11} + y_{12}\right)$$

$$= \frac{1}{2}(58 + 2 \cdot 62 + 2 \cdot 64 + \cdots + 2 \cdot 56 + 66)$$

$$= 796$$

Using T to approximate $\int_a^b f(x)dx$, we have

$$av(f) = \frac{1}{b-a} \cdot T$$

$$= \frac{1}{12} \cdot 796$$

$$\approx 66.33$$

Rounding to be consistent with the data given, we estimate the average temperature as 66 degrees.

Exercises for Alternate Example 2

In Exercises 7–12 estimate the given integral by referring to the appropriate table and using the Trapezoidal Rule with the given value of n.

Table for f

x	0	0.25	0.5	0.75	1.0	1.25	1.5	1.75	2.0	2.25	2.5	2.75	3.0
$f(x)$	1	0.7	0.3	−0.4	−1.5	−3.2	−5.6	−8.8	−13	−18.3	−25	−33	−42.5

Table for g

x	−2	−1.5	−1	−0.5	0	0.5	1	1.5	2	2.5	3	3.5	4
$f(x)$	−1	0.75	2	2.75	3	2.75	2	0.75	−1	−3.25	−6	−9.25	−13

7. $\int_0^3 f(x)\,dx,\ n = 3$ **8.** $\int_0^3 f(x)\,dx,\ n = 6$ **9.** $\int_0^3 f(x)\,dx,\ n = 12$ **10.** $\int_{-2}^4 g(x)\,dx,\ n = 2$

11. $\int_{-2}^4 g(x)\,dx,\ n = 4$ **12.** $\int_{-2}^4 g(x)\,dx,\ n = 12$

Alternate Example 3   **Applying Simpson's Rule**

Use Simpson's Rule with $n = 4$ to approximate $\int_0^2 3x^2\,dx$.

SOLUTION

Simpson's Rule states that to approximate $\int_a^b f(x)\,dx$, use

Table 5.4

x	$y = 3x^2$
0	0
$\frac{1}{2}$	$\frac{3}{4}$
1	3
$\frac{3}{2}$	$\frac{27}{4}$
2	12

$$S = \frac{h}{3}\left(y_0 + 4y_1 + 2y_2 + 4y_3 + \cdots + 2y_{n-2} + 4y_{n-1} + y_n\right)$$

where $[a, b]$ is partitioned into an even number n of subintervals of equal length $h = \dfrac{b-a}{n}$.

Partition $[0, 4]$ into four subintervals and evaluate $y = 3x^2$ at the partition points (Table 5.4).

Then apply Simpson's Rule with $n = 4$ and $h = \dfrac{1}{2}$.

$$S = \frac{h}{3}\left(y_0 + 4y_1 + 2y_2 + 4y_3 + y_4\right)$$

$$= \frac{1}{6}\left(0 + 4\left(\frac{3}{4}\right) + 2(3) + 4\left(\frac{27}{4}\right) + 12\right)$$

$$= \frac{1}{6}\left(0 + 3 + 6 + 27 + 12\right)$$

$$= 8$$

Exercises for Alternate Example 3

In Exercises 13–18, use Simpson's Rule with the given n to approximate each integral. Then use NINT to find the exact value.

13. $\int_0^2 \left(\sqrt[3]{1 - \frac{x^2}{8}}\right) dx,\ n = 4$
14. $\int_0^1 -e^{-x^2} dx,\ n = 4$
15. $\int_0^2 \frac{3\,dx}{x^3 + 1},\ n = 8$
16. $\int_0^1 2\sqrt{x - x^2}\ dx,\ n = 4$

17. $\int_0^4 \frac{4\,dx}{2 + x},\ n = 6$
18. $\int_1^2 \frac{5\,dx}{x},\ n = 4$

∎

Chapter 6

Differential Equations and Mathematical Modeling

6.1 Slope Fields and Euler's Method

Alternate Example 1 **Solving a Differential Equation**

Find all the functions y that satisfy $\dfrac{dy}{dx} = \csc^2 x + 2x + 5$.

SOLUTION

The solution to this differential equation can be any antiderivative of

$\dfrac{dy}{dx} = \csc^2 x + 2x + 5$. Taking the antiderivative of this function gives us

$y = -\cot x + x^2 + 5x + C$, where C is an arbitrary constant.

Exercises for Alternate Example 1

In Exercises 1–6, find the general solution to the exact differential equation.

1. $\dfrac{dy}{dx} = x^2 + 4x + 1$

2. $\dfrac{dy}{dx} = -6x^2 - \sec x \tan x$

3. $\dfrac{dy}{du} = (u^2 - 1)(2u)$

4. $\dfrac{dy}{dx} = 6x^5 + \dfrac{1}{x}$

5. $\dfrac{dy}{dx} = 3\sin x + 5\cos x$

6. $\dfrac{dy}{dx} = 3^x \ln 3 - \dfrac{1}{\sqrt{1-x^2}}$

Alternate Example 2 **Solving an Initial Value Problem**

Find the particular solution to the equation $\dfrac{dy}{dx} = x^2 + 1$, whose graph passes through the point $(0, 1)$.

SOLUTION

To solve this initial value problem, we first antidifferentiate to obtain the general

solution: $y = \dfrac{x^3}{3} + x + C$. Next we substitute $x = 0$ and $y = 1$ (the initial condition) to

find C:

$$(1) = \frac{(0)^3}{3} + (0) + C$$

$$C = 1$$

Using this value for C in the general solution gives us the particular solution

$$y = \frac{x^3}{3} + x + 1.$$

Exercises for Alternate Example 2

In Exercises 7–12, solve the initial value problem explicitly.

7. $\dfrac{dy}{dx} = 1 + \cos x$ and $y = 4$ when $x = 0$

8. $\dfrac{dy}{dt} = \dfrac{1}{t^2} + t$ and $y = 1$ when $t = 2$

9. $\dfrac{dy}{dx} = -\pi \sin \pi x$ and $y = 0$ when $x = 0$

10. $\dfrac{dv}{dt} = 3t^2 + 2t + 1$ and $v = 0$ when $t = 1$

11. $\dfrac{dy}{dx} = 10 + 3\sqrt{x}$ and $y = 60$ when $x = 4$

12. $\dfrac{dy}{dx} = \dfrac{4x}{(1+x^2)^2}$ and $y = 0$ when $x = 1$

Alternate Example 8 Matching Slope Fields with Differential Equations

Use slope analysis to match each of the following differential equations with one of the slope fields (a) through (d) in figure 6.1. (Do not use your graphing calculator.)

1. $\dfrac{dy}{dx} = y + 2$ **2.** $\dfrac{dy}{dx} = x + 2$ **3.** $\dfrac{dy}{dx} = 1 + \cos x$ **4.** $\dfrac{dy}{dx} = 1 - y^2$

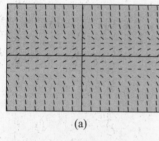

(a)

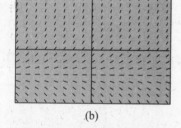

(b)

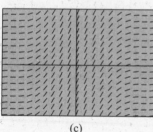

(c)

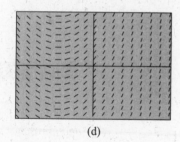

(d)

Figure 6.1 Slope fields

SOLUTION

1. To match Equation 1, we look for a graph that has zero slope when $y = -2$. That is graph (b).

2. To match Equation 2, we look for a graph that has zero slope when $x = -2$. That is graph (d).

3. To match Equation 3, we look for a graph in which the slope field does not change as y changes and is periodic. That is graph (c).

4. To match Equation 4, we look for a graph that has zero slope when $y = 1$ and when $y = -1$. That is graph (a).

Exercises for Alternate Example 8

In Exercises 13–18, use slope analysis to match of the differential equations with one of the slope fields (a) through (f).

13. $\dfrac{dy}{dx} = \sin x$ **14.** $\dfrac{dy}{dx} = 1 - x^2$ **15.** $\dfrac{dy}{dx} = x(3 - y)$ **16.** $\dfrac{dy}{dx} = y(3 - y)$

17. $\dfrac{dy}{dx} = \dfrac{-x}{2y}$ **18.** $\dfrac{dy}{dx} = \dfrac{-2x}{y}$

(a)

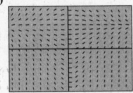

(b)

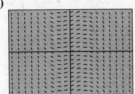

(c)

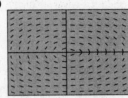

(d)

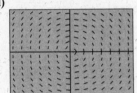

(e)

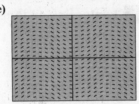

(f)

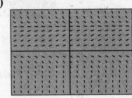

Alternate Example 9 **Applying Euler's Method**

Let f be the function that satisfies the initial value problem $\dfrac{dy}{dx} = y + x^2$ and $f(0) = 1$. Use Euler's method and increments of $\Delta x = 0.2$ to approximate $f(1)$.

SOLUTION

We use Euler's method to construct an approximation of the curve from $x = 0$ to $x = 1$ (Figure 6.2). Each segment extends from a point (x, y) to $(x + \Delta x, y + \Delta y)$, where

$\Delta x = 0.2$ and $\Delta y = \left(\dfrac{dy}{dx}\right)\Delta x$. The following table shows how we construct each new point

from the previous one. This leads us to an approximation $f(1) \approx 2.76264$, or $f(1) \approx 2.763$.

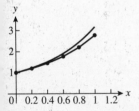

Figure 6.2 Euler's method is used to construct an approximate solution to an initial value problem between $x = 0$ and $x = 1$.

(x, y)	$\dfrac{dy}{dx} = y + x^2$	Δx	$\Delta y = \left(\dfrac{dy}{dx}\right)\Delta x$	$(x + \Delta x, y + \Delta y)$
$(0, 1)$	1	0.2	0.2	$(0.2, 1.2)$
$(0.2, 1.2)$	1.24	0.2	0.248	$(0.4, 1.448)$
$(0.4, 1.448)$	1.608	0.2	0.3216	$(0.6, 1.7696)$
$(0.6, 1.7696)$	2.1296	0.2	0.425592	$(0.8, 2.19552)$
$(0.8, 2.19552)$	2.83552	0.2	0.567104	$(1, 2.762624)$
$(1, 2.762624)$	3.762624	0.2	0.7525248	$(1.2, 3.5151488)$

Exercises for Alternate Example 9

In Exercises 19–21, use Euler's method with increments of $\Delta x = 0.2$ to approximate the value for the solution of the given initial-value problem.

19. Find $f(1)$ if $\dfrac{dy}{dx} = 2x + y$ and $y = 0$ when $x = 0$

20. Find $f(1)$ if $\dfrac{dy}{dx} = \dfrac{x}{y}$ and $y = 1$ when $x = 0$

21. Find $f(0.4)$ if $\dfrac{dy}{dx} = 2xy^2$ and $y = 1$ when $x = 0$

In Exercises 22–24, use Euler's method with increments of $\Delta x = 0.1$ to approximate the value for the solution of the given initial-value problem.

22. Find $f(0.5)$ if $\dfrac{dy}{dx} = x + y$ and $y = 1$ when $x = 0$

23. Find $f(0.5)$ if $\dfrac{dy}{dx} = x^2 + y^2$ and $y = 1$ when $x = 0$

24. Find $f(0.4)$ if $\dfrac{dy}{dx} = 2xy^2$ and $y = 1$ when $x = 0$

6.2 Antidifferentiation by Substitution

Alternate Example 1 Evaluating an Indefinite Integral

Evaluate $\displaystyle\int (3\sin x + 5\cos x)\,dx$.

SOLUTION

$$\int (3\sin x + 5\cos x)\,dx = 3(-\cos x) + 5\sin x + C$$

$$= -3\cos x + 5\sin x + C$$

You can check by differentiating

$$\frac{d}{dx}(-3\cos x + 5\sin x + C) = 3\sin x + 5\cos x .$$

Exercises for Alternate Example 1

In Exercises 1–6, evaluate the indefinite integral.

1. $\displaystyle\int x^3\,dx$

2. $\displaystyle\int (x^5 + 6x^2 + x - 1)\,dx$

3. $\displaystyle\int \frac{1}{\sec x}\,dx$

4. $\displaystyle\int (\csc^2 x + 3x^2)\,dx$

5. $\displaystyle\int \frac{e^{2u}}{e^u}\,du$

6. $\displaystyle\int \frac{3}{1+t^2}\,dt$

Alternate Example 5 **Using Substitution**

Evaluate $\int \dfrac{x^2}{(x^3-8)^5}\,dx$.

SOLUTION

Use the substitution $u = x^3 - 8$. Then $du = 3x^2\,dx$, so $x^2\,dx = \dfrac{du}{3}$.

$$\int \frac{x^2}{(x^3-8)^5}\,dx = \int \frac{1}{(x^3-8)^5}\cdot x^2\,dx$$

$$= \frac{1}{3}\int \frac{1}{(x^3-8)^5}\cdot 3x^2\,dx \qquad \text{Set up the substitution with a factor of 3.}$$

$$= \frac{1}{3}\int \frac{1}{u^5}\cdot du \qquad \text{Substitute } u \text{ for } x^3-8 \text{ and } du \text{ for } 3x^2 dx.$$

$$= \frac{1}{3}\int u^{-5}\cdot du$$

$$= \frac{1}{3}\left(\frac{u^{-4}}{-4}\right)+C \qquad\qquad \int u^n\,du = \frac{u^{n+1}}{n+1}+C$$

$$= -\frac{1}{12}(x^3-8)^{-4}+C \qquad \text{Re-substitute } x^3-8 \text{ for } u.$$

Exercises for Alternate Example 5

In Exercises 7–12, use substitution to evaluate the integral.

7. $\int \dfrac{x}{\sqrt{1-4x^2}}\,dx$ **8.** $\int 2t\sqrt{1+t^2}\,dx$ **9.** $\int \sin 4x\,dx$ **10.** $\int \cos(7t+5)\,dt$

11. $\int \dfrac{\ln x}{3x}\,dx$ **12.** $\int xe^{3x^2}\,dx$

Alternate Example 7 **Setting Up a Substitution with a Trigonometric Identity**

Find the indefinite integrals. In each case you can use a trigonometric identity to set up a substitution.

(a) $\int \sin^3 x\,dx$ **(b)** $\int \sec^6 x\,dx$ **(c)** $\int \dfrac{\tan x}{\cos^2 x}\,dx$

SOLUTION

(a) We can use the trigonometric identity $\sin^2 x = 1 - \cos^2 x$ to find this integral.

$$\int \sin^3 x\, dx = \int (\sin^2 x)(\sin x)\, dx$$

$$= \int (1 - \cos^2 x)(\sin x)\, dx \qquad \text{Rewrite using trigonometric identity.}$$

$$= -\int (1 - \cos^2 x)(-\sin x)\, dx$$

$$= -\int (1 - u^2)\, du \qquad \text{Let } u = \cos x \text{ and } du = -\sin x\, dx$$

$$= \left[-u - \frac{u^3}{3} + C \right]$$

$$= \frac{u^3}{3} - u + C$$

$$= \frac{\cos^3 x}{3} - \cos x + C \qquad \text{Resubstitute after antidifferentiating.}$$

(b) We can use the trigonometric identity $\sec^2 x = 1 + \tan^2 x$.

$$\int \sec^6 x\, dx = \int \sec^4 x \sec^2 x \, dx$$

$$= \int (\sec^2 x)^2 \sec^2 x \, dx$$

$$= \int (1 + \tan^2 x)^2 \sec^2 x \, dx \qquad \text{Rewrite using trigonometric identity.}$$

$$= \int (1 + u^2)^2 \, du \qquad \text{Let } u = \tan u \text{ and } du = \sec^2 x\, dx.$$

$$= \int (1 + 2u^2 + u^4)\, du$$

$$= u + \frac{2}{3}u^3 + \frac{1}{5}u^5 + C$$

$$= \tan x + \frac{2}{3}\tan^3 x + \frac{1}{5}\tan^5 x + C \qquad \text{Resubstitute after antidifferentiating.}$$

(c) We can use the trigonometric identity $\dfrac{1}{\cos^2 x} = \sec^2 x$ to find this integral.

$$\int \frac{\tan x}{\cos^2 x}\, dx = \int \tan x \sec^2 x \, dx \qquad \text{Rewrite using trigonometric identity.}$$

$$= \int u\, du \qquad \text{Let } u = \tan u \text{ and } du = \sec^2 x\, dx.$$

$$= \frac{u}{2} + C$$

$$= \frac{\tan^2 x}{2} + C \qquad \text{Re-substitute after antidifferentiating.}$$

Exercises for Alternate Example 7

In Exercises 13–18, find each indefinite integral using a trigonometric identity to set up a u-substitution.

13. $\displaystyle\int \sin^5 x\, dx$ **14.** $\displaystyle\int \tan^2 x \sec^4 x\, dx$ **15.** $\displaystyle\int \sin^4 x \cos^5 x\, dx$ **16.** $\displaystyle\int \tan^2 x\, dx$

17. $\displaystyle\int \frac{\sin x}{\cos^2 x}\, dx$ **18.** $\displaystyle\int \frac{\cot^3 x}{\csc x}\, dx$

Evaluating a Definite Integral by Substitution

Evaluate $\displaystyle\int_{0}^{1} \frac{dx}{1+x}$.

SOLUTION

Let $u = 1 + x$ and $du = dx$. Then $u(0) = 1 + 0 = 1$ and $u(1) = 1 + 1 = 2$.

So

$$\int_{0}^{1} \frac{dx}{1+x} = \int_{1}^{2} \frac{du}{u} \qquad \text{Substitute u-interval for x-interval.}$$

$$= \Big[\ln|u|\Big]_{1}^{2}$$

$$= \ln 2 - \ln 1 = \ln 2$$

Exercises for Alternate Example 8

In Exercises 19–24, make a *u*-substitution and then evaluate the definite integral.

19. $\displaystyle\int_{1}^{3} \frac{x}{x+1}\,dx$

20. $\displaystyle\int_{0}^{2} t(t^2 - 1)^7\,dt$

21. $\displaystyle\int_{\pi/4}^{\pi/3} \csc\frac{x}{2}\cot\frac{x}{2}\,dx$

22. $\displaystyle\int_{\sqrt{\pi/2}}^{\sqrt{\pi}} \theta^3 \cos(\theta^2)\,d\theta$

23. $\displaystyle\int_{0}^{\pi/2} \frac{\sin x}{\sqrt{1+\cos x}}\,dx$

24. $\displaystyle\int_{0}^{1/2} \frac{r}{\sqrt{1-r^2}}\,dr$

6.3 Antidifferentiation by Parts

Using Integration by Parts

Evaluate $\displaystyle\int x\cos(5x-1)\,dx$.

SOLUTION

We use the formula $\displaystyle\int u\,dv = uv - \int v\,du$ with $u = x$ and $dv = \cos(5x{-}1)\,dx$.

To complete the formula, we take the differential of u and find the simplest antiderivative of $dv = \cos(5x - 1)\,dx$.

$$du = dx \quad \text{and} \quad v = \frac{1}{5}\sin(5x - 1)$$

Then,

$$\int x\cos(5x - 1)\,dx = \frac{1}{5}x\sin(5x - 1) - \frac{1}{5}\int \sin(5x - 1)\,dx$$

$$= \frac{1}{5}x\sin(5x - 1) - \frac{1}{5}\cdot\frac{1}{5}\int \sin(5x - 1)\cdot 5\,dx$$

$$= \frac{1}{5}x\sin(5x - 1) + \frac{1}{5}\cdot\frac{1}{5}\cos(5x - 1) + C$$

$$= \frac{1}{5}x\sin(5x - 1) + \frac{1}{25}\cos(5x - 1) + C$$

Exercises for Alternate Example 1

In Exercises 1–6, find the indefinite integral.

1. $\int \dfrac{\ln x}{x^2}\,dx$ **2.** $\int \ln(x^2+1)\,dx$ **3.** $\int \tan^{-1}r\,dr$ **4.** $\int x^3 e^{x^2}\,dx$ **5.** $\int x^2 \cos 2x\,dx$ **6.** $\int r\tan^{-1}r\,dr$

Alternate Example 2   **Repeated Use of Integration by Parts**

Evaluate $\int x^2 \sin x\,dx$.

SOLUTION

Let $u = x^2, dv = \sin x\,dx, du = 2x\,dx$, and $v = -\cos x$. Then

$$\int x^2 \sin x\,dx = -x^2 \cos x - \int (-\cos x)2x\,dx$$
$$= -x^2 \cos x + 2\int x\cos x\,dx$$

To evaluate the integral on the right, we integrate by parts again with

$u = x, dv = \cos x\,dx, du = dx$, and $v = \sin x$. Then

$$\int x\cos x\,dx = x\sin x - \int \sin x\,dx$$
$$= x\sin x + \cos x$$

Hence,

$$\int x^2 \sin x\,dx = -x^2 \cos x + 2(x\sin x + \cos x) + C$$
$$= -x^2 \cos x + 2x\sin x + 2\cos x + C$$

Exercises for Alternate Example 2

In Exercises 7–12, find the indefinite integral

7. $\int e^x \sin x\,dx$ **8.** $\int \sin(\ln t)\,dt$ **9.** $\int x^3 e^{2x}\,dx$ **10.** $\int x^2 e^{3x}\,dx$ **11.** $\int (\ln x)^2\,dx$ **12.** $\int (\ln t)^3\,dt$

Alternate Example 6   **Using Tabular Integration**

Evaluate $\int x^2 \sin 4x\,dx$.

SOLUTION

With $f(x) = x^2$ and $g(x) = \sin 4x$, we list:

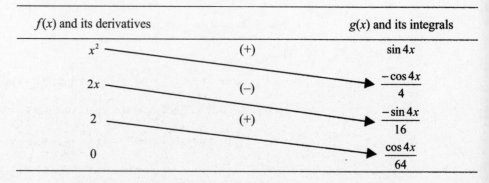

$f(x)$ and its derivatives		$g(x)$ and its integrals
x^2	(+)	$\sin 4x$
$2x$	(−)	$\dfrac{-\cos 4x}{4}$
2	(+)	$\dfrac{-\sin 4x}{16}$
0		$\dfrac{\cos 4x}{64}$

We combine the products of the functions connected by the arrows according to the operation signs above the arrows to obtain

$$-\frac{1}{4}x^2\cos 4x + \frac{1}{8}x\sin 4x + \frac{1}{32}\cos 4x + C$$

Exercises for Alternate Example 6

In Exercises 13–18, use tabular integration to find the antiderivative

13. $\int x^2\cos x\,dx$ **14.** $\int x^2\cos 4x\,dx$ **15.** $\int x^3 e^x\,dx$ **16.** $\int x^3 e^{-2x}\,dx$

17. $\int e^{3x}\sin 2x\,dx$ **18.** $\int e^{2x}\cos x\,dx$ ■

6.4   Exponential Growth and Decay

Alternate Example 1   **Solving by Separation of Variables**

Solve for y if $\dfrac{dy}{dx} = 6y^2 x$ and $y = \dfrac{1}{25}$ when $x = 1$.

SOLUTION

The equation is separable because it can be written in the form $\dfrac{dy}{dx} = f(y)g(x)$, where

$f(y) = y^2$ and $g(x) = 6x$. We separate the variables and antidifferentiate as follows:

$$y^{-2}dy = 6x\,dx \qquad\qquad \text{Separate the variables.}$$

$$\int y^{-2}dy = \int 6x\,dx \qquad\qquad \text{Prepare to antidifferentiate.}$$

$$-\frac{1}{y} = 3x^2 + C \qquad\qquad \text{Note that only one constant is needed.}$$

We then apply the initial condition to find C.

$$-\frac{1}{1/25} = 3(1)^2 + C \Rightarrow C = -28$$

Using this value for C, we can solve for y.

$$-\frac{1}{y} = 3x^2 - 28$$

$$\frac{1}{y} = 28 - 3x^2$$

$$y = \frac{1}{28 - 3x^2}$$

This solution is valid for the continuous section of the function that goes through the

point (1, 1/25), that is, on the interval $-\sqrt{\dfrac{28}{3}} < x < \sqrt{\dfrac{28}{3}}$.

Exercises for Alternate Example 1

In Exercises 1–6, use separation of variables to solve the initial value problem. Indicate the domain over which the solution is valid.

1. $\dfrac{dy}{dx} = yx$ and $y = 2$ when $x = 0$

2. $\dfrac{dy}{dt} = te^y$ and $y = 0$ when $t = 1$

3. $\dfrac{dy}{dx} = xy^3$ and $y = 1$ when $x = 0$

4. $\dfrac{dy}{dx} = \dfrac{-x}{y+1}$ and $y = -3$ when $x = 0$

5. $\dfrac{dy}{dx} = \dfrac{xy^3}{\sqrt{1+x^2}}$ and $y = -1$ when $x = 0$

6. $\dfrac{dy}{dt} = 0.02y$ and $y = 4$ when $t = 0$

Alternate Example 2 **Compounding Interest Continuously**

Suppose you deposit $800 in an account that pays 7.5% annual interest. How much will you have 8 years later if the interest is **(a)** compounded continuously? **(b)** compounded quarterly?

SOLUTION

Here $A_0 = 800$ and $r = 0.075$. The amount in the account to the nearest cent after 8 years is

(a) $A(8) = 800e^{(0.075)(8)} = 1457.70$

(b) $A(8) = 800\left(1 + \dfrac{0.075}{4}\right)^{(4)(8)} = 1449.62$

Exercises for Alternate Example 2

In Exercises 7–10, for each interest rate r, find the amount, to the nearest cent, that you will have in 15 years if you deposit $1500 and the interest is compounded **(a)** continuously and **(b)** quarterly.

7. $r = 4.25\%$ **8.** $r = 2.35\%$

9. $r = 5.00\%$ **10.** $r = 19.9\%$

In Exercises 11–14, for each interest rate r, find the amount, to the nearest cent, that you have in 7 years if you deposit $1500 and the interest is compounded **(a)** continuously and **(b)** monthly.

11. $r = 4.25\%$ **12.** $r = 2.35\%$

13. $r = 5.00\%$ **14.** $r = 19.9\%$

Alternate Example 5 **Using Carbon-14 Dating**

Scientists who use carbon-14 dating use 5700 years for its half-life. Find the age of a sample in which 20% of the radioactive nuclei originally present have decayed.

SOLUTION

We model the exponential decay in base $1/2$: $A = A_0(1/2)^{t/5700}$. We seek the value of t for which $0.8A_0 = A_0(1/2)^{t/5700}$, or $0.8 = (1/2)^{t/5700}$

Solving algebraically with logarithms,

$$0.8 = (1/2)^{t/5700}$$

$$\ln(0.8) = (t/5700)\ln(1/2)$$

$$t = 5700\left(\dfrac{\ln(0.8)}{\ln(0.5)}\right)$$

$$t \approx 1835.$$

Interpreting the answer, we conclude that the sample is about 1835 years old.

Exercises for Alternate Example 5

In Exercises 15–20, use the decay equation for carbon-14 to find the age of a sample assuming the indicated amount of radioactive nuclei originally present have decayed.

15. 1% nuclei decayed   **16.** 2% nuclei decayed   **17.** 50% nuclei decayed   **18.** 75% nuclei decayed

19. 98% nuclei decayed   **20.** 99% nuclei decayed

6.5 Logistic Growth

Alternate Example 1 **Finding a Partial Fraction Decomposition**

Write the function $f(x) = \dfrac{5x+4}{x^2 - 2x - 8}$ as a sum of rational functions with linear denominators.

SOLUTION

Since $f(x) = \dfrac{5x+4}{(x+2)(x-4)}$ we will find numbers A and B so that

$$f(x) = \frac{A}{(x+2)} + \frac{B}{(x-4)}.$$

Note that $\dfrac{A}{(x+2)} + \dfrac{B}{(x-4)} = \dfrac{A(x-4)+B(x+2)}{(x+2)(x-4)}$, so it follows that

$$5x + 4 = A(x-4) + B(x+2) \qquad (1)$$

Setting $x = 4$ in equation (1), we get

$$24 = A(0) + B(6), \text{ so } B = 4.$$

Setting $x = -2$ in equation (1), we get

$$-6 = A(-6) + B(0), \text{ so } A = 1.$$

Therefore $f(x) = \dfrac{5x+4}{(x+2)(x-4)} = \dfrac{1}{(x+2)} + \dfrac{4}{(x-4)}.$

Exercises for Alternate Example 1

In Exercises 1–6, write the function as a sum of rational functions with linear denominators

1. $f(x) = \dfrac{1}{x^2 - 4}$

2. $f(x) = \dfrac{x-3}{x^2 + 9x + 20}$

3. $f(x) = \dfrac{5x-3}{x^2 - 2x - 3}$

4. $f(x) = \dfrac{2-x}{x^2 + x}$

5. $f(x) = \dfrac{3x+11}{x^2 + 5x + 6}$

6. $f(x) = \dfrac{x+5}{x^2 + x - 2}$

Alternate Example 2 **Antidifferentiating with Partial Fractions**

Find $\displaystyle \int \frac{x^4 - 4x^2 + x + 1}{x^2 - 4}\, dx$.

SOLUTION

First we note that the degree of the denominator is not less than the degree of the numerator. We use the division algorithm to find the quotient and remainder.

$$
\begin{array}{r}
x^2 \\
x^2-4\overline{)\,x^4-4x^2+x+1} \\
\underline{x^4-4x^2} \\
x+1
\end{array}
$$

Thus

$$
\int \frac{x^4-4x^2+x+1}{x^2-4}\,dx = \int\left(x^2+\frac{x+1}{x^2-4}\right)dx
$$

$$
= \frac{1}{3}x^3 + \int \frac{x+1}{(x+2)(x-2)}\,dx
$$

$$
= \frac{1}{3}x^3 + \int \frac{A}{(x+2)}+\frac{B}{(x-2)}\,dx
$$

We know that $A(x-2)+B(x+2)=x+1$.

Setting $x=2$,

$$
A(0)+B(4)=3,\ \text{so}\ B=\frac{3}{4}.
$$

Setting $x=-2$,

$$
A(-4)+B(0)=-1,\ \text{so}\ A=\frac{1}{4}.
$$

Thus

$$
\int \frac{x^4-4x^2+x+1}{x^2-4}\,dx = \frac{1}{3}x^3 + \int\left(\frac{1/4}{(x+2)}+\frac{3/4}{(x-2)}\right)dx
$$

$$
= \frac{1}{3}x^3 + \frac{1}{4}\int \frac{1}{x+2}\,dx + \frac{3}{4}\int \frac{1}{x-2}\,dx
$$

$$
= \frac{1}{3}x^3 + \frac{1}{4}\ln|x+2| + \frac{3}{4}\ln|x-2| + C
$$

$$
= \frac{1}{3}x^3 + \frac{1}{4}\ln\left|(x+2)(x-2)^3\right| + C
$$

Exercises for Alternate Example 2

In Exercises 7–12, antidifferentiate using partial fraction decomposition.

7. $\displaystyle\int \frac{dx}{x^2-9}$
8. $\displaystyle\int \frac{4dx}{3x^2+x-14}$
9. $\displaystyle\int \frac{x+3}{2x^2-9x-5}\,dx$
10. $\displaystyle\int \frac{x}{x^2-3x-4}\,dx$

11. $\displaystyle\int \frac{x^2}{x^2-1}\,dx$
12. $\displaystyle\int \frac{x^3+2x}{x-1}\,dx$

Alternate Example 3   Finding Three Partial Fractions

Find the general solution to $\dfrac{dy}{dx} = \dfrac{x+1}{x^3 + x^2 - 6x}$.

SOLUTION

The denominator factors as follows:

$$x^3 + x^2 - 6x = x(x^2 + x - 6)$$
$$= x(x-2)(x+3)$$

$$y = \int \frac{x+1}{x^3 + x^2 - 6x}\,dx = \int \left(\frac{A}{x} + \frac{B}{x-2} + \frac{C}{x+3} \right) dx$$

We know that $A(x-2)(x+3) + B(x)(x+3) + C(x)(x-2) = x+1$

Setting $x = 0$:

$$A(-2)(3) + B(0) + C(0) = 1,\ \text{so}\ A = -\frac{1}{6}.$$

Setting $x = 2$:

$$A(0) + B(2)(5) + C(0) = 3,\ \text{so}\ B = \frac{3}{10}$$

Setting $x = -3$:

$$A(0) + B(0) + C(-3)(-5) = -2\ \text{so}\ C = -\frac{2}{15}$$

Thus

$$\int \frac{x+1}{x^3 + x^2 - 6x}\,dx = \int -\frac{1/6}{x}\,dx + \int \frac{3/10}{x-2}\,dx - \int \frac{2/15}{x+3}\,dx$$

$$= -\frac{1}{6}\int \frac{1}{x}\,dx + \frac{3}{10}\int \frac{1}{x-2}\,dx - \frac{2}{15}\int \frac{1}{x+3}\,dx$$

$$= -\frac{1}{6}\ln|x| + \frac{3}{10}\ln|x-2| - \frac{2}{15}\ln|x+3| + C$$

Exercises for Alternate Example 3

In Exercises 13–18, find the general solution using partial fractions.

13. $\dfrac{dy}{dx} = \dfrac{2x+1}{x^3 + x^2 - 6x}$

14. $\dfrac{dy}{dx} = \dfrac{x^2 + 2}{x(x+2)(x-1)}$

15. $\dfrac{dy}{dx} = \dfrac{x^2 + 2x + 1}{x(2x-1)(x+2)}$

16. $\dfrac{dy}{dx} = \dfrac{2x^2 + 1}{(x-1)(x-2)(x-3)}$

17. $\dfrac{dy}{dx} = \dfrac{x^2 - 4}{(x-1)(x-3)(x+1)}$

18. $\dfrac{dy}{dx} = \dfrac{3x+6}{x^3 + 2x^2 - 3x}$

Chapter 7

Applications of Definite Integrals

7.1 Integral as Net Change

| **Alternate Example 2** | **Finding Position from Displacement** |

The velocity in cm/sec of a particle moving along a horizontal s-axis for $0 \le t \le 8$ is

$$\frac{ds}{dt} = v(t) = \left(t^2 - \frac{8}{(t+1)^2} \right).$$

Suppose the initial position of the particle is $s(0) = 12$. What is the particle's position at **(a)** $t = 3$ sec? **(b)** $t = 6$ sec?

SOLUTION

Solve Analytically (a) The position at $t = 3$ is the initial position $s(0)$ plus the displacement (the amount, Δs, that the position changed from $t = 0$ to $t = 3$). When velocity is constant during a motion, we can find the displacement (change in position) with the formula

Displacement = rate of change × time.

But in our case the velocity varies, so we resort instead to partitioning the time interval $[0, 3]$ into subintervals of length Δt, so short that the velocity is effectively constant on each subinterval. If Δt is any time in the kth subinterval, the particle's velocity throughout that interval will be close to $v(\Delta t)$. The change in the particle's position during the brief time this constant velocity applies is $v(t_k) \Delta t$.

If $v(t_k)$ is negative, the displacement is negative and the particle will move left. If $v(t_k)$ is positive, the particle will move right. The sum $\sum v(t_k) \Delta t$ of all these small position changes approximates the displacement for the time interval $[0, 3]$.

The sum $\sum v(t_k) \Delta t$ is a Riemann sum for the continuous function $v(t)$ over $[0, 3]$. As the norms of the partitions go to zero, the approximations improve and the sums converge to the integral of v over $[0, 3]$, giving

$$\text{Displacement} = \int_0^3 v(t)\,dt$$

$$= \int_0^3 \left(t^2 - \frac{8}{(t+1)^2} \right) dt$$

$$= \left[\frac{1}{3}t^3 + \frac{8}{(t+1)} \right]_0^3$$

$$= \left[\frac{1}{3}(3)^3 + \frac{8}{(3+1)} \right] - \left[\frac{1}{3}0^3 + \frac{8}{(0+1)} \right]$$

$$= 9 + 2 - 8$$

$$= 3$$

During the first three seconds of motion, the particle moves 3 cm to the right. It starts at $s(0) = 12$, so its position at $t = 3$ is

New position = initial position + displacement
$$= 12 + 3$$
$$= 15.$$

(b) If we model the displacement from $t = 0$ to $t = 6$ in the same way, we arrive at.

$$\text{Displacement} = \int_0^6 v(t)dt$$

$$= \left[\frac{1}{3}t^3 + \frac{8}{(t+1)} \right]_0^6$$

$$= \left[\frac{1}{3}(6)^3 + \frac{8}{(6+1)} \right] - \left[\frac{1}{3}0^3 + \frac{8}{(0+1)} \right]$$

$$= 72 + \frac{8}{7} - 8$$

$$= 65.14$$

The motion has the net effect of displacing the particle 65.14 cm to the right of its starting point. The particle's final position is

Final position = initial position + displacement
$$= s(0) + 65.14$$
$$= 12 + 65.14$$
$$= 77.14$$

Support Graphically The position of the particle at any time t is given by

$$s(t) = \int_0^t \left(t^2 - \frac{8}{(t+1)^2} \right) dt + 12,$$

because $s'(t) = v(t)$ and $s(0) = 12$. Figure 7.1 shows the graph of $s(t)$ given by the parameterization

$$x(t) = \text{NINT}\ (v(u),\, u,\, 0,\, t) + 12,\ y(t) = t,\ 0 \le t \le 8$$

(a) Figure 7.1a supports that the position of the particle at $t = 3$ is 15.

(b) Figure 7.1b shows the position of the particle is 77.14 at $t = 6$. Therefore, the displacement is $77.14 - 12 \approx 65.14$.

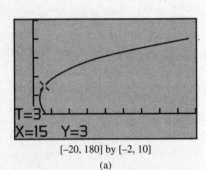

[–20, 180] by [–2, 10]

(a)

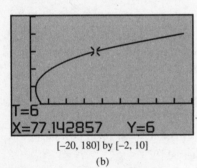

[–20, 180] by [–2, 10]

(b)

Figure 7.1 By parameterizing the function, you can "see" the left and right motion of the particle.

Exercises for Alternate Example 2

In Exercises 1–6, the function $v(t)$ is the velocity in m/sec of a particle moving along the x-axis and starting at the position, $s(0) = 8$. Use analytical methods to do each of the following:

(a) Determine when the particle is moving to the right, to the left, and stopped.

(b) Find the particle's displacement for the given time interval and its final position.

(c) Find the total distance traveled by the particle.

1. $v(t) = 6t - 12,\ 0 \le t \le 4$

2. $v(t) = 2t - \dfrac{16}{t^2},\ \ 1 \le t \le 4$

3. $v(t) = 4\cos(2t),\ 0 \le t \le \pi/2$

4. $v(t) = \dfrac{2t}{\sqrt{2t^2 + 1}},\ 0 \le t \le 2$

5. $v(t) = t^2 - 7t + 12,\ 0 \le t \le 4$

6. $v(t) = 6\sin(t)\cos^2(t),\ 0 \le t \le \pi$

Alternate Example 4 **Modeling the Effects of Acceleration**

An object moving with initial velocity of 8 mph accelerates at the rate of $a(t) = 3.2t$ mph per second for 12 seconds.

(a) How fast is the object going when the 12 seconds are up? **(b)** How far did the object travel during those 12 seconds?

SOLUTION

(a) We first model the effect of the acceleration on the object's velocity.

Step 1: *Approximate the net change in velocity as a Riemann sum.* When acceleration is constant,

velocity change = acceleration × time applied.   [rate of change × time]

To apply this formula, we partition [0, 12] into short subintervals of length Δt. On each subinterval the acceleration is nearly constant, so if t_k is any point in the kth subinterval, the change in velocity imparted by the acceleration in the subinterval is approximately

$$a\left(t_k\right)\Delta t \quad \text{mph}. \qquad \left[\frac{\text{mph}}{\text{sec}} \times \sec\right]$$

The net change in velocity for $0 \le t \le 12$ is approximately

$$\sum a\left(t_k\right)\Delta t \quad \text{mph}.$$

Step 2: *Write a definite integral.* The limit of these sums as the norms of the partitions go to zero is

$$\int_0^{12} a(t)dt \;.$$

Step 3: *Evaluate the integral.* Using an antiderivative, we have

$$\text{Net velocity change} = \int_0^{12} 3.2t \, dt$$

$$= \left[1.6t^2\right]_0^{12}$$

$$= 230.4 \quad \text{mph}.$$

So, how fast is the object going when the 12 seconds are up? Its initial velocity is 8 mph and the acceleration adds another 230.4 mph for a total of 238.4 mph.

(b) There is nothing special about the upper limit 12 in the preceding calculation. Applying the acceleration for any length of time t adds

$$\int_0^t 3.2u \, du \qquad \text{(}u \text{ is just a dummy variable here.)}$$

to the object's velocity, giving

$$v(t) = 8 + \int_0^t 3.2u \, du$$

$$= 8 + 1.6t^2 \quad \text{mph}.$$

The distance traveled from $t = 0$ to $t = 12$ sec is

$$\int_0^{12} |v(t)| \, dt = \int_0^{12} \left(8 + 1.6t^2\right) dt \qquad \text{Extension of Alternate Example 3}$$

$$= \left[8t + 0.53t^3\right]_0^{12}$$

$$= 1017.6 \quad \text{mph} \times \text{seconds}.$$

Miles-per-hour seconds is not a distance unit that we normally work with. To convert to miles we multiply by hours/second = 1/3600, obtaining

$$1017.6 \cdot \frac{\text{mi}}{\text{hr}} \cdot \sec \cdot \frac{1 \text{ hour}}{3600 \text{ sec}} = 0.283 \text{ mile}$$

The object traveled 0.283 mi during the 12 seconds of acceleration.

Exercises for Alternate Example 4

In Exercises 7–12, an object starting at $s(0) = 0$, moving with initial velocity of $v(0) = 10$ mph accelerates at the rate of $a(t)$ mph per second for t seconds. Determine how fast the object is going when the t seconds are up and how far the object traveled during those t seconds.

7. $a(t) = 3t, t = 4$ **8.** $a(t) = 6t^2,\ t = 2$ **9.** $a(t) = e^t,\ t = 3$ **10.** $a(t) = \dfrac{1}{\sqrt{t+1}},\ t = 4$

11. $a(t) = \cos t,\ t = \pi/2$ **12.** $a(t) = 2 - \sin t,\ t = \pi$

■

Alternate Example 5   Potato Consumption

From 1970 to 1980, the rate of potato consumption in a particular country was $C(t) = 2.8 + 1.8^t$ millions of bushels per year, with t being years since the beginning of 1970. How many bushels were consumed from the beginning of 1972 to the end of 1973?

SOLUTION

We seek the cumulative effect of the consumption rate for $2 \le t \le 4$.

Step 1: *Riemann sum.* We partition $[2, 4]$ into subintervals of length Δt and let t_k be a time in the kth subinterval. The amount consumed during this interval is approximately

$$A(t_k) = C\left(t_k\right) \Delta t \text{ million bushels.}$$

The consumption for for $2 \le t \le 4$ is approximately

$$\sum C\left(t_k\right) \Delta t \text{ million bushels.}$$

Step 2: *Definite integral.* The amount consumed from $t = 2$ to $t = 4$ is the limit of these sums as the norms of the partitions go to zero.

$$\int_2^4 C(t)\, dt = \int_2^4 (2.8 + 1.8^t)\, dt \text{ million bushels}$$

Step 3: *Evaluate.* Evaluating numerically, we obtain
$$\text{NINT } (2.8 + 1.8^t, t, 2, 4) = 17.95 \text{ million bushels.}$$

Exercises for Alternate Example 5

In Exercises 13–20, $C(t)$ gives the rate of consumption of different commodities from 1970 to 1980, with t being years since the beginning of 1970. How much of each commodity was consumed from the beginning of 1972 to the end of 1973?

13. $C(t) = 1.8 + 2.8^t$ **14.** $C(t) = 3.4 + 1.2^t$ **15.** $C(t) = 4.2 + 1.4^t$ **16.** $C(t) = 2.5 + 1.8^t$

17. $C(t) = 30.5\, e^{t/10}$ **18.** $C(t) = 4.3\, e^{2t}$ **19.** $C(t) = 7.4 + 2.3 \sin\left(\dfrac{\pi t}{12}\right)$ **20.** $C(t) = 4.7 - 1.2 \cos\left(\dfrac{\pi t}{12}\right)$

■

Alternate Example 7 **A Bit of Work**

It takes a force of 16 N to stretch a spring 4 m beyond its natural length. How much work is done in stretching the spring 9 m from its natural length?

SOLUTION

We let $F(x)$ represent the force in newtons required to stretch the spring x meters from its natural length. By Hooke's Law, $F(x) = kx$ for some constant k. We are told that

$$F(4) = 16$$
$$ = 4k$$

so $k = 4$ N/m and $F(x) = 4x$ for this particular spring.

We construct an integral for the work done in applying F over the interval from $x = 0$ to $x = 9$.

Step 1: *Riemann sum.* We partition the interval into subintervals on each of which F is so nearly constant that we can apply the constant-force formula ($W = Fd$) for work. If x_k is any point in the kth subinterval, the value of F throughout the interval is approximately $F(x_k) = 4x_k$. The work done by F across the interval is approximately $4x_k \Delta x$, where Δx is the length of the interval. The sum

$$\sum F\left(x_k\right) \Delta x = \sum 4x_k \Delta x$$

approximates the work done by F from $x = 0$ to $x = 4$.

Steps 2 and 3: *Integrate.* The limit of the sum as the norms of the partitions go to zero is

$$\int_0^9 F(x)\,dx = \int_0^9 (4x)\,dx$$

$$= \left[2x^2\right]_0^9$$

$$= 162 \quad \text{N} \cdot \text{m}.$$

Exercises for Alternate Example 7

In Exercises 21–26, you are given the force, F newtons, it takes to stretch a spring 10 meters beyond its natural length. How much work is done in stretching the spring x meters from its natural length?

21. $F = 10$, $x = 16$ **22.** $F = 20$, $x = 8$ **23.** $F = 30$, $x = 12$ **24.** $F = 32$, $x = 20$ **25.** $F = 38$, $x = 6$

26. $F = 47$, $x = 30$ ■

7.2 Areas in the Plane

Alternate Example 2 **Area of an Enclosed Region**

Find the area of the region enclosed by the parabola $y = -3x^2 + 5$ and the line $y = 2x$.

SOLUTION

We graph the curves to view the region (Figure 7.2).

The limits of integration are found by solving the system of equations

$$\begin{cases} y = -3x^2 + 5 \\ y = 2x \end{cases}$$

which results in the equation

$$-3x^2 + 5 = 2x$$

Solving this equation either algebraically or by calculator gives the solutions $x = 1$ and $x = -5/3$.

Since the parabola lies above the line on $\left[-\dfrac{5}{3}, 1 \right]$, the area integrand is $-3x^2 + 5 - 2x$.

$$A = \int_{-5/3}^{1} \left(-3x^2 - 2x + 5 \right) dx$$

$$= \left[-x^3 - x^2 + 5x \right]_{-5/3}^{1}$$

$$= \left[-1^3 - 1^2 + 5(1) \right] - \left[-\left(-\frac{5}{3} \right)^3 - \left(-\frac{5}{3} \right)^2 + 5\left(-\frac{5}{3} \right) \right]$$

$$= 3 - \frac{125}{27} + \frac{25}{9} + \frac{25}{3}$$

$$= 9.48$$

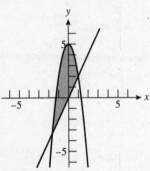

Figure 7.2 The region bounded by $y = -3x^2 + 5$ and the line $y = 2x$.

Exercises for Alternate Example 2

In Exercises 1–6, find the area of the region enclosed by the two curves, $f(x)$ and $g(x)$.

1. $f(x) = x^2 + 6$ and $g(x) = 5x$

2. $f(x) = x^2$ and $g(x) = \sqrt{x}$

3. $f(x) = 4 - x^2$ and $g(x) = x^2 - 4$

4. $f(x) = x^3$ and $g(x) = x$

5. $f(x) = 2^x$ and $g(x) = 2x$

6. $f(x) = \sin x$ and $g(x) = 3 \sin x$, $0 \le x \le \pi$

$\blacksquare$

Alternate Example 4   **Finding Area Using Subregions**

Find the area of the region R in the first quadrant that is bounded above by $y = 3\sqrt{x}$ and below by the *x*-axis and the line $y = 3x - 6$.

SOLUTION

The region is shown in Figure 7.3.

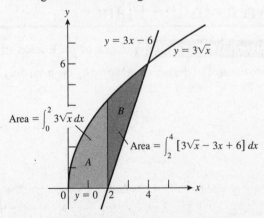

Figure 7.3 Region R split into subgroups A and B.

First find the point of intersection of the line and the curve by equating the the functions:

$$3\sqrt{x} = 3x - 6$$
$$9x = (3x - 6)^2$$
$$9x = 9(x - 2)^2$$
$$x = (x - 2)^2$$
$$x^2 - 4x + 4 - x = 0$$
$$x^2 - 5x + 4 = 0$$
$$x = 1 \text{ or } x = 4$$

$x = 1$ is an extraneous solution. So the intersection is $x = 4$ and $y = 6$.

While it appears that no single integral can give the area of R (the bottom boundary is defined by two different curves), we can split the region at $x = 2$ into two regions A and B. The area of R can be found as the sum of the areas of A and B.

$$\text{Area of } R = \underbrace{\int_0^2 3\sqrt{x}\, dx}_{\text{Area of } A} + \underbrace{\int_2^4 \left[\left(3\sqrt{x}\right) - \left(3x - 6\right)\right] dx}_{\text{Area of } B}$$

$$= \left[2x^{3/2}\right]_0^2 + \left[2x^{3/2} - \frac{3}{2}x^2 + 6x\right]_2^4$$

$$= \left[2(2)^{3/2}\right] + \left[2(4)^{3/2} - \frac{3}{2}(4)^2 + 6(4) - \left(2(2)^{3/2} - \frac{3}{2}(2)^2 + 6(2)\right)\right]$$

$$= 16 - 24 + 24 + 6 - 12$$

$$= 10 \text{ units squared}$$

Exercises for Alternate Example 4

In Exercises 7–12, find the area of the region enclosed by the two curves, $f(x)$ and $g(x)$, and the axis specified.

7. $f(x) = 3\sqrt{x}$, $g(x) = 4 - x$, x-axis

8. $f(x) = 5\sqrt{x}$, $g(x) = 4x - 6$, y-axis

9. $f(x) = 2 - x$, $g(x) = x$, y-axis

10. $f(x) = \sqrt{2 - x}$, $g(x) = x^3$, x-axis

11. $f(x) = 2 - x$, $g(x) = x^2$, y-axis

12. $f(x) = \sin x$, $g(x) = \cos x$, y-axis, $0 \le x \le \pi/4$

■

Alternate Example 5 **Integrating with Respect to *y***

Find the area of the region R in the first quadrant that is bounded above by $y = 3\sqrt{x}$ and below by the x-axis and the line $y = 3x - 6$ (the region in Alternate Example 4) by integrating with respect to y.

SOLUTION

We remarked in solving Alternate Example 4 that it appears that no single integral can give the area of R; however, notice how appearances change when we think of our rectangles being summed over y. The interval of integration is $[0, 6]$, and the rectangles run between the same two curves on the entire interval. There is no need to split the region (Figure 7.4).

We need to solve for x in terms of y in both equations:

$$y = 3x - 6 \qquad \text{becomes} \qquad x = \frac{1}{3}y + 2,$$

$$y = 3\sqrt{x} \qquad \text{becomes} \qquad x = \frac{1}{9}y^2, \quad y \ge 0.$$

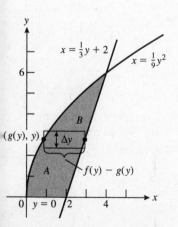

Figure 7.4 It takes two integrations to find the area of this region if we integrate with respect to x. It takes only one if we integrate with respect to y

We must still be careful to subtract the lower number from the higher number when forming the integrand. In this case, the higher numbers are the higher x-values, which are on the line $x = \frac{1}{3}y + 2$ because the line lies to the right of the parabola. So,

$$\text{Area of } R = \int_0^6 \left(\left(\frac{1}{3}y + 2 \right) - \left(\frac{1}{9}y^2 \right) \right) dy$$

$$= \int_0^6 \left(\frac{1}{3}y + 2 - \frac{1}{9}y^2 \right) dy$$

$$= \left[\frac{1}{6}y^2 + 2y - \frac{1}{27}y^3 \right]_0^6$$

$$= \frac{1}{6}(6)^2 + 2(6) - \frac{1}{27}(6)^3$$

$$= 6 + 12 - 8$$

$$= 10 \text{ units squared}$$

Exercises for Alternate Example 5

In Exercises 13–18, find the area enclosed by the two curves, $f(x)$ and $g(x)$, and the axis specified by integrating with respect to y.

13. $f(x) = 3\sqrt{x}$, $g(x) = 4 - x$, y-axis

14. $f(x) = 5\sqrt{x}$, $g(x) = 4x - 6$, x-axis

15. $f(x) = 2 - x$, $g(x) = x$, y-axis

16. $f(x) = \sqrt{2-x}$, $g(x) = x^3$, y-axis

17. $f(x) = 2 - x$, $g(x) = x^2$, x-axis

18. $f(x) = \sin x$, $g(x) = \cos x$, x-axis, $0 \le x \le \dfrac{\pi}{2}$

Alternate Example 6   Making the Choice

Find the area of the region enclosed by the graphs of $y = -x^3$ and $x = 2y^2 - 3$.

SOLUTION

We can produce a graph of the region on a calculator by graphing the three curves

$$y = -x^3, y = \sqrt{\frac{3+x}{2}}, \text{ and } y = -\sqrt{\frac{3+x}{2}} \text{ (Figure 7.5).}$$

This conveniently gives us all of our bounding curves as functions of x. If we integrate in terms of x, however, we need to split the region at $x = a$ (Figure 7.6).

On the other hand, we can integrate from $y = b$ to $y = d$ and handle the entire region at once. We solve the cubic for x in terms of y:

$$y = -x^3 \qquad \text{becomes} \quad x = (-y)^{1/3} = -(y)^{1/3}$$

To find the limits of integration, we solve the following system

$$\begin{cases} x = -(y)^{1/3} \\ x = 2y^2 - 3 \end{cases}$$

$$-(y)^{1/3} = 2y^2 - 3$$

This equation gives $y = 1$ as the upper limit b. Having $b = 1$, we need to find the other limit which is the other answer of the equation. It is easy to see that the upper limit is $d = 1$, but a calculator is needed to find that the lower limit $d = -1.43673029$. We store this value as B.

The cubic lies to the right of the parabola, so

$$\text{Area} = \text{NINT}\left(-y^{1/3} - \left(2y^2 - 3 \right), y, B, 1 \right)$$

$$= 5.132295399.$$

The area is about 5.13.

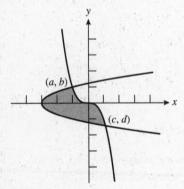

Figure 7.5 The region enclosed by $y_1 = -x^3$, $y_2 = \sqrt{(3+x)/2}$, and $y_3 = -\sqrt{(3+x)/2}$.

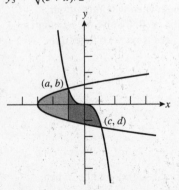

Figure 7.6 If we integrate with respect to x, we must split the region at $x = a$.

Exercises for Alternate Example 6

In Exercises 19–24, find the area of the region enclosed by the graphs of the given lines and curves.

19. $y = 3x^3$ and $x = 3y^2 - 5$ **20.** $y = 4x^3$ and $x = 5y^2 - 2$ **21.** $y = 4 - x^2$, $x = 2 - y$

22. $y = \sqrt{2+x}$, $x = 2y - 2$ **23.** $y = |x|$, $x = y^2 - 2$ **24.** $y = \sin\dfrac{\pi x}{2}$ and $x = y$ ■

7.3 Volumes

Alternate Example 1 **A Square-Based Pyramid**

A pyramid 5 m high has congruent triangular sides and a square base that is 5 m on each side. Each cross section of the pyramid is parallel to the base is a square. Find the volume of the pyramid.

SOLUTION

We follow the steps for the method of slicing.

1. *Sketch.* We draw the pyramid with its vertex at the origin and its altitude along the interval $0 \leq x \leq 5$. We sketch a typical cross section at a point x between 0 and 5 (Figure 7.7).

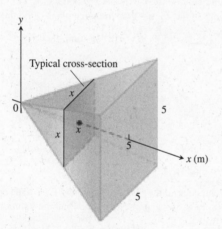

Figure 7.7 The cross section of the pyramid in Alternate Example 1.

2. *Find a formula for A(x).* The cross section at x is a square x meters on a side, so $A(x) = x^2$.

3. *Find the limits of integration.* The squares go from $x = 0$ to $x = 5$.

4. *Integrate to find the volume.*

$$V = \int_0^5 A(x)\,dx$$

$$= \int_0^5 (x^2)\,dx$$

$$= \left[\frac{1}{3}x^3 \right]_0^5$$

$$= \frac{125}{3}$$

$$= 41.67\,\text{m}^3$$

Exercises for Alternate Example 1

For Exercises 1 and 2, a pyramid h meters high has congruent triangular sides and a square base that is d meters on each side. Each cross section of the pyramid is parallel to the base is a square. Find the volume of the solid analytically.

1. $h = 8$ and $d = 8$

2. $h = 12$ and $d = 12$

For Exercises 3 and 4, the solid lies between planes perpendicular to the x-axis at $x = a$ and $x = b$. The cross sections perpendicular to the axis on $a \le x \le b$ are squares whose bases run from $y = f(x)$ to $y = g(x)$ in the xy-plane. Find the volume of the solid analytically.

3. $f(x) = |2 - x|$ and $g(x) = 2 - |2 - x|$, $(a, b) = (1, 3)$

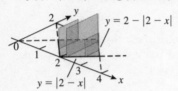

4. $f(x) = 4 - x^2$ and $g(x) = x^2 - 4$, $(a, b) = (-2, 2)$

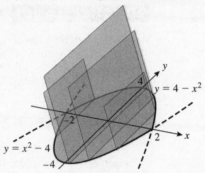

For Exercises 5 and 6 the solid lies between planes perpendicular to the x-axis at $x = a$ and $x = b$. The cross sections perpendicular to the axis on $a \le x \le b$ are equilateral triangles whose bases run from $y = f(x)$ to $y = g(x)$ in the xy-plane. Find the volume of the solid analytically.

5. $f(x) = |2 - x|$ and $g(x) = 2 - |2 - x|$, $(a, b) = (1, 3)$

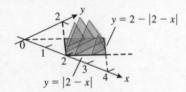

6. $f(x) = 4 - x^2$ and $g(x) = x^2 - 4$, $(a, b) = (-2, 2)$

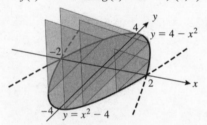

For Exercises 7 and 8, the solid lies between planes perpendicular to the x-axis at $x = a$ and $x = b$. The cross sections perpendicular to the axis on $a \le x \le b$ semicircles whose diameters run from $y = f(x)$ to $y = g(x)$ in the xy-plane. Find the volume of the solid analytically.

7. $f(x) = |2 - x|$ and $g(x) = 2 - |2 - x|$, $(a, b) = (1, 3)$

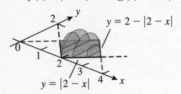

8. $f(x) = 4 - x^2$ and $g(x) = x^2 - 4$, $(a, b) = (-2, 2)$

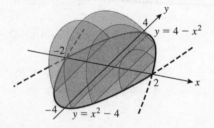

Alternate Example 2 A Solid of Revolution

The region between the graph of $f(x) = 2 + x \sin x$ and the x-axis over the interval $[-2, 2]$ is revolved about the x-axis to generate a solid. Find the volume of the solid.

SOLUTION

Revolving the region (Figure 7.8) about the x-axis generates the vase-shaped solid in Figure 7.9. The cross section at a typical point x is circular, with radius equal to $f(x)$. Its area is

$$A(x) = \pi \left(f(x) \right)^2.$$

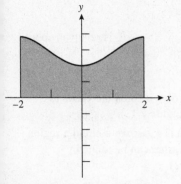

Figure 7.8 The region between $f(x) = 2 + x \sin x$ and the x-axis over the interval $[-2, 2]$.

The volume of the solid is

$$V = \int_{-2}^{2} A(x)\,dx$$

$$= \int_{-2}^{2} \pi \left(2 + x \sin x\right)^2 dx$$

$$= \text{NINT}\left(\pi \left(2 + x \sin x\right)^2, x, -2, 2\right)$$

$$\approx 108.6 \text{ units cubed.}$$

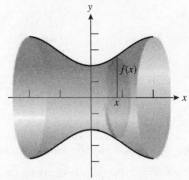

Figure 7.9 The region in Figure 7.8 is revolved about x-axis to generate a solid. A typical cross section is circular, with radius $f(x) = 2 + x \sin x$.

Exercises for Alternate Example 2

In each of Exercises 9–11, the region between the graph of $f(x)$ and the x-axis over the interval $[a, b]$ is revolved about the x-axis to generate a solid. Find the volume of each solid.

9. $f(x) = \sqrt{2 + x}$, $[-2, 0]$

10. $f(x) = 15 - 2x - x^2$, $[-5, 3]$

11. $f(x) = |1 - x^2|$, $[-2, 2]$

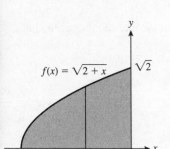

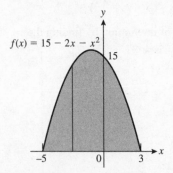

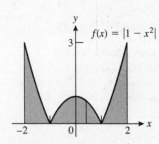

In each of Exercises 12–14, the region between the graph of $f(y)$ and the y-axis over the interval $[a, b]$ is revolved about the x-axis to generate a solid. Find the volume of each solid.

12. $f(y) = 4 - y^2$, $[0, 2]$

13. $f(y) = -1 + \sqrt{16 - y}$, $[0, 15]$

14. $f(y) = 4 + y$, $[0, 4]$

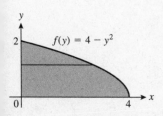

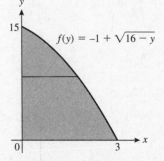

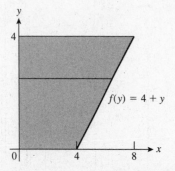

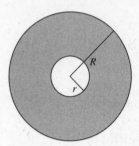

Alternate Example 3   Washer Cross Sections

The region bounded by the curve $y = x^2 + 1$ and the line $y = -x + 3$ is revolved about the x-axis to generate a solid. Find the volume of the solid.

SOLUTION

The curve and the line are shown in Figure 7.10. We revolve it about the x-axis to generate a solid with a cone-shaped cavity in its center (Figure 7.11).

Each cross section perpendicular to the axis of revolution is a *washer*, a circular region with a circular region cut from its center. The area of a washer can be found by subtracting the inner area from the outer area (Figure 7.12).

Figure 7.10 The curve $y = x^2 + 1$ and the line $y = -x + 3$.

Figure 7.12 A washer cross section of the solid shown in Figure 7.11.

In our region the line $y = -x + 3$ defines the outer radius $R(x)$, and the inner radius $r(x)$ is defined by the curve $y = x^2 + 1$. So

$$A(x) = \pi\left(R(x)\right)^2 - \pi\left(r(x)\right)^2$$
$$= \pi\left(\left(R(x)\right)^2 - \left(r(x)\right)^2\right)$$
$$= \pi\left((-x+3)^2 - (x^2+1)^2\right)$$
$$= \pi\left((x^2 - 6x + 9) - (x^4 + 2x^2 + 1)\right)$$
$$= \pi(8 - 6x - x^2 - x^4)$$

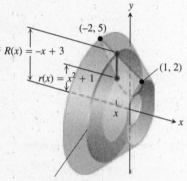

Washer cross section
Outer radius: $R(x) = -x + 3$
Inner radius: $r(x) = x^2 + 1$

Figure 7.11 The curve $y = x^2 + 1$ and the line $y = -x + 3$ rotated about the x-axis to form a solid.
Source: Weir/Giordano/Hass, THOMAS *CALCULUS* 11th edition (page 403).
(c) 2005 Pearson Education, Inc.
Reproduced by permission of Pearson Education, Inc.

Find the limits of integration by finding the x-coordinates of the intersections of the line and the curve as follows:

$$x^2 + 1 = -x + 3$$
$$x^2 + x - 2 = 0$$
$$(x + 2)(x - 1) = 0$$
$$x = -2, \; x = 1$$

The volume is

$$V = \int_a^b A(x)\,dx$$

$$= \int_{-2}^{1} \pi(8 - 6x - x^2 - x^4)\,dx$$

$$= \pi\left[8x - 3x^2 - \frac{x^3}{3} - \frac{x^5}{5}\right]_{-2}^{1}$$

$$= \frac{67\pi}{15} - \left(-\frac{284\pi}{15}\right)$$

$$= \frac{117\pi}{5}$$

Exercises for Alternate Example 3

In Exercises 15–20, the region in the first quadrant enclosed by the *y*-axis and the graphs of $f(x)$ and $g(x)$ is revolved about the *x*-axis to form a solid. Find its volume.

15. $f(x) = 6 \cos x, g(x) = 6 \sin x$ **16.** $f(x) = 8 \cos x, g(x) = 8 \sin x$ **17.** $f(x) = 4 - x^2, g(x) = 1 - (1 - x)^2$

18. $f(x) = x^3, g(x) = \sqrt{x}$ **19.** $f(x) = x^2 + 6, g(x) = 5x$ **20.** $f(x) = x^4 - 4x^2 + 4, g(x) = x^2$ ■

Alternate Example 6   Mathematician's Paperweight

A mathematician has a paperweight made so that its base is the shape of the region between the *x*-axis and one arch of the curve $y = 6 \sin x$ (linear units in inches). Each cross section cut perpendicular to the *x*-axis (and hence to the *xy*-plane) is a semicircle whose diameter runs from the *x*-axis to the curve. (Think of the cross section as a semicircular fin sticking up out of the plane.) Find the volume of the paperweight.

SOLUTION

The paperweight is not easily drawn, but we know what it looks like. Its base is the region in Figure 7.13, and the cross sections perpendicular to the base are semicircular fins like those in Figure 7.14.

The semicircle at each point *x* has

$$\text{Radius} = \frac{6 \sin x}{2}$$
$$= 3 \sin x$$

and area

$$A(x) = \frac{1}{2} \pi \left(3 \sin x\right)^2$$

The volume of the paperweight is

$$V = \int_0^\pi A(x)\, dx$$

$$= \int_0^\pi \left[\frac{1}{2} \pi (3 \sin x)^2\right] dx$$

$$= \frac{9\pi}{2} \int_0^\pi (\sin x)^2\, dx$$

$$= \frac{9\pi}{2} \text{ NINT} \left((\sin x)^2, x, 0, \pi\right)$$

$$\approx \frac{9\pi}{2} (1.570796327)$$

The number in parentheses looks like half of π, an observation that can be confirmed analytically, and which we support numerically by dividing by π to get 1.5. The volume of the paperweight is

$$\frac{9\pi}{2}\left(\frac{\pi}{2}\right) = \frac{9\pi^2}{4}$$
$$\approx 22.21 \text{ in.}^3$$

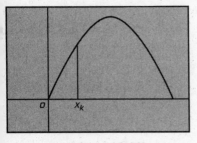

[−1, 3.5] by [−0.8, 2.2]

Figure 7.13 The base of the paperweight in Alternate Example 6. The segment perpendicular to the *x*-axis at x_k is the diameter of a semicircle that is perpendicular to the base.

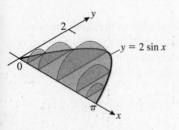

Figure 7.14 Cross sections perpendicular to the region in Figure 7.13 are semicircular.

Exercises for Alternate Example 6

In Exercises 21–26, find the volume of the solid analytically. The base of the solid is the shape of the region between the x-axis and one arch of the curve y (linear units in inches). Each cross section cut perpendicular to the x-axis (and hence to the xy-plane) is the given figure whose base runs from the x-axis to the curve. (Think of the cross section as a fin sticking up out of the plane.)

21. $y = 4 \sin x$ (cross sections are semicircles)

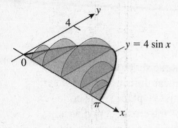

22. $y = 8 \sin x$ (cross sections are equilateral triangles)

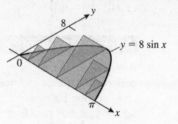

23. $y = 10 \sin x$ (cross sections are squares)

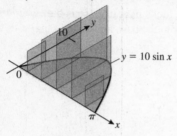

24. $y = 4 - (x - 2)^2$ (cross sections are semicircles)

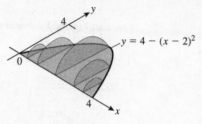

25. $y = 5 - |x|$ (cross sections are equilateral triangles)

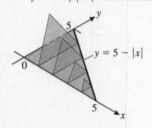

26. $y = 16 - x^4$ (cross sections are squares)

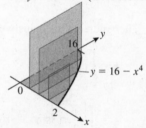

7.4 Lengths of Curves

Alternate Example 1 **The Length of a Sine Wave**

What is the length of the curve $y = 3 \sin x$ from $x = 0$ to $x = 2\pi$?

SOLUTION

We answer this question with integration, following our usual plan of breaking the whole into measurable parts. We partition $[0, 2\pi]$ into intervals so short that the pieces of curve (call them "arcs") lying directly above the intervals are nearly straight. That way, each arc is nearly the same as the line segment joining its two ends and we can take the length of the segment as an approximation to the length of the arc.

Figure 7.15 shows the segment approximating the arc above the subinterval $[x_{k-1}, x_k]$.

The length of the segment is $\sqrt{\Delta x_k{}^2 + \Delta y_k{}^2}$.

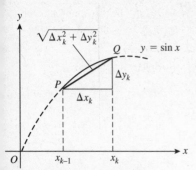

Figure 7.15 The line segment approximating the arc PQ of the sine curve above the subinterval $[x_{k-1}, x_k]$

The sum

$$\sum \sqrt{\Delta x_k^2 + \Delta y_k^2}$$

over the entire partition approximates the length of the curve. All we need now is to find the limit of this sum as the norms of the partitions go to zero. However, the sums as written are not Riemann sums. They do not have the form $\sum f(c_k)\,\Delta x$. We can rewrite them as Riemann sums if we multiply and divide each square root by Δx_k.

$$\sum \sqrt{\Delta x_k^2 + \Delta y_k^2} = \sum \frac{\left(\sqrt{\Delta x_k^2 + \Delta y_k^2}\right)\Delta x_k}{\Delta x_k}$$

$$= \sum \frac{\left(\sqrt{\Delta x_k^2 + \Delta y_k^2}\right)\Delta x_k}{\sqrt{\Delta x_k^2}}$$

$$= \sum \sqrt{\frac{\Delta x_k^2 + \Delta y_k^2}{\Delta x_k^2}}\,(\Delta x_k)$$

$$= \sum \sqrt{1 + \frac{\Delta y_k^2}{\Delta x_k^2}}\,(\Delta x_k)$$

$$= \sum \sqrt{1 + \left(\frac{\Delta y_k}{\Delta x_k}\right)^2}\,(\Delta x_k)$$

This is better, but we still need to write the last square root as a function evaluated at some c_k in the kth subinterval. For this, we call on the Mean Value Theorem for differentiable functions (Section 4.2), which says that since $3\sin x$ is continuous on $[x_{k-1}, x_k]$ and is differentiable on $[x_{k-1}, x_k]$, there is a point c_k in $[x_{k-1}, x_k]$ at which $\dfrac{\Delta y_k}{\Delta x_k} = 3\sin' c_k$ (Figure 7.16). That gives us

$$\sum \sqrt{1 + \left(\left(3\sin c_k\right)'\right)^2}\,\Delta x,$$

which is a Riemann sum.

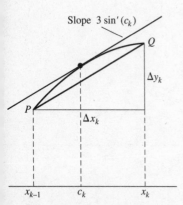

Figure 7.16 The portion of the curve above $[x_{k-1}, x_k]$. At some c_k in the interval, $3\sin'(c_k) = \dfrac{\Delta y_k}{\Delta x_k}$, the slope of segment PQ.

Now we take the limit as the norms of the subdivisions go to zero and find that the length of one wave of the sine function is

$$\sum \sqrt{1 + \left(\left(3\sin c_k\right)'\right)^2}\,dx = \int_0^{2\pi} \sqrt{1 + \left(3\cos x\right)^2}\,dx$$

$$\approx 13.97 \qquad \text{Using NINT}$$

Exercises for Alternate Example 1

In Exercises 1–6, what is the length of each curve y from $x = a$ to $x = b$?

1. $y = 2\sin x$ from $x = 0$ to $x = 2\pi$ **2.** $y = 5\sin x$ from $x = 0$ to $x = 2\pi$ **3.** $y = x^3$ from $x = 0$ to $x = 2$

4. $y = \sqrt{x - 3}$ from $x = 3$ to $x = 10$ **5.** $y = e^{3x}$ from $x = 0$ to $x = 1$ **6.** $y = x\sin x$ from $x = 0$ to $x = \pi$

Alternate Example 2 **Applying the Definition**

Find the length of the curve

$$y = \frac{3\sqrt{5}}{4}x^{3/2} - 2 \quad \text{for } 0 \le x \le 2.$$

SOLUTION

Differentiate both sides of the equation of the curve.

$$\frac{dy}{dx} = \frac{3\sqrt{5}}{4}\left(\frac{3}{2}\right)x^{1/2}$$

$$= \frac{9\sqrt{5}}{8}x^{1/2},$$

which is continuous on $[0, 2]$. Therefore,

$$L = \int_0^2 \sqrt{1 + \left(\frac{dy}{dx}\right)^2}\, dx$$

$$= \int_0^2 \sqrt{1 + \left(\frac{9\sqrt{5}}{8}x^{1/2}\right)^2}\, dx$$

$$= \int_0^2 \sqrt{1 + \frac{405}{64}x}\, dx$$

$$= \frac{2}{3}\cdot\frac{64}{405}\left[\left(1 + \frac{405}{64}x\right)^{3/2}\right]_0^2$$

$$= \frac{128}{1215}\left[\left(1 + \frac{405}{64}(2)\right)^{3/2} - \left(1 + \frac{405}{64}(0)\right)^{3/2}\right]$$

$$= \frac{128}{1215}\left[\left(1 + \frac{405}{32}\right)^{3/2} - 1\right]$$

$$\approx 5.21$$

Exercises for Alternate Example 2

In Exercises 7–12, find the length of each curve y for $a \le x \le b$.

7. $y = \dfrac{5\sqrt{7}}{3}x^{3/2} - 9$ for $0 \le x \le 5$ **8.** $y = \dfrac{2\sqrt{6}}{5}x^{3/2} - 2$ for $0 \le x \le 6$ **9.** $y = (x+5)^{3/2}$ for $-5 \le x \le 0$

10. $y = 2x^{4/5}$ for $0 \le x \le 2$ **11.** $y = (x-5)^{4/3}$ for $5 \le x \le 6$ **12.** $y = \ln x$ for $1 \le x \le 2$ ■

Alternate Example 3 **A Vertical Tangent**

Find the length of the curve $y = 2x^{1/5}$ between $(-32, -4)$ and $(32, 4)$.

SOLUTION

The derivative

$$\frac{dy}{dx} = \frac{2}{5}x^{-4/5}$$

is not defined at $x = 0$. Graphically, there is a vertical tangent at $x = 0$, where the derivative becomes infinite (Figure 7.17). If we change to x as a function of y, the tangent at the origin will be horizontal (Figure 7.18) and the derivative will be zero instead of undefined. Solving $y = 2x^{1/5}$ for x gives $x = \frac{1}{32}y^5$, and so $\frac{dx}{dy} = \frac{5}{32}y^4$.

$$L = \int_{-4}^{4} \sqrt{1 + \left(\frac{dx}{dy}\right)^2}\, dy$$

$$= \int_{-4}^{4} \sqrt{1 + \left(\frac{5}{32}y^4\right)^2}\, dy$$

$$\approx 67.17 \qquad\qquad \text{Using NINT}$$

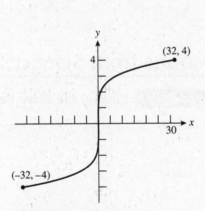

Figure 7.17 The graph of $y = 2x^{1/5}$ has a vertical tangent line at the origin where dy/dx does not exist.

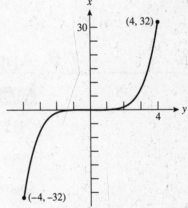

Figure 7.18 The curve in Figure 7.16 plotted with x as a function of y. The tangent at the origin is now horizontal.

Exercises for Alternate Example 3

In Exercises 13–18, find the length of each curve on the interval indicated.

13. $y = 4x^{1/3}$, $-8 \le x \le 8$

14. $y = 7x^{1/5}$, $-32 \le x \le 32$

15. $y = \frac{1}{8}x^{3/5}$, $-32 \le x \le 32$

16. $y = \frac{1}{9}x^{2/3}$, $-27 \le x \le 27$

17. $y = x^{1/3} - x^{2/3}$, $-8 \le x \le 0$

18. $y = x^{4/5} + x^{2/5}$, $0 \le x \le 32$

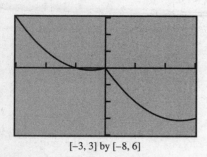

[–3, 3] by [–8, 6]

Figure 7.19 The graph of $y = x^2 - 3|x| - 2x$ from $x = -3$ to $x = 3$ has a corner at $x = 0$, where neither $\dfrac{dy}{dx}$ nor $\dfrac{dx}{dy}$ exist. We find the lengths of the two smooth pieces and add them together.

Alternate Example 4 **Getting Around a Corner**

Find the length of the curve $y = x^2 - 3|x| - 2x$ from $x = -3$ to $x = 3$.

SOLUTION

We should always be alert for abrupt slope changes when absolute value is involved. We graph the function to check (Figure 7.18).

There is clearly a corner at $x = 0$ where neither $\dfrac{dy}{dx}$ or $\dfrac{dx}{dy}$ can exist. To find the length, we split the curve at $x = 0$ to write the function without absolute values:

$$x^2 - 3|x| - 2x = \begin{cases} x^2 + x & \text{if } x < 0 \\ x^2 - 5x & \text{if } x \geq 0 \end{cases}$$

Then,

$$L = \int_{-4}^{0} \sqrt{1 + (2x + 1)^2}\, dx + \int_{0}^{4} \sqrt{1 + (2x - 5)^2}\, dx$$

$$= 23.39 \qquad \text{Using NINT}$$

Exercises for Alternate Example 4

In Exercises 19–24, find the length of each curve from $x = a$ to $x = b$.

19. $y = 2x^2 - 5|x| - 7x$, $-3 \leq x \leq 3$ **20.** $y = x^2 - 2|x| - 5x$, $-4 \leq x \leq 4$ **21.** $y = x^3 + 5|x - 1|$, $-1 \leq x \leq 2$

22. $y = |4 - x^2|$, $0 \leq x \leq 3$ **23.** $y = |\sin x|$, $-\pi \leq x \leq \pi$ **24.** $y = \sqrt{\cos x}$, $-\pi/2 \leq x\, \pi/2$ ■

7.5 Applications from Science and Statistics

Alternate Example 1 **Finding the Work Done by a Force**

Find the work done by the force $F(x) = \cos(3\pi x)$ newtons along the x-axis from $x = 0$ meters to $x = \dfrac{3}{2}$ meters.

SOLUTION

$$W = \int_{0}^{3/2} \cos(3\pi x)\, dx = \left[\frac{1}{3\pi} \sin(3\pi x) \right]_{0}^{3/2} = \frac{1}{3\pi} \sin\left(\frac{9\pi}{2} \right) = \frac{1}{3\pi}\ \text{J}$$

Exercises for Alternate Example 1

In Exercises 1–8, find the work done by the force $F(x)$ newtons along the x-axis from $x = a$ meters to $x = b$ meters.

1. $F(x) = \cos(5\pi x)$ from $x = 0$ meters to $x = 5/2$ meters   **2.** $F(x) = \cos(\pi x + 4)$ from $x = 0$ meters to $x = 3/2$ meters

3. $F(x) = \sin(7\pi x)$ from $x = 0$ meters to $x = 1/2$ meters   **4.** $F(x) = x\sqrt{x^2 + 9}$ from $x = 0$ meters to $x = 7/2$ meters

5. $F(x) = x \sin x$ from $x = 0$ meters to $x = 5/2$ meters   **6.** $F(x) = xe^{x^2}$ from $x = 0$ meters to $x = 3/2$ meters

7. $F(x) = e^x \cos x$ from $x = 0$ meters to $x = 1/2$ meters   **8.** $F(x) = 1/(x + 1)$ from $x = 0$ meters to $x = 3/2$ meters   ■

Alternate Example 2 **Work Done Lifting**

A leaky bucket weighs 28 newtons (N) empty. It is lifted from the ground at a constant rate to a point 18 m above the ground by a rope weighing 0.8 N/m. The bucket starts with 90 N of water, but it leaks at a constant rate and just finishes draining as the bucket reaches the top. Find the amount of work done

(a) lifting the bucket alone;

(b) lifting the water alone;

(c) lifting the rope alone;

(d) lifting the bucket, water, and rope together.

SOLUTION

(a) *The bucket alone.* This is easy because the bucket's weight is constant. To lift it, you must exert a force of 28 N through the entire 18-meter interval.

$$\text{Work} = (28 \text{ N}) \times (18 \text{ m})$$
$$= 504 \text{ N} \cdot \text{m}$$
$$= 504 \text{ J}$$

Figure 7.20 shows the graph of force vs. distance applied. The work corresponds to the area under the force graph.

(b) *The water alone.* The force needed to lift the water is equal to the water's weight, which decreases steadily from 90 N to 0 N over the 18-m lift. When the bucket is x meters off the ground, the water weighs

$$F(x) = \underset{\substack{\text{original} \\ \text{weight} \\ \text{of water}}}{90} \left(\underset{\substack{\text{proportion} \\ \text{left at} \\ \text{elevation } x}}{\frac{18 - x}{18}} \right) =$$

$$= 90 \left(1 - \frac{x}{18} \right)$$

$$= 90 - 5x \text{ N}$$

The work done is (Figure 7.21)

$$W = \int_{a}^{b} F(x)\,dx$$

$$= \int_{0}^{18} (90 - 5x)\,dx$$

$$= \left[90x - \frac{5}{2}x^2 \right]_{0}^{18}$$

$$= 1620 - 810$$

$$= 810 \text{ J}$$

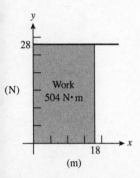

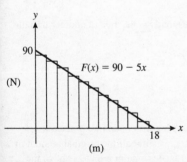

Figure 7.20 The work done by a constant 28 N force lifting a bucket 18 m is 504 N·m.

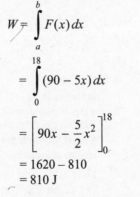

Figure 7.21 The force required to lift the water varies with distance but the work still corresponds to the area under the force graph.

(c) *The rope alone.* The force needed to lift the rope is also variable, starting at $(0.8)(18) = 14.4$ N when the bucket is on the ground and ending at 0 N when the bucket and rope are all at the top. As with the leaky bucket, the rate of decrease is constant. At elevation x meters, the $(18 - x)$ meters of rope still there to lift weigh $F(x) = (0.8)(18 - x)$ N. Figure 7.22 shows the graph of F. The work done lifting the rope is

$$W = \int_a^b F(x)\,dx$$

$$= \int_0^{18} (0.8)(18 - x)\,dx$$

$$= \int_0^{18} (14.4 - 0.8x)\,dx$$

$$= \left[14.4x - 0.4x^2 \right]_0^{18}$$

$$= 259.2 - 129.6$$

$$= 129.6 \ \text{N} \cdot \text{m}$$

$$= 129.6 \ \text{J}$$

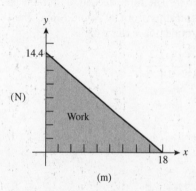

Figure 7.22 The work done lifting the rope to the top corresponds to the area of another triangle.

(d) *The bucket, water, and rope together.* The total work is
$$504 + 810 + 129.6 = 1443.6 \ \text{J}$$

Exercises for Alternate Example 2

In Exercises 9–11, a leaky bucket weighs p newtons (N) empty. It is lifted from the ground at a constant rate to a point h meters above the ground by a rope weighing 0.6 N/m. The bucket starts with q newtons (N) of water, but it leaks at a constant rate and just finishes draining as the bucket reaches the top. Find the amount of work done.

(a) lifting the bucket alone;

(b) lifting the water alone;

(c) lifting the rope alone;

(d) lifting the bucket, water, and rope together.

  9. $p = 22,\quad q = 55,\quad h = 12$

10. $p = 24,\quad q = 50,\quad h = 14$

11. $p = 18,\quad q = 65,\quad h = 16$

In Exercises 12–14, suppose a bucket containing q newtons of water is pulled up so that there is still half the original amount of water in the bucket when it reaches a point h meters above the ground. How much work is done lifting the water? (Do not include the rope and bucket.)

12. $q = 55,\quad h = 12$

13. $q = 50,\quad h = 14$

14. $q = 65,\quad h = 16$

Alternate Example 3 Work Done Pumping

The conical tank in Figure 7.23 is filled to within 2 ft of the top with olive oil weighing 64 lb/ft³. How much work does it take to pump the oil to the rim of the tank?

SOLUTION

We imagine the oil partitioned into thin slabs by planes perpendicular to the y-axis at the points of a partition of the interval $[0, 8]$. (The 8 represents the top of the oil, not the top of the tank.)

The typical slab between the planes at y and $y + \Delta y$ has a volume of about

$$\Delta V = \pi \,(\text{radius})^2(\text{thickness})$$

$$= \pi \left(\frac{1}{2} y\right)^2 \Delta y$$

$$= \left(\frac{\pi y^2}{4}\right) \Delta y \ \text{ft}^3.$$

The force $F(y)$ required to lift this slab is equal to its weight,

$$F(y) = 64 \,\Delta V \qquad \text{Weight} = (\text{weight per unit volume}) \times \text{volume}$$

$$= 64 \left(\frac{\pi y^2}{4}\right) \Delta y$$

$$= (16\pi y^2)\Delta y \ \text{lb}.$$

The distance through which $F(y)$ must act to lift this slab to the level of the rim of the cone is about $(10 - y)$ ft, so the work done lifting the slab is about

$$\Delta W = (16\pi y^2)(10 - y)\Delta y \ \text{ft} \cdot \text{lb}.$$

The work done lifting all the slabs from $y = 0$ to $y = 8$ to the rim is approximately

$$W \approx \sum (16\pi y^2)(10 - y)\Delta y \ \text{ft} \cdot \text{lb}.$$

This is a Riemann sum for the function $(16\pi y^2)(10 - y)$ on the interval from $y = 0$ to $y = 8$. The work of pumping the oil to the rim is the limit of these sums as the norms of the partitions go to zero.

$$W = \int_0^8 \left(16\pi y^2\right)(10 - y)\,dy$$

$$= 16\pi \int_0^8 \left(10y^2 - y^3\right)dy$$

$$= 16\pi \left[\frac{10}{3} y^3 - \frac{1}{4} y^4\right]_0^8$$

$$= 16\pi \left[\frac{10}{3}(8)^3 - \frac{1}{4}(8)^4\right]$$

$$\approx 34{,}314.57 \ \text{ft} \cdot \text{lb}$$

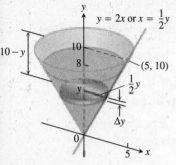

$y = 2x$ or $x = \frac{1}{2}y$

$(5, 10)$

$10 - y$

$\frac{1}{2}y$

Δy

Figure 7.23 The conical tank in Alternate Example 3.

Exercises for Alternate Example 3

In Exercises 15–18, the conical tank in Figure 7.23 is filled to within x feet of the top with olive oil weighing m pounds per cubic foot. How much work does it take to pump the oil to the rim of the tank?

15. $x = 2$, $m = 65$ lb/ft^3 **16.** $x = 2$, $m = 60$ lb/ft^3 **17.** $x = 1$, $m = 65$ lb/ft^3

18. $x = 1$, $m = 60$ lb/ft^3

In Exercises 19–20, a cylindrical tank with height 20 feet and diameter 10 feet is filled to within x feet of the top with olive oil weighing m pounds per cubic foot. How much work does it take to pump the oil to the rim of the tank?

19. $x = 3$, $m = 78$ lb/ft^3 **20.** $x = 4$, $m = 80$ lb/ft^3

Alternate Example 7 Weights of Potato Chip Bags

Suppose that bags of potato chips marked as "20 ounces" actually have weights that are normally distributed about a mean weight of 20.1 ounces and a standard deviation of 0.1 ounce.

(a) What percentage of all such bags of potato chips can be expected to weigh between 20 and 21 ounces?

(b) What percentage would we expect to weigh less than 20 ounces?

(c) What is the probability that a bag weighs exactly 20 ounces?

SOLUTION

We can use a normal probability density function for this distribution (Figure 7.24).

$$f(x) = \frac{1}{\sigma\sqrt{2\pi}} e^{-(x-\mu)^2/(2\sigma)^2} = \frac{1}{0.1\sqrt{2\pi}} e^{-(x-20.1)^2/0.02}$$

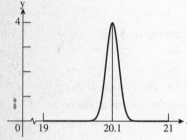

(a) The probability that a randomly selected bag of these potato chips weighs between 20 and 21 ounces is the area under the curve from 20 to 21. That is,

NINT($f(x), x, 19, 21$) ≈ 0.8413

So, we can predict that 84.13% of all such bags will weigh between 20 and 21 ounces.

(b) The percentage that would weigh less than 20 ounces could be approximated by

NINT($f(x), x, 19, 20$) ≈ 0.1587

So, we would expect about 15.87% of the bags to weigh less than 20 ounces.

Figure 7.24 The normal pdf for the potato chip weights in Alternate Example 7. The mean is at the center.

(c) Since the area under a point is zero, the probability that a bag weighs exactly any fixed amount, including 20 ounces, is zero. Remember that we are assuming that there are an infinite number of possible potato chip weights along a continuous, unbroken interval, and 20 is but one of an infinite number of them.

Exercises for Alternate Example 7

In Exercises 21–26, you are given the mean (μ) and standard deviation (σ) of a distribution that can be assumed to be normal. In each case, determine the probability requested.

21. SAT scores, $\mu = 500$, $\sigma = 100$, probability of score greater than 600

22. Heights of men, $\mu = 68$ inches, $\sigma = 2.5$ inches, probability of between 66 and 72 inches

23. Unemployment rate, $\mu = 7.9\%$, $\sigma = 1.6\%$, probability of less than 6%

24. Diameter of hail, $\mu = 0.5$ inch, $\sigma = 0.1$ inch, probability of greater than 0.7 inches

25. Weights of apples, $\mu = 5$ ounces, $\sigma = 1.2$ ounces, probability of between 4 and 6 ounces

26. Emergency Medical team time to respond, $\mu = 17$ minutes, $\sigma = 3$ minutes, probability more than 22 minutes

Chapter 8

Sequences, L'Hôpital's Rule, and Improper Integrals

8.1 Sequences

Alternate Example 2 **Defining a Sequence Recursively**

Find the first four terms and the tenth term for the sequence defined recursively by the conditions:

$$b_1 = 6$$
$$b_n = 2b_{n-1} - 3 \quad \text{for all } n \geq 2.$$

SOLUTION

We proceed one term at a time, starting with $b_1 = 6$ and obtaining each succeeding term by doubling the term just before it and subtracting 3 from the result:

$$b_1 = 6$$
$$b_2 = 2b_1 - 3 = 2(6) - 3 = 9$$
$$b_3 = 2b_2 - 3 = 2(9) - 3 = 15$$
$$b_4 = 2b_3 - 3 = 2(15) - 3 = 27$$

and so forth.

Continuing in this way we arrive at $b_{10} = 1539$.

Exercises for Alternate Example 2

In Exercises 1–8, given b_1 and b_n, find the first three terms and the seventh term for each sequence.

1. $b_1 = 5, \ b_n = b_{n-1} - 5 \quad \text{for all } n \geq 2$

2. $b_1 = 1, \ b_n = 2b_{n-1} + 1 \quad \text{for all } n \geq 2$

3. $b_1 = 2, \ b_n = 2(b_{n-1} - 1) \quad \text{for all } n \geq 2$

4. $b_1 = 1, \ b_n = 2b_{n-1} + 3 \quad \text{for all } n \geq 2$

5. $b_1 = 11, b_n = 2(b_{n-1} - 1) \quad \text{for all } n \geq 2$

6. $b_1 = 4, b_n = b_{n-1} + 6 \quad \text{for all } n \geq 2$

7. $b_1 = -4, b_n = 3b_{n-1} \quad \text{for all } n \geq 2$

8. $b_1 = 7, b_n = b_{n-1} + 11 \quad \text{for all } n \geq 2$

Alternate Example 4 **Defining Geometric Sequences**

For each of the following geometric sequences, find **(a)** the common ratio, **(b)** the eighth term, **(c)** a recursive rule for the nth term, and **(d)** an explicit rule for the nth term.

Sequence 1: $4, \ -12, \ 36, \ -108, \ldots$

Sequence 2: $5^{-3}, \ 5^{-5}, \ 5^{-7}, \ 5^{-9}, \ldots$

SOLUTION

Sequence 1:

(a) The ratio between successive terms is -3

(b) $a_8 = (4)(-3)^7 = -8748$

(c) The sequence is defined by $a_1 = 4$ and $a_n = -3a_{n-1}$ for $n \geq 2$.

(d) The sequence is defined explicitly by $a_n = 4(-3)^{n-1}$

Sequence 2:

(a) The ratio between successive terms is 5^{-2}.

(b) $a_8 = (5^{-3})(5^{-2})^7 = 5^{-17}$

(c) The sequence is defined by $a_1 = 5^{-3}$ and $a_n = (5^{-2})a_{n-1}$ for $n \geq 2$.

(d) The sequence is defined explicitly by $a_n = (5^{-3})(5^{-2})^{n-1} = 5^{-2n-1}$

Exercises for Alternate Example 4

In Exercises 9–14, for each geometric sequence, find **(a)** the common ratio, **(b)** the eighth term, **(c)** a recursive rule for the nth term, and **(d)** an explicit rule for the nth term.

9. Sequence 1:   1, 5, 25, 125, ...   and   Sequence 2: $(-2)^{-2}, (-2)^{-3}, (-2)^{-4}, (-2)^{-5}, \ldots$

10. Sequence 1:   11, –11, 11, –11, ...   and   Sequence 2: $3^{-3}, 3^{-6}, 3^{-9}, 3^{-12}, \ldots$

11. Sequence 1:   –3, 9, –27, 81, ...   and   Sequence 2: $7^3, 7^7, 7^{11}, 7^{15}, \ldots$

12. Sequence 1:   10, –20, 40, –80, ...   and   Sequence 2: $11^3, 11^5, 11^7, 11^9, \ldots$

13. Sequence 1:   4, 20, 100, 500 , ...   and   Sequence 2: $55^{-5}, 55^{-15}, 55^{-25}, 55^{-35}, \ldots$

14. Sequence 1:   6, 24, 96, 384, ...   and   Sequence 2: $2^{11}, 2^{22}, 2^{33}, 2^{44}, \ldots$

Alternate Example 8   **Finding the Limit of a Sequence**

Determine whether the sequence converges or diverges. If it converges, find its limit.

$$a_n = \frac{6n + 7}{5n}$$

SOLUTION

It appears from the graph of the sequence in Figure 8.1 that the limit exists.

Analytically, using Properties of Limits, we have

$$\lim_{n\to\infty} \frac{6n + 7}{5n} = \lim_{n\to\infty} \left(\frac{6n}{5n} + \frac{7}{5n} \right)$$

$$= \lim_{n\to\infty} \left(\frac{6}{5} + \frac{7}{5n} \right)$$

$$= \lim_{n\to\infty} \left(\frac{6}{5} \right) + \lim_{n\to\infty} \left(\frac{7}{5n} \right)$$

$$= \frac{6}{5} + 0$$

$$= \frac{6}{5}$$

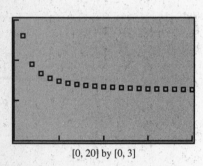

[0, 20] by [0, 3]

Figure 8.1 The graph of the sequence in Alternate Example 8.

Exercises for Alternate Example 8

In each of Exercises 15–20, determine whether the given sequence converges or diverges. If it converges, find its limit.

15. $a_n = \dfrac{-5n + 7}{-7n}$ 16. $a_n = \dfrac{-3n^2 + 3}{2n^2 + 10n + 4}$ 17. $a_n = \dfrac{n - 7}{-11n}$ 18. $a_n = \dfrac{1 + 2n}{2n^2 + 1}$

19. $a_n = \dfrac{5n + 1}{55n}$ 20. $a_n = \dfrac{\pi n^2 + \pi n}{n}$

Alternate Example 10   Using the Sandwich Theorem

Show that the sequence $\left\{\dfrac{\sin^3 n}{n^3}\right\}$ converges and find its limit.

SOLUTION

Because $\left|\sin n\right| \le 1$ for all x, it follows that

$$\left|\frac{\sin^3 n}{n^3}\right| = \frac{\left|\sin^3 n\right|}{\left|n^3\right|} \le \frac{1}{n^3}$$

for all integers $n \ge 1$. Thus,

$$-\frac{1}{n^3} \le \frac{\sin^3 n}{n^3} \le \frac{1}{n^3}.$$

Then, $\displaystyle\lim_{n\to\infty} \frac{\sin^3 n}{n^3} = 0$ because $\displaystyle\lim_{n\to\infty}\left(-\frac{1}{n^3}\right) = \lim_{n\to\infty}\left(\frac{1}{n^3}\right) = 0$ and the sequence $\left\{\dfrac{\sin^3 n}{n^3}\right\}$

converges.

Exercises for Alternate Example 10

In Exercises 21–26, use the Sandwich Theorem to show that the sequence converges, and then find its limit.

21. $\left\{\dfrac{n!}{(2n)!}\right\}$ **22.** $\left\{3n\sin\dfrac{1}{n}\right\}$ **23.** $\left\{n - n\cos\dfrac{1}{n}\right\}$ **24.** $\left\{\dfrac{\sin^2 n}{n}\right\}$ **25.** $\left\{\dfrac{\tan^{-1} n}{n}\right\}$

26. $\left\{\dfrac{\cos\sqrt{4n}}{\ln n}\right\}$

$\blacksquare$

8.2 L'Hôpital's Rule

Alternate Example 2   Applying a Stronger Form of L'Hôpital's Rule

Evaluate $\displaystyle\lim_{x\to 0} \frac{\sqrt{x + 9} - 3 - \dfrac{x}{6}}{4x^2}$.

SOLUTION

Substituting $x = 0$ leads to the indeterminate form $0/0$ because the numerator and denominator of the fraction are 0 when 0 is substituted for x. So we apply l'Hôpital's Rule.

$$\lim_{x\to 0} \frac{\sqrt{x + 9} - 3 - x/6}{4x^2} = \lim_{x\to 0} \frac{(1/2)(x + 9)^{-1/2} - 1/6}{8x} \qquad \text{Differentiate the numerator and denominator.}$$

Substituting 0 for x leads us to 0 in both the numerator and denominator of the second fraction, so we differentiate again.

$$\lim_{x\to 0} \frac{\sqrt{x + 9} - 3 - x/6}{4x^2} = \lim_{x\to 0} \frac{(1/2)(x + 9)^{-1/2} - \dfrac{1}{6}}{8x} = \lim_{x\to 0} \frac{(-1/4)(x + 9)^{-3/2}}{8}$$

This third limit is equal to

$$\frac{(-1/4)(9)^{-3/2}}{8}$$

$$= \frac{-1}{32(27)}$$

$$= -\frac{1}{864}.$$

Thus,

$$\lim_{x \to 0} \frac{\sqrt{x+9} - 3 - x/6}{4x^2} = -\frac{1}{864}.$$

Exercises for Alternate Example 2

In Exercises 1–8, evaluate each limit.

1. $\lim_{x \to 0} \dfrac{\sqrt{16+x} - 4 - x/8}{6x^2}$

2. $\lim_{x \to \pi/4} \dfrac{\sin x - \cos x}{x - \pi/4}$

3. $\lim_{x \to 0} \dfrac{\sqrt{x+9} - 3 - x/2}{-x}$

4. $\lim_{\theta \to \pi} \dfrac{\pi - \theta}{\sin \theta}$

5. $\lim_{x \to 0} \dfrac{\sin x}{\tan 2x}$

6. $\lim_{x \to \pi/2} \dfrac{\cos^2 x}{2x - \pi}$

7. $\lim_{x \to 0} \dfrac{7(\sin x - x)}{x^3}$

8. $\lim_{x \to 2} \dfrac{\sqrt{x^2+5} - 3}{x^2 - 4}$

Alternate Example 5 Working with Indeterminate Form ∞/∞

Identify the indeterminate form and evaluate the limit using l'Hôpital's Rule. Support your answer graphically.

$$\lim_{x \to \infty} \frac{-3 \ln x}{x\sqrt{x}}$$

SOLUTION

$\lim_{x \to \infty} \dfrac{-3 \ln x}{x\sqrt{x}}$ is of indeterminate form $\dfrac{\infty}{\infty}$.

Differentiate the denominator and numerator.

$$\lim_{x \to \infty} \frac{-3 \ln x}{x\sqrt{x}} = \lim_{x \to \infty} \frac{-3/x}{(3/2)x^{1/2}}$$

$$= \lim_{x \to \infty} \frac{-3}{(3/2)x^{3/2}}$$

$$= -\frac{1}{2} \lim_{x \to \infty} \frac{1}{x^{3/2}}$$

$$= 0$$

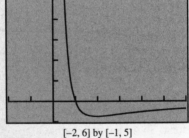

[−2, 6] by [−1, 5]

Figure 8.2 A graph of $\dfrac{-3 \ln x}{x\sqrt{x}}$.

The graph in Figure 8.2 supports the result.

Exercises for Alternate Example 5

In Exercises 9–14, identify the indeterminate form and evaluate the limit using l'Hôpital's Rule. Support your answer graphically

9. $\lim_{x \to \infty} \dfrac{3x^3 + 2x^2 + 4}{x+1}$

10. $\lim_{x \to \infty} \dfrac{x^2 + 1}{x^3 + 8}$

11. $\lim_{x \to \pi/2} \dfrac{\sec x}{1 + \tan x}$

12. $\lim_{x \to \infty} \dfrac{3 \ln x}{7x\sqrt{3x}}$

13. $\lim_{x \to \infty} \dfrac{\ln(x^2)}{\ln(2^x)}$

14. $\lim_{x \to \infty} \dfrac{\ln x}{x\sqrt{5x}}$

Alternate Example 8   **Working with Indeterminate Form 1^{∞}**

Find $\lim\limits_{x \to \infty} \left(1 - \dfrac{3}{x} \right)^{2x}$.

SOLUTION

Let $f(x) = \left(1 - \dfrac{3}{x} \right)^{2x}$. Then taking logarithms of both sides converts the indeterminate

form 1^{∞} to 0/0 form to which we apply l'Hôpital's Rule.

$$\ln f(x) = \ln \left(1 - \frac{3}{x} \right)^{2x}$$

$$= 2x \ln \left(1 - \frac{3}{x} \right)$$

$$= \frac{2 \ln \left(1 - \dfrac{3}{x} \right)}{\dfrac{1}{x}}$$

We apply l'Hôpital's Rule to the last expression above.

$$\lim_{x \to \infty} \ln f(x) = \lim_{x \to \infty} \frac{2 \ln \left(1 - \dfrac{3}{x} \right)}{\dfrac{1}{x}} \qquad \text{The right side is of the form } \frac{0}{0}.$$

$$= \lim_{x \to \infty} \frac{2 \left(\dfrac{3}{x^2} \Big/ \left(1 - \dfrac{3}{x} \right) \right)}{-x^{-2}} \qquad \text{Differentiate the numerator and denominator.}$$

$$= \lim_{x \to \infty} \frac{2 \left(\dfrac{3}{x^2 - 3x} \right)}{-\dfrac{1}{x^2}}.$$

$$= \lim_{x \to \infty} -\frac{6x^2}{x^2 - 3x}$$

$$= \lim_{x \to \infty} \frac{-6x}{x - 3}$$

Note that $\lim\limits_{x \to \infty} \dfrac{-6x}{x - 3} \to \dfrac{\infty}{\infty}$, so we can apply l'Hôpital's rule.

$$\lim_{x \to \infty} \frac{-6x}{x - 3} = \lim_{x \to \infty} \frac{-6}{1} \qquad \text{Differentiate the numerator and denominator.}$$

$$= -6$$

Therefore,

$$\lim_{x \to \infty} \left(1 - \frac{3}{x}\right)^{2x} = \lim_{x \to \infty} f(x)$$

$$= \lim_{x \to \infty} e^{\ln f(x)} = e^{\lim_{x \to \infty} \ln f(x)}$$

$$= e^{-6}$$

Exercises for Alternate Example 8

In Exercises 15–20, find each limit

15. $\lim_{x \to \infty} \left(1 - \frac{5}{x}\right)^{5x}$ **16.** $\lim_{x \to \infty} \left(1 - \frac{7}{x}\right)^{2x}$ **17.** $\lim_{x \to \infty} \left(1 - \frac{4}{x}\right)^{3x}$ **18.** $\lim_{x \to 0^+} (1 + x)^{1/x}$

19. $\lim_{x \to 1^+} x^{\frac{1}{1-x}}$ **20.** $\lim_{x \to 0} (e^x + x)^{1/x}$

Alternate Example 10 **Working with Indeterminate Form ∞^0**

Find $\lim_{x \to \infty} x^{-1/x}$.

SOLUTION

Let $f(x) = x^{-1/x}$. Then,

$$\ln f(x) = \ln x^{-1/x}$$

$$= -\frac{1}{x} \ln x$$

Applying l'Hôpital's Rule to $\ln f(x)$, we obtain

$$\lim_{x \to \infty} \ln f(x) = \lim_{x \to \infty} \left[\left(-\frac{1}{x}\right) \ln x\right]$$

$$= \lim_{x \to \infty} \left(-\frac{\ln x}{x}\right) \qquad \frac{\infty}{\infty}$$

$$= \lim_{x \to \infty} \left(-\frac{1/x}{1}\right) \qquad \text{Differentiate the numerator and denominator.}$$

$$= \lim_{x \to \infty} \left(-\frac{1}{x}\right)$$

$$= 0$$

Therefore,

$$\lim_{x \to \infty} \ln f(x) = 0 \text{ and this implies that}$$

$$\lim_{x \to \infty} x^{-1/x} = \lim_{x \to \infty} e^{\ln f(x)} = e^{\lim_{x \to \infty} \ln f(x)}$$

$$= e^0$$

$$= 1.$$

Exercises for Alternate Example 10

In Exercise 21–26, find each limit.

21. $\lim_{x\to\infty} x^{1/x}$ **22.** $\lim_{x\to\infty} (2x)^{3/x}$ **23.** $\lim_{x\to\infty} (1+2x)^{1/(2\ln x)}$ **24.** $\lim_{x\to\infty} x^{1/\ln x}$ **25.** $\lim_{x\to\infty} 2(3x)^{3/x}$

26. $\lim_{x\to\infty} 3(5x)^{5/x}$

■

8.3 Relative Rates of Growth

Alternate Example 1 Comparing Functions Such as e^x and x^2 as $x \to \infty$

Show that e^{2x} grows faster than x^3 as $x \to \infty$.

SOLUTION

We need to show that $\lim_{x\to\infty} \frac{e^{2x}}{x^3} = \infty$. Notice that this limit is of indeterminate type ∞/∞, so we can appy l'Hôpital's Rule and take the derivative of the numerator and the derivative of the denominator. In fact, we have to apply l'Hôpital's Rule three times.

$$\begin{aligned}\lim_{x\to\infty} \frac{e^{2x}}{x^3} &= \lim_{x\to\infty} \frac{2e^{2x}}{3x^2} \\ &= \lim_{x\to\infty} \frac{4e^{2x}}{6x} \\ &= \lim_{x\to\infty} \frac{8e^{2x}}{6} \\ &= \infty.\end{aligned}$$

Exercises for Alternate Example 1

In Exercises 1–8, show that $f(x)$ grows faster than $g(x)$ as $x \to \infty$.

1. $f(x) = 9e^x$ and $g(x) = x^3$

2. $f(x) = -2e^{4x}$ and $g(x) = 4x^5$

3. $f(x) = 4e^{4x}$ and $g(x) = x^3 + 10^6 x^2$

4. $f(x) = e^{8x}$ and $g(x) = x^{100,000}$

5. $f(x) = e^{6x}$ and $g(x) = e^{\sin x}$

6. $f(x) = e^{3x}$ and $g(x) = 1/x^2$

7. $f(x) = e^{5x}$ and $g(x) = (\pi/2)^x$

8. $f(x) = e^{2x}$ and $g(x) = 2x^2 + 3x + 1$

■

Alternate Example 2 Comparing ln $5x$ with $5x$ and x^3 as $x \to \infty$

Show that ln $5x$ grows slower than **(a)** $5x$ and **(b)** x^3

SOLUTION

(a) Solve Analytically

$$\begin{aligned}\lim_{x\to\infty} \frac{\ln 5x}{5x} &= \lim_{x\to\infty} \frac{1/x}{5} \qquad \text{l'Hôpital's rule} \\ &= \lim_{x\to\infty} \frac{1}{5x} \\ &= 0\end{aligned}$$

Support Graphically Figure 8.3 suggests that the graph of the function $f(x) = \frac{\ln 5x}{5x}$ drops dramatically toward the x-axis as x grows larger.

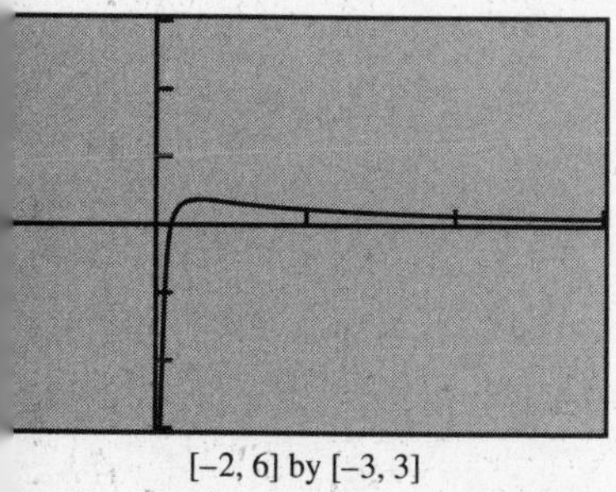

[–2, 6] by [–3, 3]

Figure 8.3 The x-axis is a horizontal asymptote of the function $f(x) = \frac{\ln 5x}{5x}$.

(b)
$$\lim_{x\to\infty}\frac{\ln 5x}{x^3} = \lim_{x\to\infty}\frac{1/x}{3x^2} \qquad \text{l'Hôpital's rule}$$

$$= \lim_{x\to\infty}\frac{1}{3x^3}$$

$$= 0$$

Exercises for Alternate Example 2

In Exercises 9–14, show that $f(x)$ grows slower than $g(x)$ as $x\to\infty$.

9. $f(x) = \ln 7x$ and $g(x) = 3x$

10. $f(x) = \ln 5x$ and $g(x) = x^4$

11. $f(x) = 4\ln x$ and $g(x) = 0.00002x$

12. $f(x) = \ln 6x^2$ and $g(x) = \sqrt[3]{6x+1}$

13. $f(x) = \ln(11x + 1)$ and $g(x) = 7x(\sin^2 x + 1)$

14. $f(x) = \ln(65x^{85})$ and $g(x) = x$

Alternate Example 3   Comparing x with $2x - 3\sin x$ as $x\to\infty$

Show that x grows at the same rate as $(2x - 3\sin x)$ as $x\to\infty$.

SOLUTION

We need to show that $\displaystyle\lim_{x\to\infty}\frac{2x - 3\sin x}{x}$ is finite and not 0. The limit can be computed directly.

$$\lim_{x\to\infty}\frac{2x - 3\sin x}{x} = \lim_{x\to\infty}\left(2 - \frac{3\sin x}{x}\right)$$

$$= 2.$$

Exercises for Alternate Example 3

In Exercises 15–20, show that $f(x)$ grows at the same rate as $g(x)$ when $x\to\infty$.

15. $f(x) = 3x^2$ and $g(x) = 11x^2$

16. $f(x) = 3x^3$ and $g(x) = 3x^3 + 7x^2 + 2$

17. $f(x) = 5x^4$ and $g(x) = 7x^4 - 3\sin x$

18. $f(x) = 3x^2$ and $g(x) = \sqrt{x^4 + x}$

19. $f(x) = 3x$ and $g(x) = \sqrt{4x^2 + 3\sin x}$

20. $f(x) = 3x^4$ and $g(x) = x^4 + \cos x$

Alternate Example 4   Comparing Logarithmic Functions as $x\to\infty$

Let a and b be numbers greater than 1. Show that $\log_a(x + b)$ and $\log_b(2x + 3b)$ grow at the same rate as $x\to\infty$.

SOLUTION

$$\lim_{x\to\infty}\frac{\log_a(x + b)}{\log_b(2x + 3b)} = \lim_{x\to\infty}\frac{\dfrac{\ln(x + b)}{\ln a}}{\dfrac{\ln(2x + 3b)}{\ln b}}$$

$$= \lim_{x\to\infty}\frac{(\ln b)\big[\ln(x + b)\big]}{(\ln a)\big[\ln(2x + 3b)\big]}$$

L'Hôpital's rule applies, so we differentiate the numerator and denominator of the fraction above.

$$\lim_{x \to \infty} \frac{\log_a(x+b)}{\log_b(2x+3b)} = \lim_{x \to \infty} \frac{\dfrac{\ln b}{x+b}}{\dfrac{2\ln a}{2x+3b}}$$

$$= \lim_{x \to \infty} \frac{(\ln b)(2x+3b)}{(2\ln a)(x+b)}$$

$$= \lim_{x \to \infty} \left[\left(\frac{\ln b}{2\ln a} \right) \left(\frac{2x+3b}{x+b} \right) \right]$$

$$= \lim_{x \to \infty} \left[\left(\frac{\ln b}{2\ln a} \right) \left(\frac{2+\dfrac{3b}{x}}{1+\dfrac{b}{x}} \right) \right]$$

$$= \left[\left(\frac{\ln b}{2\ln a} \right) \left(\frac{2}{1} \right) \right]$$

$$= \frac{\ln b}{\ln a}$$

The limiting value is finite and nonzero therefore the two functions grow at the same rate as $x \to \infty$.

Exercises for Alternate Example 4

In Exercises 21–26, show that $f(x)$ and $g(x)$ grow at the same rate as $x \to \infty$.

21. $f(x) = \ln(4x+1), \quad g(x) = \ln(3x+9)$

22. $f(x) = \ln(9x+3), \quad g(x) = \ln(9x+6)$

23. $f(x) = x^2 + 2, \quad g(x) = \sqrt{4x^4 + 5}$

24. $f(x) = \sqrt{7x+3}, \quad g(x) = \sqrt{2x}$

25. $f(x) = 6x^3, \quad g(x) = \sqrt{4x^6 + 8x^2}$

26. $f(x) = 9x+1, \quad g(x) = \sqrt[3]{27x^3 + 8x^2}$

8.4 Improper Integrals

Alternate Example 3 **Using Partial Fractions With Improper Integrals**

Evaluate $\displaystyle\int_0^\infty \frac{5\,dx}{x^2 + 8x + 12}$ or show that it diverges.

SOLUTION

By definition, $\displaystyle\int_0^\infty \frac{5\,dx}{x^2 + 8x + 12} = \lim_{b \to \infty} \int_0^b \frac{5\,dx}{x^2 + 8x + 12}$. We use partial fractions to integrate the definite integral. Set

$$\frac{5}{x^2 + 8x + 12} = \frac{5}{(x+2)(x+6)}$$

$$= \frac{A}{x+2} + \frac{B}{x+6}$$

and solve for A and B.

$$\frac{5}{(x + 2)(x + 6)} = \frac{A(x + 6) + B(x + 2)}{(x + 2)(x + 6)}$$

$$= \frac{xA + 6A + xB + 2B}{(x + 2)(x + 6)}$$

$$= \frac{x(A + B) + (6A + 2B)}{(x + 2)(x + 6)}$$

Thus, $A + B = 0$ and $6A + 2B = 5$. Solving this system of equations, we obtain $A = \dfrac{5}{4}$ and

$B = -\dfrac{5}{4}$. Therefore,

$$\frac{5}{x^2 + 8x + 12} = \frac{5}{4(x + 2)} - \frac{5}{4(x + 6)}$$

and

$$\int_0^b \frac{5\,dx}{x^2 + 8x + 12} = \int_0^b \left[\frac{5}{4(x + 2)} - \frac{5}{4(x + 6)} \right] dx$$

$$= \frac{5}{4} \int_0^b \left[\frac{1}{(x + 2)} - \frac{1}{(x + 6)} \right] dx$$

$$= \frac{5}{4} \left[\int_0^b \frac{dx}{(x + 2)} - \int_0^b \frac{dx}{(x + 6)} \right]$$

$$= \frac{5}{4} \left[\ln(x + 2) \Big|_0^b - \ln(x + 6) \Big|_0^b \right]$$

$$= \frac{5}{4} \left[\ln(b + 2) - \ln 2 - \ln(b + 6) + \ln 6 \right]$$

$$= \frac{5}{4} \left[\ln \frac{b + 2}{b + 6} + \ln \frac{6}{2} \right]$$

$$= \frac{5}{4} \left[\ln \frac{b + 2}{b + 6} + \ln 3 \right].$$

So,

$$\lim_{b \to \infty} \frac{5}{4} \left[\ln \frac{b + 2}{b + 6} + \ln 3 \right] = \left(\frac{5}{4} \right) \lim_{b \to \infty} \left[\ln \frac{b + 2}{b + 6} + \ln 3 \right]$$

$$= \left(\frac{5}{4} \right) \ln 3 + \left(\frac{5}{4} \right) \lim_{b \to \infty} \left(\ln \frac{b + 2}{b + 6} \right)$$

$$= \left(\frac{5 \ln 3}{4} \right) + \left(\frac{5}{4} \right) \lim_{b \to \infty} \left(\ln \frac{1 + 2/b}{1 + 6/b} \right)$$

$$= \left(\frac{5 \ln 3}{4} + \frac{5}{4} \right) \ln 1$$

$$= \left(\frac{5 \ln 3}{4} \right) + \left(\frac{5}{4} \right) \cdot 0$$

$$= \left(\frac{5 \ln 3}{4} \right)$$

and

$$\int_0^\infty \frac{5dx}{x^2 + 8x + 12} = \frac{5\ln 3}{4}.$$

Exercises for Alternate Example 3

In Exercises 1–6, evaluate each integral or state that it diverges

1. $\displaystyle\int_0^\infty \frac{-4dx}{x^2 + 11x + 30}$

2. $\displaystyle\int_0^\infty \frac{11dx}{x^2 + 3x + 2}$

3. $\displaystyle\int_4^\infty \frac{2x+1}{x^2 - 3x}dx$

4. $\displaystyle\int_0^\infty \frac{-8dx}{x^2 + 3x + 2}$

5. $\displaystyle\int_0^\infty \frac{-7dx}{x^2 + 4x + 3}$

6. $\displaystyle\int_0^\infty \frac{5dx}{x^2 + 16x + 63}$

■

Alternate Example 4 Using L'Hôpital's Rule with Improper Integrals

Evaluate $\displaystyle\int_1^\infty -3xe^{-2x}\,dx$ or state that it diverges.

SOLUTION

By definition $\displaystyle\int_1^\infty -3xe^{-2x}\,dx = \lim_{b\to\infty}\int_1^b -3xe^{-2x}\,dx$. We use integration by parts to evaluate

the definite integral. Let
$$u = -3x \text{ and } dv = e^{-2x}dx$$
Then
$$du = -3dx \text{ and } v = -\frac{1}{2}e^{-2x}$$

Therefore,

$$\int_1^b -3xe^{-2x}\,dx = (-3x)\left(-\frac{1}{2}e^{-2x}\right)\Bigg|_1^b - \int_1^b -3\left(-\frac{1}{2}e^{-2x}\right)dx$$

$$= \frac{3}{2}xe^{-2x}\Bigg|_1^b + \frac{3}{4}e^{-2x}\Bigg|_1^b = \frac{3}{2}e^{-2x}\left(x+\frac{1}{2}\right)\Bigg|_1^b = \frac{3}{2}e^{-2b}\left(b+\frac{1}{2}\right) - \frac{3}{2}e^{-2}\left(\frac{3}{2}\right).$$

$$= \frac{3b}{2e^{2b}} + \frac{3}{4e^{2b}} - \frac{9}{4e^2}$$

Now, $\displaystyle\lim_{b\to\infty}\left(\frac{3b}{2e^{2b}} + \frac{3}{4e^{2b}} - \frac{9}{4e^2}\right) = -\frac{9}{4e^2}.$

Thus, $\displaystyle\int_1^\infty -3xe^{-2x}\,dx = -\frac{9}{4e^2}.$

Exercises for Alternate Example 4

In Exercises 7–12, evaluate each integral or state that it diverges.

7. $\displaystyle\int_1^\infty xe^{-5x}dx$

8. $\displaystyle\int_1^\infty -8xe^{-8x}dx$

9. $\displaystyle\int_0^\infty 2x\ln(x+1)dx$

10. $\displaystyle\int_1^\infty -xe^{-6x}dx$

11. $\displaystyle\int_2^\infty (x+2)\ln(3x)dx$

12. $\displaystyle\int_1^\infty -11xe^{4x}dx$

Alternate Example 6   Infinite Discontinuity at an Interior Point

Evaluate. $\displaystyle\int_0^5 \frac{dx}{(x-3)^{2/3}}$.

SOLUTION

The integral has a vertical asymptote at $x=3$ and is continuous on $[0, 3)$ and $(3, 5]$. We know that if $f(x)$ is continuous on $[a, c)\cup(c, b]$, then

$$\int_a^b f(x)dx = \int_a^c f(x)dx + \int_c^b f(x)dx.$$

Using this definition,

$$\int_0^5 \frac{dx}{(x-3)^{2/3}} = \int_0^3 \frac{dx}{(x-3)^{2/3}} + \int_3^5 \frac{dx}{(x-3)^{2/3}} .$$

Next, we evaluate each improper integral on the right-hand side of this equation.

$$\int_0^3 \frac{dx}{(x-3)^{2/3}} = \lim_{c\to3^-} \int_0^c \frac{dx}{(x-3)^{2/3}}$$

$$= \lim_{c\to3^-} 3(x-3)^{1/3}\Big|_0^c$$

$$= \lim_{c\to3^-} 3(c-3)^{1/3} - \lim_{c\to3^-} 3(0-3)^{1/3}$$

$$= -3\sqrt[3]{-3}$$

Also,

$$\int_3^5 \frac{dx}{(x-3)^{2/3}} = \lim_{c\to3^+} \int_c^5 \frac{dx}{(x-3)^{2/3}} = \lim_{c\to3^+} 3(x-3)^{1/3}\Big|_c^5$$

$$= \lim_{c\to3^+} 3(5-3)^{1/3} - \lim_{c\to3^+} 3(c-3)^{1/3}$$

$$= 3\sqrt[3]{2} .$$

We conclude that

$$\int_0^5 \frac{dx}{(x-3)^{2/3}} = -3\sqrt[3]{-3} + 3\sqrt[3]{2} .$$

Exercises for Alternate Example 6

In Exercises 13–18, evaluate each integral.

13. $\displaystyle\int_0^9 \frac{dx}{(x-9)^{2/3}}$

14. $\displaystyle\int_{-6}^0 \frac{dx}{(x+3)^{2/3}}$

15. $\displaystyle\int_0^4 \frac{dx}{4-x^2}$

16. $\displaystyle\int_{-3}^3 \frac{3x^2\,dx}{\sqrt[3]{x^3+1}}$

17. $\displaystyle\int_0^\pi \frac{\sin x\,dx}{\cos x}$

18. $\displaystyle\int_0^9 \frac{e^{\sqrt{x}}\,dx}{\sqrt{x}}$

■

Alternate Example 9 **Finding Circumference**

Use the arc length formula (Section 7.4) to show that the circumference of the circle $x^2 + y^2 = 81$ is 18π.

SOLUTION

If a smooth curve begins at (a, c) and ends at (b, d), $a < b$, $c < d$, then the arc length of the curve is:

$$L = \int_a^b \sqrt{1 + \left(\frac{dy}{dx}\right)^2}\, dx \text{ if } y \text{ is a smooth function of } x \text{ on } [a, b];$$

$$L = \int_c^d \sqrt{1 + \left(\frac{dx}{dy}\right)^2}\, dy \text{ if } y \text{ is a smooth function of } x \text{ on } [c, d].$$

One fourth of the circle is given by $y = \sqrt{81 - x^2}$, $0 \le x \le 9$. Its arc length is

$$L = \int_0^9 \sqrt{1 + (y')^2}\, dx\,, \text{ where } y' = -\frac{x}{\sqrt{81 - x^2}}\,.$$

The integral is improper because y' is not defined at $x = 9$. We evaluate it as a limit.

$$L = \int_0^9 \sqrt{1 + (y')^2}\, dx$$

$$= \int_0^9 \sqrt{1 + \left(-\frac{x}{\sqrt{81 - x^2}}\right)^2}\, dx$$

$$= \int_0^9 \sqrt{1 + \frac{x^2}{81 - x^2}}\, dx$$

$$= \int_0^9 \sqrt{\frac{81}{81 - x^2}}\, dx \qquad \text{Combine terms under the square root}$$

$$= \lim_{b \to 9^-} \int_0^b \sqrt{\frac{81}{81 - x^2}}\, dx$$

$$= \lim_{b \to 9^-} \int_0^b \sqrt{\frac{1}{1 - (x/9)^2}}\, dx$$

$$= \lim_{b \to 9^-} 9\left(\sin^{-1}\frac{x}{9}\right)\Big]_0^b$$

$$= \lim_{b \to 9^-} 9\left(\sin^{-1}\frac{b}{9} - \sin^{-1}\frac{0}{9}\right)$$

$$= \frac{9\pi}{2} \qquad\qquad \sin^{-1}\frac{9}{9} - \sin^{-1}\frac{0}{9} = \frac{\pi}{2}$$

The circumference of the quarter circle is $\dfrac{9\pi}{2}$. Therefore, the circumference of the circle

is $4\left(\dfrac{9\pi}{2}\right) = 18\pi$.

Exercises for Alternate Example 9

In Exercises 19–24, use the arc length formula (Section 7.4) to show that the circumference of the given circle D is C.

19. $D: x^2 + y^2 = 16$ $C = 8\pi$ 20. $D: x^2 + y^2 = 49$ $C = 14\pi$ 21. $D: x^2 + y^2 = 144$ $C = 24\pi$

22. $D: x^2 + y^2 = 25$ $C = 10\pi$ 23. $D: x^2 + y^2 = 121$ $C = 22\pi$ 24. $D: x^2 + y^2 = 36$ $C = 12\pi$

Chapter 9 | Infinite Series

9.1 Power Series

Alternate Example 1 | Identifying a Divergent Series

Does the series $\pi - 2\pi + 3\pi - 4\pi + 5\pi - 6\pi + 7\pi - 8\pi + \cdots$ converge?

SOLUTION

You may be tempted to sum the terms of this series in pairs as

$$(\pi - 2\pi) + (3\pi - 4\pi) + (5\pi - 6\pi) + (7\pi - 8\pi)\cdots = -\pi - \pi - \pi - \pi - \cdots$$

and conclude that the series does not converge. In fact, it is true that the series diverges, but not by the reasoning shown above.

This is an infinite sum, and the associative property cannot be used because this strategy requires an infinite number of pairings. We must show divergence by calculating the sequence of partial sums.

The partial sums of the series are as follows:

$$\pi = \pi$$
$$\pi - 2\pi = -\pi$$
$$\pi - 2\pi + 3\pi = \pi$$
$$\pi - 2\pi + 3\pi - 4\pi = -\pi$$

The partial sums are oscillating between π and $-\pi$. This is an infinite series, not a finite sum, so if it has a sum it has to be the limit of its sequence of partial sums

$$\pi, -\pi, \pi, -\pi, \pi, -\pi, \pi, -\pi, \cdots$$

Since this sequence has no limit, the series has no sum. It diverges.

Exercises for Alternate Example 1

In Exercises 1–6, compute the limit of the partial sums to determine whether each series diverges or converges.

1. $5 + 25 + 125 + 625 + \cdots + 5^n + \cdots$

2. $\dfrac{1}{1 \times 2} + \dfrac{1}{2 \times 3} + \dfrac{1}{3 \times 4} + \cdots + \dfrac{1}{n \times (n+1)} + \cdots$

3. $\dfrac{1}{1} + \dfrac{1}{4} + \dfrac{1}{9} + \cdots + \dfrac{1}{n^2} + \cdots$

4. $6 + 18 + 54 + 192 + \cdots + 2(3^n) + \cdots$

5. $2 + 4 + 8 + 16 + \cdots + 2^n + \cdots$

6. $3 - 5 + 7 - 9 + \cdots$

Alternate Example 2 | Identifying a Convergent Series

Does the series

$$\frac{7}{10} + \frac{7}{100} + \frac{7}{1000} + \cdots + \frac{7}{10^n} + \cdots$$

converge?

SOLUTION

Here is the sequence of partial sums, written in decimal form.

$$0.7, \; .77, 0.777, 0.7777, \ldots$$

This sequence has a limit $0.\overline{7}$, which we recognize as the fraction 7/9. The series converges to the sum 7/9.

Exercises for Alternate Example 2

In Exercises 7–12, compute the limit of the partial sums to determine whether each series converges or diverges.

7. $\dfrac{5}{100} + \dfrac{5}{1000} + \dfrac{5}{10000} + \cdots + \dfrac{5}{10^{n+1}} + \cdots$

8. $\dfrac{11}{1} + \dfrac{11}{100} + \dfrac{11}{10000} + \cdots + \dfrac{11}{10^{2n}} + \cdots$

9. $\dfrac{1}{10} + \dfrac{10}{1} + \dfrac{1}{100} + \dfrac{100}{1} + \cdots + \dfrac{1}{10^n} + \dfrac{10^n}{1} + \cdots$

10. $\dfrac{9}{1000} + \dfrac{9}{100000} + \dfrac{9}{10000000} + \cdots + \dfrac{9}{10^{2n+1}} + \cdots$

11. $\dfrac{6}{1} + \dfrac{6}{10} + \dfrac{6}{100} + \cdots + \dfrac{6}{10^n} + \cdots$

12. $\dfrac{1}{9} + \dfrac{10^2}{9} + \dfrac{10^3}{9} + \cdots + \dfrac{10^n}{9} + \cdots$

Alternate Example 4 Finding a Power Series by Differentiation

Given that $\dfrac{1}{2-x}$ is represented by the power series

$$\frac{1}{2} + \frac{x}{4} + \frac{x^2}{8} + \frac{x^3}{16} + \cdots + \frac{x^n}{2^{n+1}} + \cdots$$

on the interval $(-2, 2)$, find a power series to represent $\dfrac{1}{(2-x)^2}$.

SOLUTION

Notice that $\dfrac{1}{(2-x)^2}$ is the derivative of $\dfrac{1}{(2-x)}$. To find the power series, we differentiate both sides of the equation

$$\frac{1}{2-x} = \frac{1}{2} + \frac{x}{4} + \frac{x^2}{8} + \frac{x^3}{16} + \cdots + \frac{x^n}{2^{n+1}} + \cdots$$

$$\frac{d}{dx}\left(\frac{1}{2-x}\right) = \frac{d}{dx}\left(\frac{1}{4} + \frac{x}{4} + \frac{x^2}{8} + \cdots + \frac{x^n}{2^{n+1}} + \cdots\right)$$

$$\frac{1}{(2-x)^2} = \frac{1}{4} + \frac{x}{4} + \frac{3x^2}{16} + \cdots + \frac{nx^{n-1}}{2^{n+1}} + \cdots$$

What about the interval of convergence? Since the original series converges for $-2 < x < 2$, it would seem that the differentiated series ought to converge on the same open interval. The graphs (shown in Figure 9.1) of the partial sums

$$\frac{1}{4} + \frac{x}{4} + \frac{3x^2}{16}$$

$$\frac{1}{4} + \frac{x}{4} + \frac{3x^2}{16} + \frac{x^3}{8}$$

suggest that this is the case (although such empirical evidence does not constitute a proof).

Partial Sums

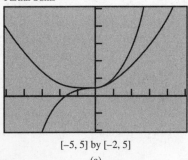

[–5, 5] by [–2, 5]

(a)

$y = \dfrac{1}{(2-x)^2}$

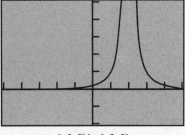

[–5, 5] by [–2, 5]

(b)

Figure 9.1 (a) The polynomial partial sums of the power series we derived for (b) $\dfrac{1}{(2-x)^2}$ seem to converge on the open interval $(-2, 2)$.

Exercises for Alternate Example 4

In Exercises 13–18, use the power series and the function $f(x)$ that it represents to find a power series that represents $f'(x)$.

13. $\displaystyle\sum_{n=0}^{\infty} \frac{(-1)^n (x-1)^{n+1}}{(n+1)};\ f(x) = \ln x$

14. $\displaystyle\sum_{n=1}^{\infty} n(-1)^n x^{n-1};\ f(x) = \ln(x+1)$

15. $\displaystyle\frac{1}{2}\sum_{n=0}^{\infty}\left(-\frac{x}{2}\right)^n;\ f(x) = \frac{1}{x+2}$

16. $\displaystyle\sum_{n=1}^{\infty} \frac{n(n+1)(-1)^{n+1}}{2} x^{n-1};\ f(x) = \frac{1}{(x+1)^3}$

17. $\displaystyle\sum_{n=1}^{\infty} \frac{(-1)^{n+1}}{n} x^{n-1};\ f(x)\frac{1}{x}\ln(x+1)$

18. $\displaystyle\sum_{n=0}^{\infty} x^{2n};\ f(x) = \frac{1}{1-x^2}$

Partial Sums

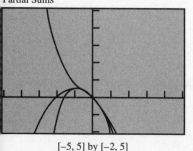

[−5, 5] by [−2, 5]

(a)

$y = \ln(1-x)$

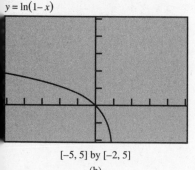

[−5, 5] by [−2, 5]

(b)

Figure 9.2 The graphs of the partial sums

$$-\left(x+\frac{x^2}{2}\right),\ -\left(x+\frac{x^2}{2}+\frac{x^3}{3}\right),$$

$$-\left(x+\frac{x^2}{2}+\frac{x^3}{3}+\frac{x^4}{4}\right)\ \text{closing in on (b)}$$

the graph of $\ln(1-x)$ over $(-1, 1)$.

Alternate Example 5   Finding a Power Series by Integration

Given that

$$\frac{1}{1-x} = 1 + x + x^2 + x^3 + \cdots + x^n + \cdots,\qquad -1 < x < 1$$

find a power series to represent $\ln(1-x)$.

SOLUTION

Recall that $1/(1-x)$ is the derivative of $-\ln(1-x)$ for $-1 < x < 1$. We can therefore integrate the series for $1/(1-x)$ to obtain a series for $-\ln(1-x)$ for $-1 < x < 1$. (No absolute value bars are necessary because $(1-x)$ is positive for $-1 < x < 1$.)

$$\frac{1}{1-x} = 1 + x + x^2 + x^3 + \cdots + x^n + \cdots$$

Thus, $\displaystyle\int_0^x \frac{dt}{1-t} = \int_0^x (1 + t + t^2 + t^3 + \cdots + t^n + \cdots)$ t is a dummy variable.

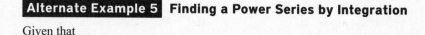

$$-\ln(1-t)\Big]_0^x = \left(t + \frac{t^2}{2} + \frac{t^3}{3} + \frac{t^4}{4} + \cdots + \frac{t^n}{n} + \cdots\right)\Bigg]_0^x$$

$$-\ln(1-x) = \left(x + \frac{x^2}{2} + \frac{x^3}{3} + \frac{x^4}{4} + \cdots + \frac{x^n}{n} + \cdots\right)$$

$$\ln(1-x) = -\left(x + \frac{x^2}{2} + \frac{x^3}{3} + \frac{x^4}{4} + \cdots + \frac{x^n}{n} + \cdots\right)$$

It would seem logical for the new series to converge where the original series converges, on the open interval $(-1, 1)$. The graphs of the partial sums in Figure 9.2 support this idea.

Exercises for Alternate Example 5

In exercises 19–24, use the series and the function $f(x)$ that it represents to find a power series to represent $g(x) = \int_0^x f(x)$.

19. $x - \dfrac{x^3}{3!} + \dfrac{x^5}{5!} - \dfrac{x^7}{7!} + \cdots;\ f(x) = \sin x$ $\qquad\qquad$ $g(x) = \cos x$

20. $1 + 2x + 3x^2 + 4x^3 + \cdots;\ f(x) = \dfrac{1}{(1-x)^2}$ $\qquad$ $g(x) = \dfrac{1}{1-x}$

21. $1 - \dfrac{x^2}{2!} + \dfrac{x^4}{4!} - \cdots;\ f(x) = \cos x$ $\qquad\qquad$ $g(x) = \sin x$

22. $1 - 2x + 4x^2 - 8x^3 + \cdots;\ f(x) = \dfrac{1}{1+2x}$ $\qquad\quad$ $g(x) = \dfrac{1}{2}\ln(1+2x)$

23. $-1 + x^2 - x^4 + x^6;\ f(x) = \dfrac{-1}{x^2+1}$ $\qquad\qquad$ $g(x) = -\tan^{-1} x$

24. $2x - \dfrac{8x^3}{3!} + \dfrac{32x^5}{5!} - \dfrac{128x^7}{7!} + \cdots;\ f(x) = \sin(2x)$ $\quad$ $g(x) = -\dfrac{1}{2}\cos(2x)$

9.2 Taylor Series

Alternate Example 1 **Approximating ln $(2x + 3)$ by a Polynomial**

Construct a polynomial $P(x) = a_0 + a_1x + a_2x^2 + a_3x^3$ that matches the behavior of $\ln(2x + 3)$ at $x = 0$ through its first four derivatives. That is,

$$P(0) = \ln(2x + 3) \qquad \text{at } x = 0$$

$$P'(0) = \left(\ln(2x + 3)\right)' \qquad \text{at } x = 0$$

$$P''(0) = \left(\ln(2x + 3)\right)'' \qquad \text{at } x = 0$$

$$P'''(0) = \left(\ln(2x + 3)\right)''' \qquad \text{at } x = 0$$

$$P^{(4)}(0) = \left(\ln(2x + 3)\right)^{(4)} \qquad \text{at } x = 0$$

SOLUTION

This is just like Exploration 1 in section 9.2, except that first we need to find out what the numbers are.

$$P(0) = \ln(2x + 3)\big|_{x=0}$$

$$= \ln 3$$

$$P'(0) = \dfrac{2}{2x + 3}\bigg|_{x=0}$$

$$= \dfrac{2}{3}$$

$$P''(0) = \dfrac{-4}{(2x + 3)^2}\bigg|_{x=0}$$

$$= -\dfrac{4}{9}$$

$$P'''\left(0\right) = \left.\frac{16}{(2x+3)^3}\right|_{x=0}$$

$$= \frac{16}{27}$$

$$P^{(4)}(0) = \left.\frac{-96}{(2x+3)^4}\right|_{x=0}$$

$$= -\frac{32}{27}$$

In working through Exploration 1, you probably noticed that the coefficient of the term x^n in the polynomial we seek is $P^{(n)}$ divided by $n!$. The polynomial is

$$P(x) = \ln 3 + \frac{2}{3}x - \frac{2}{9}x^2 + \frac{8}{81}x^3 - \frac{4}{81}x^4.$$

Exercises for Alternate Example 1

In Exercises 1–6, construct a polynomial $P(x) = a_0 + a_1x + a_2x^2 + a_3x^2 + a_4x^4$ that matches the behavior of $F(x)$ at $x = 0$ through its first four derivatives

1. $F(x) = \dfrac{1}{x+1}$ **2.** $F(x) = \sin x^2$ **3.** $F(x) = \sin x$ **4.** $F(x) = \tan x$ **5.** $F(x) = \sqrt[3]{x+1}$

6. $F(x) = \cos 3x$

■

Alternate Example 2   Constructing a Power Series for cos *x*

Construct the seventh order Taylor polynomial series for cos x at $x = 0$

SOLUTION

We need to evaluate cos x and its first seven derivatives at $x = 0$. Fortunately, this is not hard to do.

$$\cos(0) = 1$$

$$\cos'(0) = -\sin(0)$$

$$= 0$$

$$\cos''(0) = -\cos(0)$$

$$= -1$$

$$\cos'''(0) = \sin(0)$$

$$= 0$$

$$\cos^{(4)}(0) = \cos(0)$$

$$= 1$$

$$\cos^{(5)}(0) = -\sin(0)$$

$$= 0$$

$$\cos^{(6)}(0) = -\cos(0)$$

$$= -1$$

$$\cos^{(7)}(0) = \sin(0)$$

$$= 0$$

The pattern 1, 0, –1, 0 will keep repeating forever.

The unique seventh order Taylor polynomial that matches all these derivatives at $x = 0$ is

$$P_7(x) = 1 + 0x - \frac{1}{2!}x^2 + \frac{0}{3!}x^3 + \frac{1}{4!}x^4 + \frac{0}{5!}x^5 - \frac{1}{6!}x^6 + \frac{0}{7!}x^7$$

$$= 1 - \frac{x^2}{2!} + \frac{x^4}{4!} - \frac{x^6}{6!}$$

P_7 is the seventh order Taylor polynomial for $\cos x$ at $x = 0$. (It also happens to be of seventh degree, but that does not always happen. For example, you can see that P_8 for $\sin x$ will be the same polynomial as P_7.)

To form the Taylor polynomial we just keep going on:

$$\cos x = 1 - \frac{x^2}{2!} + \frac{x^4}{4!} - \frac{x^6}{6!} + \frac{x^8}{8!} + \cdots + \frac{(-1)^n x^{2n}}{(2n)!} + \cdots$$

Exercises for Alternate Example 2

In Exercises 7–12, construct the sixth order Taylor polynomial and the Taylor series for $f(x)$ at $x = 0$

7. $f(x) = e^x$ **8.** $f(x) = e^{-x}$ **9.** $f(x) = \cos(2x + \pi)$ **10.** $f(x) = \dfrac{1}{1-x}$ **11.** $f(x) = e^{3x}$

12. $f(x) = \dfrac{1}{x+1}$

Alternate Example 3   **Approximating a Function Near 0**

Find the fourth order Taylor polynomial that approximates $y = \sin 2x$ near 0.

SOLUTION

The polynomial we want is $P_4(x)$, the Taylor polynomial for $\sin 2x$ at $x = 0$. Instead of writing out derivatives, remember that we can use a known power series to generate another, as we did in Section 9.1. We can expand $\sin x$ as

$$\sin x = x - \frac{x^3}{3!} + \frac{x^5}{5!} - \frac{x^7}{7!} + \cdots + \frac{(-1)^n x^{2n+1}}{(2n+1)!} + \cdots$$

Therefore,

$$\sin 2x = 2x - \frac{(2x)^3}{3!} + \frac{(2x)^5}{5!} - \frac{(2x)^7}{7!} + \cdots + \frac{(-1)^n (2x)^{2n+1}}{(2n+1)!} + \cdots$$

So,

$$P_4(x) = 2x - \frac{(2x)^3}{3!}$$

$$= 2x - \frac{4x^3}{3}$$

The graph in Figure 9.3 shows how well the polynomial approximates the sine function near $x = 0$.

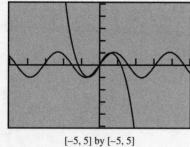

[–5, 5] by [–5, 5]

Figure 9.3 The graphs of $y = 2x - \dfrac{4x^3}{3}$ and $y = \sin 2x$.

Exercises for Alternate Example 3

In Exercises 13–18, find the fourth order Taylor polynomial that approximates $f(x)$ near 0 given the series $g(x)$.

13. $f(x) = \cos \sqrt{x}$ $g(x) = \cos x = 1 - \dfrac{x^2}{2!} + \dfrac{x^4}{4!} - \dfrac{x^6}{6!} + \cdots$ **14.** $f(x) = \sin x^3$ $g(x) = \sin x = x - \dfrac{x^3}{3!} + \dfrac{x^5}{5!} - \cdots$

15. $f(x) = \cos x^2 \sqrt{x}$ $g(x) = \cos x = 1 - \dfrac{x^2}{2!} + \dfrac{x^4}{4!} - \dfrac{x^6}{6!} + \cdots$ **16.** $f(x) = e^{2x}$ $g(x) = e^x = 1 + x + \dfrac{x^2}{2!} + \dfrac{x^3}{3!} + \cdots$

17. $f(x) = 2\cos(5x)$ $g(x) = \cos x = 1 - \dfrac{x^2}{2!} + \dfrac{x^4}{4!} - \dfrac{x^6}{6!} + \cdots$ **18.** $f(x) = \cos x \sqrt{x}$ $g(x) = \cos x = 1 - \dfrac{x^2}{2!} + \dfrac{x^4}{4!} - \dfrac{x^6}{6!} + \cdots$ ■

Alternate Example 4   **A Taylor Series at $x = a$**

Find the Taylor series generated by $f(x) = e^x$ at $x = 3$.

SOLUTION

We first observe that

$$f(3) = e^3$$
$$f'(3) = e^3$$
$$f''(3) = e^3$$
$$f'''(3) = e^3$$
$$f^{(n)}(3) = e^3$$

The series, therefore, is

$$e^x = e^3 + e^3(x-3) + \frac{e^3}{2!}(x-3)^2 + \cdots + \frac{e^3}{n!}(x-3)^n + \cdots$$

$$= \sum_{n=0}^{\infty} \left(\frac{e^3}{n!}\right)(x-3)^n$$

We illustrate the convergence near $x = 3$ by sketching the graphs of $y = e^x$ and $y = P_3(x)$ in Figure 9.4.

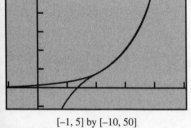

[−1, 5] by [−10, 50]

Figure 9.4 The graphs of $y = e^x$ and $y = P_3(x)$ (the third order Taylor polynomial for e^x at $x = 3$).

Exercises for Alternate Example 4

In Exercises 19–24, find the Taylor series generated by the given function at the given point a.

19. $f(x) = x^3 - 2x + 4$, $a = 3$ **20.** $f(x) = \dfrac{x}{1+x}$, $a = 0$ **21.** $f(x) = e^x$, $a = 6$ **22.** $f(x) = \dfrac{1}{x^2}$, $a = -1$

23. $f(x) = 3^x$, $a = 1$ **24.** $f(x) = \ln x$, $a = 1$ ■

9.3 Taylor's Theorem

Alternate Example 1   **Approximating a Function to Specifications**

Find a Taylor polynomial that will serve as an adequate substitute for $\sin x$ on the interval $[0, \pi]$.

SOLUTION

For this exercise, we define "adequate" to mean that the polynomial should differ from $\sin x$ by less than 0.0001 anywhere on the interval.

Another words we must choose $P_n(x)$ so that $|P_n(x) - \sin x| < 0.0001$ for every x in the interval $[0, \pi]$. How do we do this?

Recall the nine graphs of the partial sums of the Maclaurin series for $\sin x$ in Section 9.2. They show that the approximations get worse as x moves away from 0, suggesting that if we can make $|P_n(x) - \sin \pi| < 0.0001$, then P_n will be adequate throughout the interval. Since $\sin \pi = 0$, this means that we need to make $|p_n(\pi)| < 0.0001$.

We evaluate the partial sums at $x = \pi$, adding a term at a time, eventually arriving at the following:

As graphical support that the polynomial $P_{13}(x)$ is adequate throughout the interval, we graph the *absolute error* of the approximation, namely $|P_{13}(x) - \sin x|$ in the window $[0, \pi]$ by $[-0.00004, 0.00004]$ (Figure 9.5).

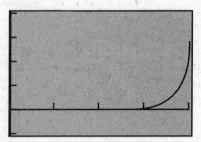

$[0, \pi]$ by $[-0.00001, 0.00004]$

Figure 9.5 The graph shows that $|p_{13}(\pi) - \sin x| < 0.0001$ throughout the interval $[0, \pi]$.

Exercises for Alternate Example 1

In exercises 1–3, find a Taylor polynomial p_n for $\sin x$ so that $|p_n(x) - \sin x| < 0.1$ for each x in the given interval.

1. $\left[-2\pi,\ 2\pi\right]$　　2. $\left[-\dfrac{3\pi}{2}, \dfrac{3\pi}{2}\right]$　　3. $[-5, 5]$

In exercises 4–6, find a Taylor polynomial p_n for e^x so that $|p_n(x) - e^x| < 0.1$ for each x in the given interval.

4. $\left[-\dfrac{1}{2}, \dfrac{1}{2}\right]$　　5. $[-\pi, \pi]$　　6. $[-e, e]$

Alternate Example 2 **Truncation Error for a Geometric Series**

Find a formula for the truncation error if we use $1 - x + x^2 - x^3 + x^4 - x^5$ to approximate $\dfrac{1}{x+1}$ over the interval $(-1, 1)$.

SOLUTION

We recognize this polynomial as the sixth partial sum of the geometric series for $1/(x+1)$. Since this series converges to $1/(x+1)$ on $(-1, 1)$, the truncation error is the absolute value of the part that we threw away, namely

$$\left| x^6 - x^7 + x^8 - x^9 + \cdots + (-1)^n x^n + \cdots \right|.$$

This is the absolute value of a geometric series with first term x^6 and $r = -x$ Therefore,

$$\left| x^6 - x^7 + x^8 - x^9 + \cdots + (-1)^n x^n + \cdots \right| = \left| \frac{x^6}{1 - (-x)} \right|$$

$$= \frac{x^6}{1 + x}.$$

Figure 9.6 shows that the error is small near 0, but increases as x gets closer to 1 or -1.

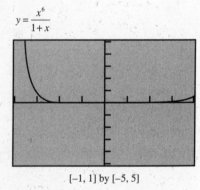

$y = \dfrac{x^6}{1+x}$

$[-1, 1]$ by $[-5, 5]$

Figure 9.6 A graph of the truncation error on $(-1, 1)$ if $P_5(x)$ is used to approximate $1/(x+1)$.

Exercises for Alternate Example 2

In Exercises 7–12, find a formula for the truncation error if we use $P_n(x)$ to approximate $g(x)$ over the given interval I.

7. $P_6(x) = 1 + x + x^2 + x^3 + x^4 + x^5 + x^6,$ $g(x) = \dfrac{1}{1-x},$ $I = (-1, 1)$

8. $P_9(x) = 1 - x + x^2 - x^3 + x^4 - x^5 + x^6 - x^7 + x^8 - x^9,$ $g(x) = \dfrac{1}{x+1},$ $I = (-1, 1)$

9. $P_5(x) = 1 + 2x + 4x^2 + 8x^3 + 16x^4 + 32x^5,$ $g(x) = \dfrac{1}{1-2x},$ $I = \left(-\dfrac{1}{2}, \dfrac{1}{2}\right)$

10. $P_4(x) = 1 - 3x + 9x^2 - 27x^3 + 81x^4,$ $g(x) = \dfrac{1}{1+3x},$ $I = \left(-\dfrac{1}{3}, \dfrac{1}{3}\right)$

11. $P_{11}(x) = 1 - x + x^2 - x^3 + x^4 - x^5 + x^6 - x^7 + x^8 - x^9 + x^{10},$ $g(x) = \dfrac{1}{x+1},$ $I = (-1, 1)$

12. $P_3(x) = \dfrac{1}{2} - \dfrac{x}{8} + \dfrac{x^2}{32} - \dfrac{x^3}{128},$ $g(x) = \dfrac{2}{x+4},$ $I = (-4, 4)$ ∎

Alternate Example 3 **Proving Convergence of a Maclaurin Series**

Prove that the series

$$\sum_{n=0}^{\infty} \frac{(-1)^n x^{2n}}{(2n)!}$$

converges to $\cos x$ for all x.

SOLUTION

We need to consider what happens to $R_n(x)$ as $n \to \infty$.

By Taylor's Theorem,

$$R_n(x) = \frac{f^{(n+1)}(c)}{(n+1)!}(x - 0)^{n+1},$$

where $f^{(n+1)}(c)$ is the $(n + 1)$st derivative of $\cos x$ evaluated at some c between x and 0. This does not seem at first glance to give us much information, but for this particular function we can say something very significant about $f^{(n+1)}(c)$: it lies between -1 and 1 inclusively. Therefore, no matter what x is, we have

$$\left| R_n(x) \right| = \left| \frac{f^{(n+1)}(c)}{(n+1)!}(x - 0)^{n+1} \right|$$

$$= \frac{\left| f^{(n+1)}(c) \right|}{(n+1)!}\left| x^{n+1} \right|$$

$$= \frac{1}{(n+1)!}\left| x^{n+1} \right|$$

$$= \frac{|x|^{n+1}}{(n+1)!}$$

What happens to $\dfrac{|x|^{n+1}}{(n+1)!}$ as $n \to \infty$? The numerator is a product of $n + 1$ factors, all of them $|x|$. The denominator is a product of $n + 1$ factors, the largest of which eventually exceeds $|x|$ and keeps on growing as $n \to \infty$. The factorial growth in the denominator, therefore, eventually outstrips the power growth in the numerator, and we have

$$\frac{|x|^{n+1}}{(n+1)!} \to 0 \text{ for all } x.$$ This means $R_n(x) \to 0$ for all x, which completes the proof.

Exercises for Alternate Example 3

In Exercises 13–18, use the Remainder Estimation Theorem to prove that the series $S(x)$ converges to $f(x)$ for all x in the domain of f.

13. $S(x) = \sum_{n=0}^{\infty} \frac{(-1)^n (2x)^{2n}}{(2n)!}$ $\qquad f(x) = \cos(2x)$

14. $S(x) = \sum_{n=0}^{\infty} \frac{(-1)^{n+1} 2(3x)^{2n+1}}{(2n+1)!}$ $\qquad f(x) = -2\sin(3x)$

15. $S(x) = \sum_{n=0}^{\infty} (-1)^n (x-1)^n$ $\qquad f(x) = \frac{1}{x}$

16. $S(x) = \sum_{n=0}^{\infty} \frac{(-1)^{n+1}(2x-1)^n}{n}$ $\qquad f(x) = \ln(2x)$

17. $S(x) = \sum_{n=0}^{\infty} \frac{x^n}{n!}$ $\qquad f(x) = e^x$

18. $S(x) = \sum_{n=0}^{\infty} \frac{(-1)^{n+1}(x-1)^n}{n}$ $\qquad f(x) = \ln x$

Alternate Example 5 Estimating a Remainder

The approximation $\ln(1+x) \approx x - (x^2/2)$ is used when x is small. Use the Remainder Estimation Theorem to get a bound for the maximum error when $|x| \le 0.05$. Support the answer graphically.

SOLUTION

In the notation of the Remainder Estimation Theorem, $f(x) = \ln(1+x)$, the polynomial is $P_2(x)$, and we need a bound for $|R_2(x)|$ On the interval $[-0.05, 0.05]$, the function

$$|f^{(3)}(t)| = \frac{2}{(1+t)^3}$$ is strictly decreasing, achieving its maximum value at the left-hand endpoint, -0.05.

We can therefore bound $|f^{(3)}(t)|$ by

$$M = \left| \frac{2}{(1+(-0.05))^3} \right|$$

$$= \frac{2{,}000{,}000}{857{,}375}.$$

We can let $r = 1$.

By the Remainder Estimation Theorem, we may conclude that

$$|R_2(x)| \le \frac{2{,}000{,}000}{857{,}375} \cdot \frac{|x^3|}{3!}$$

$$\le \frac{2{,}000{,}000}{857{,}375} \cdot \frac{|\pm 0.05^3|}{3!}$$

$$< 4.86 \times 10^{-5}.$$

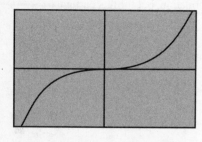

[−0.12, 0.12] by [−0.0005, 0.0005]

Figure 9.7 A graph of the error term $|R_2(x)|$. Maximum error for $|x| \le 0.05$ occurs at the left-hand endpoints of the interval.

Since $R^2(x) = \ln(1+x) - (x - x^2/2)$, it is an easy matter to produce a graph to observe the behavior of the error on the interval $[-0.1, 0.1]$ (Figure 9.7). The graph almost appears to have odd-function symmetry, but evaluation shows that $R_2(-.05) \approx -4.33 \times 10^{-5}$ and $R_2(.05) \approx 4.02 \times 10^{-5}$. The maximum absolute error on the interval is 4.33×10^{-5}, which is indeed less than the bound 4.86×10^{-5}.

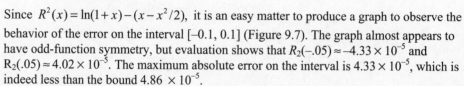

Exercises for Alternate Example 5

In Exercises 19–24, the approximation $\ln(1+x) \approx x - (x^2/2)$ is used when x is small. Use the Remainder Estimation Theorem to get a bound for the maximum error when $|x| \leq m$.

19. $m = 0.2$ **20.** $m = 0.02$ **21.** $m = 0.3$ **22.** $m = 0.03$ **23.** $m = 0.4$ **24.** $m = 0.04$ ∎

9.4 Radius of Convergence

Alternate Example 2 **Proving Convergence by Comparison**

Prove that $\displaystyle\sum_{n=0}^{\infty} \frac{x^{4n}}{(n!)^4}$ converges for all real x.

SOLUTION

Let x be any real number. The series

$$\sum_{n=0}^{\infty} \frac{x^{4n}}{(n!)^4}$$

has no negative terms.

For any n, we have

$$\frac{x^{4n}}{(n!)^4} \leq \frac{x^{4n}}{(n!)} = \frac{(x^4)^n}{n!}.$$

We recognize

$$\sum_{n=0}^{\infty} \frac{(x^4)^n}{n!}$$

as the Taylor series for e^{x^4}, which we know converges to e^{x^4} for all real numbers. Since the e^{x^4} series dominates

$$\sum_{n=0}^{\infty} \frac{x^{4n}}{(n!)^4}$$

term by term, the latter series must also converge for all real numbers by the Direct Comparison Test.

Exercises for Alternate Example 2

In Exercises 1–6, prove that each series converges for all real x.

1. $\displaystyle\sum_{n=0}^{\infty} \frac{x^{6n}}{(n!)^6}$ **2.** $\displaystyle\sum_{n=4}^{\infty} \frac{1}{(n-3)^2}$ **3.** $\displaystyle\sum_{n=1}^{\infty} \frac{1}{3^n + 3n}$ **4.** $\displaystyle\sum_{n=1}^{\infty} \frac{1}{n^2 - 11n}$ **5.** $\displaystyle\sum_{n=0}^{\infty} \frac{x^{12n}}{(n!)^{12}}$

6. $\displaystyle\sum_{n=0}^{\infty} \frac{x^{8n}}{(n!)^8}$ ∎

Alternate Example 3 **Using Absolute Convergence**

Show that

$$\sum_{n=0}^{\infty} \frac{(\cos x)^n}{3^n}$$

converges for all x.

SOLUTION

Let x be any real number. The series

$$\sum_{n=0}^{\infty} \frac{|\cos x|^n}{3^n}$$

has no negative terms, and it is term-by-term less than or equal to the series $\sum_{n=0}^{\infty} \frac{1}{3^n}$,

which we know converges to 1/2. Therefore,

$$\sum_{n=0}^{\infty} \frac{|\cos x|^n}{3^n}$$

converges by direct comparison. Since

$$\sum_{n=0}^{\infty} \frac{(\cos x)^n}{3^n}$$

converges absolutely, it converges.

Exercises for Alternate Example 3

In Exercises 7–13, show that each series converges.

7. $\sum_{n=0}^{\infty} \frac{(\cos x)^n}{(5n)!}$

8. $\sum_{n=0}^{\infty} \frac{(\sin x)^n}{n^n}$

9. $\sum_{n=0}^{\infty} \frac{(\sin x)^n}{n^2}$

10. $\sum_{n=0}^{\infty} \frac{(\cos x)^n}{n^2}$

11. $\sum_{n=0}^{\infty} \frac{(\cos x)^n}{(2n)!}$

12. $\sum_{n=0}^{\infty} \frac{(\sin x)^n}{(2n)!}$

13. $\sum_{n=0}^{\infty} \frac{(\sin x)^n}{3^n}$

Alternate Example 6   **Determining Convergence of a Series**

Determine the convergence or divergence of the series $\sum_{n=0}^{\infty} \frac{5^n}{11^n + 3}$.

SOLUTION

We use the Ratio Test.

$$\lim_{n\to\infty} \frac{a_{n+1}}{a_n} = \lim_{n\to\infty} \frac{\dfrac{5^{n+1}}{11^{n+1} + 3}}{\dfrac{5^n}{11^n + 3}}$$

$$= \lim_{n\to\infty} \left(\left(\frac{5^{n+1}}{11^{n+1} + 3} \right) \left(\frac{11^n + 3}{5^n} \right) \right)$$

$$= \lim_{n\to\infty} \left(\left(\frac{5}{11^{n+1} + 3} \right) \left(\frac{11^n + 3}{1} \right) \right)$$

$$= \lim_{n\to\infty} 5 \left(\frac{11^n + 3}{11^{n+1} + 3} \right)$$

$$= \lim_{n \to \infty} 5 \left(\frac{\dfrac{11^n + 3}{11^n}}{\dfrac{11^{n+1} + 3}{11^n}} \right) \qquad \text{Divide numerator and denominator by } 11^n.$$

$$= \lim_{n \to \infty} 5 \left(\frac{\dfrac{11^n}{11^n} + \dfrac{3}{11^n}}{\dfrac{11^{n+1}}{11^n} + \dfrac{3}{11^n}} \right)$$

$$= \lim_{n \to \infty} 5 \left(\frac{1 + \dfrac{3}{11^n}}{11 + \dfrac{3}{11^n}} \right)$$

$$= 5 \left(\frac{1}{11} \right)$$

$$= \frac{5}{11}.$$

The series converges by the Ratio Test because the ratio $\dfrac{5}{11} < 1$.

Exercises for Alternate Example 6

In exercises 14–21, determine whether the given series are divergent or convergent.

14. $\displaystyle\sum_{n=0}^{\infty} \frac{4^n}{7^n - 11}$ **15.** $\displaystyle\sum_{n=0}^{\infty} \frac{2^n}{22^n + 11}$ **16.** $\displaystyle\sum_{n=0}^{\infty} \frac{4^n}{8^n - 81}$ **17.** $\displaystyle\sum_{n=0}^{\infty} \frac{99^n}{9^n + 99}$

18. $\displaystyle\sum_{n=0}^{\infty} \frac{23^n}{32^n + 232}$ **19.** $\displaystyle\sum_{n=0}^{\infty} \frac{7^n}{77^n + 777}$ **20.** $\displaystyle\sum_{n=0}^{\infty} \frac{77^n}{7^n + 777}$ **21.** $\displaystyle\sum_{n=0}^{\infty} \frac{4^n}{40^n + 404}$

Alternate Example 7   **Summing a Telescoping Series**

Find the sum of $\displaystyle\sum_{n=2}^{\infty} \frac{2}{n^2 - 1}$.

SOLUTION

Use partial sums to find a general formula for the nth term.

$$\frac{2}{n^2 - 1} = \frac{2}{(n - 1)(n + 1)}$$

$$= \frac{A}{(n - 1)} + \frac{B}{(n + 1)}$$

$$= \frac{A(n + 1) + B(n - 1)}{(n - 1)(n + 1)}$$

Set the numerators of the fractions on both sides equal to each other.

$$A(n + 1) + B(n - 1) = 2$$
$$An + A + Bn - B = 2$$
$$n(A + B) + (A - B) = 2$$

Thus,

$$A + B = 0 \text{ and } A - B = 2.$$

Then, $A = 1$ and $B = -1$. Replacing these values in the identity above, we obtain

$$\frac{2}{n^2 - 1} = \frac{1}{(n-1)} - \frac{1}{(n+1)}.$$

Now, we compute a few partial sums to find a general formula.

$$s_1 = \left(\frac{1}{1} - \frac{1}{3}\right)$$

$$s_2 = \left(\frac{1}{1} - \frac{1}{3}\right) + \left(\frac{1}{2} - \frac{1}{4}\right)$$

$$s_3 = \left(\frac{1}{1} - \frac{1}{3}\right) + \left(\frac{1}{2} - \frac{1}{4}\right) + \left(\frac{1}{3} - \frac{1}{5}\right) = 1 + \frac{1}{2} - \frac{1}{4} - \frac{1}{5}$$

$$s_4 = \left(\frac{1}{1} - \frac{1}{3}\right) + \left(\frac{1}{2} - \frac{1}{4}\right) + \left(\frac{1}{3} - \frac{1}{5}\right) + \left(\frac{1}{4} - \frac{1}{6}\right) = 1 + \frac{1}{2} - \frac{1}{5} - \frac{1}{6}$$

$$s_n = \left(\frac{1}{1} - \frac{1}{3}\right) + \left(\frac{1}{2} - \frac{1}{4}\right) + \left(\frac{1}{3} - \frac{1}{5}\right) + \left(\frac{1}{4} - \frac{1}{6}\right) + \cdots + \left[\frac{1}{n-2} - \frac{1}{n}\right]$$

$$+ \left[\frac{1}{(n-1)} - \frac{1}{(n+1)}\right] + \left[\frac{1}{(n)} - \frac{1}{(n+2)}\right] = 1 + \frac{1}{2} - \frac{1}{n+1} - \frac{1}{n+2}$$

Then

$$\lim_{n \to \infty} s_n = \lim_{x \to \infty} \left[\frac{3}{2} - \frac{1}{n} - \frac{1}{n+1}\right]$$

$$= \frac{3}{2}.$$

Exercises for Alternate Example 7

In Exercises 22–29, find the sum of the telescoping series.

22. $\displaystyle\sum_{n=2}^{\infty} \frac{3}{n^2 + 3n + 2}$ **23.** $\displaystyle\sum_{n=1}^{\infty} \frac{1}{n^2 + 2n}$ **24.** $\displaystyle\sum_{n=2}^{\infty} \frac{-7}{n^2 - 1}$ **25.** $\displaystyle\sum_{n=1}^{\infty} \frac{4}{4n^2 - 1}$

26. $\displaystyle\sum_{n=1}^{\infty} \frac{12}{n^2 + 4n + 3}$ **27.** $\displaystyle\sum_{n=0}^{\infty} \frac{24}{9n^2 + 15n + 4}$ **28.** $\displaystyle\sum_{n=0}^{\infty} \frac{1}{16n^2 + 8n - 3}$ **29.** $\displaystyle\sum_{n=7}^{\infty} \frac{8}{n^2 + 3n + 2}$

9.5 Testing Convergence at Endpoints

Alternate Example 1 Applying the Integral Test

Does $\displaystyle\sum_{n=1}^{\infty} \frac{2}{n^2 \sqrt{n}}$ converge?

SOLUTION

The integral test applies because

$$f(x) = \frac{2}{x^2 \sqrt{x}}$$

is a continuous, positive, decreasing function of x for $x > 1$.

We have

$$\int_1^\infty \frac{2dx}{x^2\sqrt{x}} = \lim_{k\to\infty} \int_1^k 2x^{-5/2}\,dx$$

$$= \lim_{k\to\infty} \left[-\frac{4}{3}x^{-3/2} \right]_1^k$$

$$= \lim_{k\to\infty} \left[-\frac{4}{3k\sqrt{k}} + \frac{4}{3} \right]$$

$$= \frac{4}{3}.$$

Since the integral converges, so must the series.

Exercises for Alternate Example 1

In Exercises 1–6, determine whether each series converges or diverges.

1. $\displaystyle\sum_{n=1}^\infty \frac{9}{n^5\sqrt{n}}$ **2.** $\displaystyle\sum_{n=1}^\infty \frac{2n}{\sqrt[3]{n}}$ **3.** $\displaystyle\sum_{n=1}^\infty \frac{2(n^2+1)}{n^2\sqrt{n}}$ **4.** $\displaystyle\sum_{n=1}^\infty \frac{6}{n^6\sqrt{n}}$ **5.** $\displaystyle\sum_{n=1}^\infty \frac{9n^2}{\sqrt{n}}$ **6.** $\displaystyle\sum_{n=1}^\infty \frac{5}{7n^3\sqrt{n}}$ ■

Alternate Example 2   The Slow Divergence of the Harmonic Series

Approximately how many terms of the harmonic series are required to form a partial sum larger than 30?

SOLUTION

Before you set your graphing calculator to the task of finding this number, you might want to estimate how long the calculation might take. The graphs in Figure 9.8 tell the story.

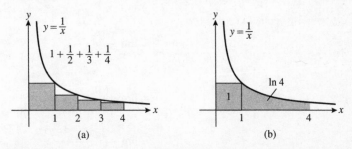

Figure 9.8 Finding an upper bound for the partial sums of the harmonic series.

Let H_n denote the nth partial sum of the harmonic series. Comparing the two graphs, we see that $H_4 < (1 + \ln 4)$ and (in general) that $H_n \le (1 + \ln n)$. If we wish H_n to be greater than 30, then

$$1 + \ln n > H_n > 30$$
$$1 + \ln n > 30$$
$$\ln n > 29$$
$$n > e^{29}.$$

The exact value of e^{29} rounds up to 3,931,334,297,000. It will take at least that many terms of the harmonic series to move the partial sums beyond 30. It would take your calculator several weeks to compute a partial sum of this many terms. Nonetheless, the harmonic series really does diverge.

Exercises for Alternate Example 2

In Exercises 19–24, approximately how many terms of the harmonic series are required to form a partial sum larger than *m*?

7. $m = 5$ **8.** $m = 10$ **9.** $m = 12$ **10.** $m = 25$ **11.** $m = 35$ **12.** $m = 40$

Alternate Example 3 Using the Limit Comparison Test.

Determine whether each series converges or diverges.

(a) $\dfrac{2}{9} + \dfrac{5}{16} + \dfrac{8}{25} + \cdots = \displaystyle\sum_{n=1}^{\infty} \dfrac{3n-1}{(n+2)^2}$

(b) $\dfrac{1}{8} + \dfrac{1}{14} + \dfrac{1}{32} + \cdots = \displaystyle\sum_{n=1}^{\infty} \dfrac{1}{3^n + 5}$

(c) $\dfrac{13}{2} + \dfrac{18}{18} + \dfrac{23}{52} + \cdots = \displaystyle\sum_{n=2}^{\infty} \dfrac{5n+3}{n^3 - 3n}$

(d) $\tan 1 + \tan\dfrac{1}{2} + \tan\dfrac{1}{3} + \cdots = \displaystyle\sum_{n=1}^{\infty} \tan\dfrac{1}{n}$

SOLUTION

(a) For *n* large,

$$\frac{3n-1}{(n+2)^2}$$

behaves like

$$\frac{3n}{n^2} = \frac{3}{n}.$$

Because the 3 in the numerator has little relevance to its behavior as $n \to \infty$, we can compare terms of the given series to the terms of $\sum(1/n)$ and try the LCT (Limit Comparison Test).

$$\lim_{n\to\infty} \frac{a_n}{b_n} = \lim_{n\to\infty} \frac{\dfrac{3n-1}{(n+2)^2}}{\dfrac{1}{n}}$$

$$= \lim_{n\to\infty} \frac{n(3n-1)}{(n+2)^2}$$

$$= \lim_{n\to\infty} \frac{3n^2 - 3n}{n^2 + 4n + 4}$$

$$= \lim_{n\to\infty} \frac{3 - \dfrac{3}{n}}{1 + \dfrac{4}{n} + \dfrac{4}{n^2}}$$

$$= 3.$$

Since the limit is positive and $\sum(1/n)$ diverges,

$$\sum_{n=1}^{\infty} \frac{3n-1}{(n+2)^2}$$

also diverges.

(b) For n large, $1/(3^n + 5)$ behaves like $1/3^n$, so we can compare the given series to $\sum (1/3^n)$.

$$\lim_{n \to \infty} \frac{a_n}{b_n} = \lim_{n \to \infty} \frac{\dfrac{1}{3^n + 5}}{\dfrac{1}{3^n}}$$

$$= \lim_{n \to \infty} \frac{3^n}{3^n + 5}$$

$$= \lim_{n \to \infty} \frac{\dfrac{3^n}{3^n}}{\dfrac{3^n}{3^n} + \dfrac{5}{3^n}}$$

$$= \frac{1}{1 + 0}$$

$$= 1.$$

Since $\displaystyle\sum_{n=1}^{\infty} \frac{1}{3^n}$ converges (geometric, $r = 1/3$), the LCT guarantees that

$$\sum_{n=1}^{\infty} \frac{1}{3^n + 5}$$

also converges.

(c) For n large,

$$\frac{5n + 3}{n^3 - 3n}$$

behaves like $5/n^2$, so we compare the given series to $\sum (1/n^2)$.

$$\lim_{n \to \infty} \frac{a_n}{b_n} = \lim_{n \to \infty} \frac{\dfrac{5n + 3}{n^3 - 3n}}{\dfrac{1}{n^2}}$$

$$= \lim_{n \to \infty} \frac{n^2(5n + 3)}{(n^3 - 3n)}$$

$$= \lim_{n \to \infty} \frac{5n^3 + 3n^2}{n^3 - 3n}$$

$$= \lim_{n \to \infty} \frac{5 + \dfrac{3}{n}}{1 - \dfrac{3}{n}}$$

$$= 5.$$

Since $\sum (5/n^2)$ converges by the p-Series test,

$$\sum_{n=2}^{\infty} \frac{5n + 3}{n^3 - 3n}$$

also, converges (by LCT).

(d) Recall that $\lim\limits_{x \to 0} \dfrac{\sin x}{x} = 1$ and $\lim\limits_{x \to 0} \dfrac{1}{\cos x} = 1$ so that

$$\lim\limits_{x \to 0} \frac{\tan x}{x} = 1.$$

We use this fact and apply the LCT to the given series and $\sum 1/n$.

$$\lim\limits_{n \to \infty} \frac{a_n}{b_n} = \lim\limits_{n \to \infty} \frac{\tan \dfrac{1}{n}}{\dfrac{1}{n}} = 1.$$

Since $\sum\limits_{n=1}^{\infty} \dfrac{1}{n}$ diverges, $\sum\limits_{n=1}^{\infty} \tan \dfrac{1}{n}$ also diverges.

Exercises for Alternate Example 3

In Exercises 13–18, determine whether the series converges or diverges.

13. $\sum\limits_{n=3}^{\infty} \dfrac{3}{(n-2)^3}$ **14.** $\sum\limits_{n=1}^{\infty} \dfrac{n^2 - 12}{6n^5 + 7n^3}$ **15.** $\sum\limits_{n=1}^{\infty} \dfrac{1}{n^2 + 9}$ **16.** $\sum\limits_{n=1}^{\infty} \dfrac{n+7}{n^2 + 19n}$

17. $\sum\limits_{n=1}^{\infty} \dfrac{1}{11a + b}$, where a and b are constants satisfying $11a + b \neq 0$ **18.** $\sum\limits_{n=1}^{\infty} \dfrac{3n^2 - 1}{6n^5 + 7n + 2}$

Alternate Example 6   **Finding Intervals of Convergence**

For what values of x do the following series converge?

(a) $\sum\limits_{n=1}^{\infty} (-1)^{n+1} \dfrac{x^{4n}}{4n}$ **(b)** $\sum\limits_{n=0}^{\infty} \dfrac{(50x)^{2n}}{(2n)!}$ **(c)** $\sum\limits_{n=0}^{\infty} \dfrac{(3n)!(x+1)^{2n}}{3n}$

SOLUTION

We apply the Ratio Test to find the interval of absolute convergence, then check the endpoints if they exist.

(a) $\lim\limits_{n \to \infty} \left| \dfrac{u_{n+1}}{u_n} \right| = \lim\limits_{n \to \infty} \dfrac{\dfrac{x^{4n+4}}{4n + 4}}{\dfrac{x^{4n}}{4n}}$

$= \lim\limits_{n \to \infty} \dfrac{x^{4n+4}(4n)}{x^{4n}(4n + 4)}$

$= \lim\limits_{n \to \infty} \dfrac{x^4(4n)}{4n + 4}$

$= \lim\limits_{n \to \infty} \left(\dfrac{4}{4} \right) x^4$

$= x^4.$

The series converges absolutely for $x^4 < 1$, i.e., on the interval $(-1, 1)$. At $x = 1$ or at $x = -1$, the series is

$$\sum \frac{(-1)^{n+1}}{4n}$$

which converges by the Alternating Series Test. (It is one fourth of the sum of the alternating harmonic series.) The interval of convergence is $[-1, 1]$.

(b) $\lim\limits_{n\to\infty} \left| \dfrac{u_{n+1}}{u_n} \right| = \lim\limits_{n\to\infty} \left| \dfrac{\dfrac{(50x)^{2n+2}}{(2n+2)!}}{\dfrac{(50x)^{2n}}{(2n)!}} \right|$

$= \lim\limits_{n\to\infty} \left| \dfrac{(2n)!(50x)^{2n+2}}{(2n+2)!(50x)^{2n}} \right|$

$= \lim\limits_{n\to\infty} \left| \dfrac{(50x)^2}{\left[(2n+2)(2n+1) \right]} \right|$

$= 0.$

The series converges absolutely for all x.

(c) $\lim\limits_{n\to\infty} \left| \dfrac{u_{n+1}}{u_n} \right| = \lim\limits_{n\to\infty} \dfrac{\dfrac{(3n+3)!(x+1)^{2n+2}}{3(n+1)}}{\dfrac{(3n)!(x+1)^{2n}}{3n}}$

$= \lim\limits_{n\to\infty} \dfrac{(3n)(3n+3)!(x+1)^{2n+2}}{3(n+1)(3n)!(x+1)^{2n}}$

$= \lim\limits_{n\to\infty} \dfrac{(3n)(3n+1)(3n+2)(3n+3)(x+1)^2}{3(n+1)}$

$= \lim\limits_{n\to\infty} \dfrac{(3n)(3n+1)(3n+2)(3n+3)(x+1)^2}{(3n+3)}$

$= \lim\limits_{n\to\infty} \left((3n)(3n+1)(3n+2)(x+1)^2 \right) = \begin{cases} \infty & x \neq -1 \\ 0 & x = -1 \end{cases}$

The series converges only at $x = -1$.

Exercises for Alternate Example 6

In Exercises 19–24, for what value of x does each series converge?

19. $\sum\limits_{n=1}^{\infty} \dfrac{(50x)^n}{(3n)!}$

20. $\sum\limits_{n=1}^{\infty} \dfrac{(x+1)^n}{7^n}$

21. $\sum\limits_{n=0}^{\infty} (n!)x^{n+1}$

22. $\sum\limits_{n=1}^{\infty} \dfrac{(x+1)^n}{3^n}$

23. $\sum\limits_{n=0}^{\infty} \dfrac{(-1)^n(x+5)^n}{6^n}$

24. $\sum\limits_{n=1}^{\infty} \dfrac{(32x)^n}{(23n)!}$

Chapter 10

Parametric, Vector, and Polar Functions

10.1 Parametric Functions

Reviewing Some Parametric Curves

Sketch the parametric curves and identify those which define y as a function of x. In each case, eliminate the parameter to find an equation that relates x and y. Determine if y is related directly to x.

(a) $x = 2 \cos t$ and $y = 2 \sin t$ for t in the interval $[0, 2\pi)$

(b) $x = 5 \cos t$ and $y = 3 \sin t$ for t in the interval $[0, 4\pi]$

(c) $x = \sqrt{\dfrac{t}{2}}$ and $y = t - 3$ for t in the interval $[0, 4]$

SOLUTION

(a) This type of the parametrization is probably the best-known one. The curve is a circle of radius 2 centered at the origin (Figure 10.1a), and it does not define y as a function of x. To eliminate the parameter, we use the identity $(\cos t)^2 + (\sin t)^2 = 1$ to eliminate t. To do so, first square both given equations, and then add them:

$$x^2 = 4(\cos t)^2$$
$$y^2 = 4(\sin t)^2$$
$$x^2 + y^2 = 4(\sin t)^2 + 4(\cos t)^2$$
$$x^2 + y^2 = 4((\sin t)^2 + (\cos t)^2)$$
$$x^2 + y^2 = 4$$

(b) This parametrization stretches the unit circle by a factor of 5 horizontally and by a factor of 3 vertically. The result is an ellipse (Figure 10.1b), which is traced twice as t covers the interval $[0, 4\pi]$. (In fact, the point $(5, 0)$ is visited three times.) It does not define y as a function of x, We use the same identity as in part (a) to write

$$\left(\frac{x}{5}\right)^2 + \left(\frac{y}{3}\right)^2 = 1.$$

(c) This parametrization produces a segment of a parabola (Figure 10.1c). It does define y as a function of x. Since $t = 2x^2$, we write $y = 2x^2 - 3$

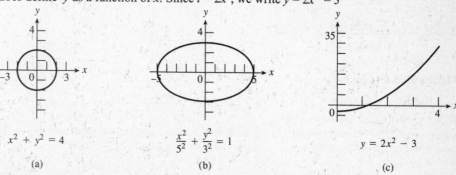

$$x^2 + y^2 = 4 \qquad \frac{x^2}{5^2} + \frac{y^2}{3^2} = 1 \qquad y = 2x^2 - 3$$

(a)   (b)   (c)

Figure 10.1 A collection of parametric curves. Each point (x, y) is determined by parametric functions of t, but only the parametrization in graph (c) determines y as a function of x.

Exercises for Alternate Example 1

In Exercises 1–8, (a) sketch the parametric curves, (b) determine if y is defined as a function of x, and (c) eliminate the parameter to find an equation that relates x and y directly.

1. $x = t + 2$ and $y = 3t - 1$ for t in the interval $[-2, 2]$

2. $x = -t$ and $y = 3t$ for t in the interval $[0,3]$

3. $x = 6 \cos t$ and $y = 6 \sin t$ for t in the interval $[0, 2\pi)$

4. $x = 2 \cos t$ and $y = \sin t$ for t in the interval $[0, 4\pi]$

5. $x = 2t$ and $y = (t-1)^2$ for t in the interval $[-4, 4]$

6. $x = t + 2$ and $y = (t+1)^2$ for t in the interval $[0,4]$

7. $x = \sqrt{t/3}$ and $y = t - 4$ for t in the interval $[0, 8]$

8. $x = \sqrt{t/5}$ and $y = t^2 - 7$ for t in the interval $[0.05, 5]$

Alternate Example 2   Analyzing a Parametric Curve

Consider the curve defined parametrically by $x = t^2 - 3$ and $y = -4 \sin t$ for $0 \le t \le \pi$.

(a) Sketch a graph of the curve in the viewing window $[-5, 9]$ by $[-6, 2]$. Indicate the direction in which it is traced.

(b) Find the lowest point on the curve. Justify your answer.

(c) Find all points of inflection on the curve. Justify your answer.

SOLUTION

(a) The curve is shown in Figure 10.2.

(b) We seek to minimize y as a function of t, so we compute $dy/dt = -4 \cos t$. Since dy/dt is negative for $0 < t \le \pi/2$ and positive for $\pi/2 < t \le \pi$, the minimum occurs when $t = \pi/2$. Substituting this t value into the parametrization, we find the lowest point to be approximately $(-0.53, -4)$.

(c) First, we compute $d^2 y / dx^2$.

$$\frac{d^2 y}{dx^2} = \frac{dy'/dt}{dx/dt} = \frac{\dfrac{d(dy/dx)}{dt}}{dx/dt}$$

$$= \frac{\dfrac{d(-4\cos t/2t)}{dt}}{2t}$$

$$= \frac{(-2\cos t/t)'}{2t}$$

$$= \frac{(2t\sin t + 2\cos t)/(t^2)}{2t}$$

$$= \frac{(t\sin t + \cos t)/(t^2)}{t}$$

$$= \frac{t\sin t + \cos t}{t^3}.$$

A graph of $y = \dfrac{t\sin t + \cos t}{t^3}$ on the interval $\left[0, \pi\right]$ shows a sign change at $t = 2.798386$.

Substituting this t value into the parametrization, we find the point of inflection to be approximately $(4.830964, -1.346034)$.

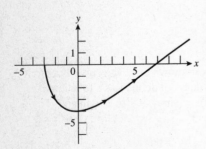

Figure 10.2 The parametric curve defined by $x = t^2 - 3$ and $y = -4\sin t$ for $0 \le t \le \pi$.

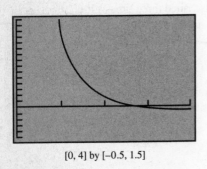

[0, 4] by [−0.5, 1.5]

Figure 10.3 The graph of $\dfrac{d^2 y}{dx^2}$ for the parametric curve $x = t^2 - 3$ and $y = -4 \sin t$ for $0 \le t \le \pi$ shows a sign change at $t = 2.798386$ indicating a point of inflection on the curve.

Exercises for Alternate Example 2

In Exercises 9–14, consider the curve defined parametrically by x and y for $0 \le t \le \pi$.

(a) Sketch a graph of each curve. Indicate the direction in which it is traced.

(b) Find the highest or lowest point of each curve.　　　(c) Find all points of inflection on each curve.

9. $x = t^2 - 1$ and $y = -2 \sin t$　　　for $0 \le t \le \pi$

10. $x = t - 3$ and $y = t^3 - t$　　　for $-2 \le t \le 2$

11. $x = \sin t$ and $y = 0.5 \cos t$　　　for $-\pi/2 \le t \le \pi/2$

12. $x = \sin^2 t$ and $y = \cos t$　　　for $0 \le t \le \pi$

13. $x = t^2 - 7$ and $y = 4 \sin t$　　　for $0 \le t \le \pi$

14. $x = \tan t$ and $y = -2 \sec t$　　　for $-1 \le t \le 1$

Alternate Example 3　Measuring a Parametric Curve

Find the length of the astroid (Figure 10.4)

$$x = 2 \cos^3 t, \quad y = 2 \sin^3 t, \quad 0 \le t \le 2\pi$$

SOLUTION

Solve Analytically The curve is traced once as t goes from 0 to 2π. Because of the curve's symmetry with respect to the coordinate axes, its length is four times the length of the first quadrant portion. We have

$$\left(\frac{dx}{dt} \right)^2 = \left(2(3)(-\sin t)(\cos^2 t) \right)^2$$

$$= 36(\sin^2 t)(\cos^4 t)$$

$$\left(\frac{dy}{dt} \right)^2 = \left(2(3)(\cos t)(\sin^2 t) \right)^2$$

$$= 36(\cos^2 t)(\sin^4 t)$$

$$\sqrt{\left(\frac{dx}{dt} \right)^2 + \left(\frac{dy}{dt} \right)^2} = \sqrt{36(\sin^2 t)(\cos^4 t) + 36(\cos^2 t)(\sin^4 t)}$$

$$= \sqrt{36(\sin^2 t)(\cos^2 t)(\sin^2 t + \cos^2 t)}$$

$$= \sqrt{36(\sin^2 t)(\cos^2 t)}$$

$$= 6| (\sin t)(\cos t) |.$$

Thus, the length of the first quadrant portion of the curve is

$$\int_0^{\pi/2} 6\left| (\sin t)(\cos t) \right| dt = 6 \int_0^{\pi/2} \left| (\sin t)(\cos t) \right| dt$$

$$= 6 \left[\frac{1}{2} \sin^2 t \right]_0^{\frac{\pi}{2}}$$

$$= 3 \left[\sin^2 t \right]_0^{\frac{\pi}{2}}$$

$$= 3.$$

The length of the asteroid is $4(3) = 12$.

Support Numerically NINT $(6|(\sin t)(\cos t)|, t, 0, 2\pi) = 12$.

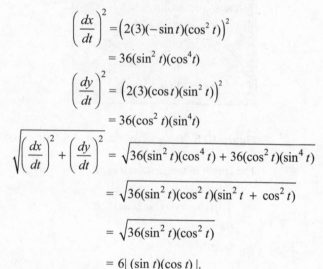

[−4.7, 4.7] by [−3.1, 3.1]

Figure 10.4 The astroid in Alternate Example 3.

Exercises for Alternate Example 3

In Exercises 15–22, find the length of the curve on the indicated interval.

15. $x = \sin t, y = \cos t, \ 0 \le t \le \pi$

16. $x = \cos t - \sin t, \ y = \sin t - \cos t, \ 0 \le t \le 2\pi$

17. $x = 3 \cos^3 t, y = 3 \sin^3 t, \ 0 \le t \le 2\pi$

18. $x = 11 \cos^3 t, y = 2 \sin^3 t, \ 0 \le t \le 2\pi$

19. $x = t, y = \ln t, \ 1 \le t \le 10$

20. $x = t + 1, y = \sqrt{2t}, \ 1 \le t \le 8$

21. $x = e^t, y = e^{-2t}, \ -2 \le t \le 2$

22. $x = t^{4/5}, \ y = t^{-1/3}, \ 1 \le t \le 2$

Alternate Example 5 **Finding Length**

Find the length of one arch of the cycloid

$$x = 5(t - \sin t), \qquad y = 5(1 - \cos t).$$

SOLUTION

Figure 10.5 shows the first arch of the cycloid and part of the next for $a = 5$. In Exploration 1, you found that the x-intercepts occur at $t = n(2\pi)$, n an integer, and that the arches are congruent.

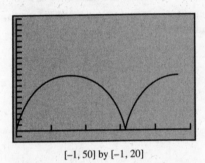

[–1, 50] by [–1, 20]

Figure 10.5 The graph of the cycloid $x = 5(t - \sin t), y = 5(1 - \cos t)$.

The length of the first arch is

$$\int_0^{2\pi} \sqrt{(dx/dt)^2 + (dy/dt)^2} \ dt \ .$$

We have

$$(dx/dt)^2 = \left(5(1 - \cos t)\right)^2$$

$$= 25(1 - \cos t)^2$$

$$= 25(1 - 2 \cos t + \cos^2 t)$$

$$= 25 - 50 \cos t + 25 \cos^2 t$$

$$(dy/dt)^2 = (5\sin t)^2$$

$$= 25 \sin^2 t$$

$$\sqrt{(dx/dt)^2 + (dy/dt)^2} = \sqrt{25 - 50\cos t + 25\cos^2 t + 25\sin^2 t}$$

$$= \sqrt{25 - 50\cos t + 25}$$

$$= \sqrt{50 - 50\cos t}$$

$$= \sqrt{25(2 - 2\cos t)}$$

$$= 5\sqrt{(2 - 2\cos t)} \ .$$

Therefore,

$$\int_0^{2\pi} \sqrt{(dx/dt)^2 + (dy/dt)^2}\, dt = \int_0^{2\pi} 5\sqrt{(2 - 2\cos t)}\, dt$$

$$= 5\int_0^{2\pi} \sqrt{(2 - 2\cos t)}\, dt$$

$$= 40.$$

The length of one arch of the cycloid is 40.

Exercises for Alternate Example 5

In Exercises 23–28, find the length of one arch of the cycloid

23. $x = 4(t - \sin t)$, $y = 4(1 - \cos t)$
24. $x = 2(t - \sin t)$, $y = 2(1 - \cos t)$
25. $x = 11(t - \sin t)$, $y = 11(1 - \cos t)$
26. $x = 3(t - \sin t)$, $y = 3(1 - \cos t)$
27. $x = 6(t - \sin t)$, $y = 6(1 - \cos t)$
28. $x = 9(t - \sin t)$, $y = 9(1 - \cos t)$

10.2 Vectors in the Plane

Alternate Example 1   Finding Magnitude and Direction

Find the magnitude and the direction angle θ of the vector $\mathbf{v} = \left\langle -5,\ \sqrt{11} \right\rangle$ (Figure 10.6).

SOLUTION

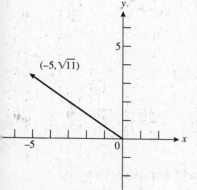

The magnitude of $\mathbf{v}$ is $|\mathbf{v}| = \sqrt{(-5 - 0)^2 + (\sqrt{11} - 0)^2} = 6$. Using triangle ratios, we see

that the direction angle θ satisfies $\cos\theta = \dfrac{-5}{6} = -0.833$ and $\sin\theta = \dfrac{\sqrt{11}}{6} = 0.55$,

So $\theta = 146.44°$ or 2.56 radians.

Figure 10.6 The vector $\mathbf{v}$ in Alternate Example 1 is represented by an arrow from the origin to the point $\left(-5, \sqrt{11}\right)$.

Exercises for Alternate Example 1

In Exercises 1–8, find the magnitude and the direction angle θ of the vector $\mathbf{v}$

1. $\mathbf{v} = \left\langle 1, \sqrt{15} \right\rangle$
2. $\mathbf{v} = \left\langle \sqrt{7}, 2 \right\rangle$
3. $\mathbf{v} = \left\langle -1, -\sqrt{15} \right\rangle$
4. $\mathbf{v} = \left\langle -3, \sqrt{7} \right\rangle$

5. $\mathbf{v} = \left\langle 3, -\sqrt{7} \right\rangle$
6. $\mathbf{v} = \left\langle 6, \sqrt{3} \right\rangle$
7. $\mathbf{v} = \left\langle -1, -\sqrt{3} \right\rangle$
8. $\mathbf{v} = \left\langle 4, -\sqrt{3} \right\rangle$

Alternate Example 3   Performing Operations on Vectors

Let $\mathbf{u} = \left\langle -4,\ 6 \right\rangle$ and $\mathbf{y} = \left\langle 3, -7 \right\rangle$. Find

(a) $2\mathbf{u} + 4\mathbf{v}$ **(b)** $2\mathbf{u} - 3\mathbf{v}$ **(c)** $\left| \dfrac{3}{2}\mathbf{u} \right|$

SOLUTION

(a) $2\mathbf{u} + 4\mathbf{v} = 2\langle -4, \ 6 \rangle + 4\langle 3, \ -7 \rangle$

$= \langle -8, \ 12 \rangle + \langle 12, \ -28 \rangle$

$= \langle -8 + 12, \ 12 - 28 \rangle$

$= \langle 4, \ -16 \rangle$

(b) $2\mathbf{u} - 3\mathbf{v} = 2\langle -4, \ 6 \rangle - 3\langle 3, \ -7 \rangle$

$= \langle -8, \ 12 \rangle - \langle 9, \ -21 \rangle$

$= \langle -8 - 9, \ 12 + 21 \rangle$

$= \langle -17, \ 33 \rangle$

(c) $\left| \dfrac{3}{2}\mathbf{u} \right| = \left| \dfrac{3}{2}\langle -4, \ 6 \rangle \right|$

$= \left| \langle -6, \ 9 \rangle \right|$

$= \sqrt{(-6)^2 + (9)^2}$

$= \sqrt{117}$

$= 3\sqrt{13}$

Exercises for Alternate Example 3

In Exercises 9–14, given $\mathbf{u} = \langle 6, \ -8 \rangle$ and $\mathbf{v} = \langle -3, 12 \rangle$, calculate each expression.

9. $4\mathbf{u} + 5\mathbf{v}$ **10.** $5\mathbf{u} + 6\mathbf{v}$ **11.** $6\mathbf{u} - 7\mathbf{v}$ **12.** $7\mathbf{u} - 8\mathbf{v}$ **13.** $\left| 3\mathbf{u} \right| - \left| 2\mathbf{v} \right|$ **14.** $\left| \dfrac{1}{2}\mathbf{u} \right| - \left| \dfrac{1}{3}\mathbf{v} \right|$

Alternate Example 4   Finding Ground Speed and Direction

A Boeing® 727® airplane, flying due east at 300 mph in still air, encounters a 60-mph tail wind acting in the direction 45° north of east. The airplane holds its compass heading due east but, because of the wind, acquires a new ground speed and direction. What are they?

SOLUTION

If $\mathbf{u}$ = the velocity of the airplane alone and $\mathbf{v}$ = the velocity of the tail wind, then $\left| \mathbf{u} \right| = 300$ and $\left| \mathbf{v} \right| = 60$ (Figure 10.7).

We need to find the magnitude and direction of the resultant vector $\mathbf{u} + \mathbf{v}$. If we let the positive x-axis represent east and the positive y-axis represent north, then the component forms of $\mathbf{u}$ and $\mathbf{v}$ are

$$\mathbf{u} = \langle 300, \ 0 \rangle \ \text{and} \ \mathbf{v} = \langle 60\cos 45°, 60\sin 45° \rangle.$$

Therefore,

$$\mathbf{u} + \mathbf{v} = \langle 300, \ 0 \rangle + \langle 60\cos 45°, 60\sin 45° \rangle$$

$$= \langle 300, \ 0 \rangle + \left\langle 60\left(\frac{\sqrt{2}}{2} \right), \ 60\left(\frac{\sqrt{2}}{2} \right) \right\rangle$$

$$= \langle 300, \ 0 \rangle + \langle 30\sqrt{2}, 30\sqrt{2} \rangle$$

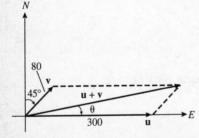

Figure 10.7 Vectors representing the velocities of the airplane and tail wind.

$$= \left\langle 300 + 30\sqrt{2}, \, 30\sqrt{2} \right\rangle$$

$$|\mathbf{u} + \mathbf{v}| = \sqrt{(300 + 30\sqrt{2})^2 + (30\sqrt{2})^2}$$

$$= \sqrt{(90000 + 18000\sqrt{2} + 1800) + (1800)}$$

$$= \sqrt{93600 + 18000\sqrt{2}}$$

$$\approx 345.04$$

and

$$\tan\theta \approx \frac{30\sqrt{2}}{300 + 30\sqrt{2}}$$

$$\theta = \tan^{-1}\frac{30\sqrt{2}}{300 + 30\sqrt{2}}$$

$$\approx 7.06°.$$

Interpret The new ground speed of the airplane is about 345.0 mph, and its new direction is about 7.06° north of east.

Exercises for Alternate Example 4

In exercises 15–20, an airplane flying in the direction described at p mph in still air, encounters an m-mph tail wind acting in the direction $d°$ north of east. The airplane holds its compass heading due east but, because of the wind, acquires a new ground speed and direction. What are they?

15. Due east, $p = 600$, $m = 80$, $d = 30°$

16. Due east, $p = 400$, $m = 50$, $d = 50°$

17. Due north, $p = 600$, $m = 80$, $d = 40°$

18. Due south, $p = 750$, $m = 65$, $d = 70°$

19. Due east, $p = 900$, $m = 90$, $d = 45°$

20. Northwest, $p = 700$, $m = 60$, $d = 60°$ ■

Alternate Example 9   Finding the Path of the Particle

A particle moves in the plane with velocity vector

$$\mathbf{v}(t) = \left\langle 2t - 4\pi\cos\pi t, \, 6t - \pi\sin\pi t \right\rangle$$

At $t = 0$, the particle is at the point $(2, 5)$. Determine the path the particle travels from $(3, 6)$ to $(18, 53)$.

SOLUTION

The velocity vector and the position at $t = 0$ are combined to give us the vector equivalent of an initial value problem. We simply find the components of the position vector separately.

$$\frac{dx}{dt} = 2t - 4\pi\cos\pi t$$

$$x = t^2 - 4\sin\pi t + C \qquad\qquad \text{Antidifferentiate}$$

$$x = t^2 - 4\sin\pi t + 2 \qquad x = 2, \text{ when } t = 0$$

$$\frac{dy}{dt} = 6t - \pi\sin\pi t$$

$$y = 3t^2 + \cos\pi t + C \qquad\qquad \text{Antidifferentiate}$$

$$y = 3t^2 + \cos\pi t + 4 \qquad y = 5, \text{ when } t = 0$$

We then graph the position $\left\langle t^2 - 4\sin\pi t + 2, \, 3t^2 + \cos\pi t + 4 \right\rangle$ parametrically from $t = 1$ to $t = 4$. The path is shown in Figure 10.8.

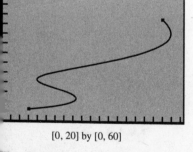

[0, 20] by [0, 60]

Figure 10.8 The path traveled by the particle as it goes from $(3, 6)$ to $(18, 53)$.

Exercises for Alternate Example 9

In Exercises 21–26, a particle moves in the plane with velocity vector $\mathbf{v}(t)$. At $t = 0$, the particle is at the point A. Determine the position vector for the particle and the range of values for the parameter t as the particle travels from M to N.

21. $\mathbf{v}(t) = \left\langle 3t^2 + 2, -2t \right\rangle$, $A(1, 8)$, $M(4, 7)$, $N(13, 4)$

22. $\mathbf{v}(t) = \left\langle 2t - \pi \cos \pi t, 2t - \pi \sin \pi t \right\rangle$, $A(2, 5)$, $M(3, 4)$, $N(27, 28)$

23. $\mathbf{v}(t) = \left\langle e^t (t+1), -4e^{-2t} \right\rangle$, $A(0, 2)$, $M\left(2e^2, \dfrac{2}{e^4} \right)$, $N\left(3e^3, \dfrac{2}{e^6} \right)$

24. $\mathbf{v}(t) = \left\langle \dfrac{-1}{(1+t)^2}, \dfrac{-1}{2(t+1)^{3/2}} \right\rangle$, $A(1,1)$, $M\left(\dfrac{1}{3}, \dfrac{1}{\sqrt{3}} \right)$, $N\left(\dfrac{1}{9}, \dfrac{1}{3} \right)$

25. $\mathbf{v}(t) = \left\langle 2t - \pi \cos \pi t, 4t - \pi \sin \pi t \right\rangle$, $A(2, 4)$, $M(6, 12)$, $N(18, 36)$

26. $\mathbf{v}(t) = \left\langle 4t - \pi \cos \pi t, 3t - \pi \sin \pi t \right\rangle$, $A(1, 2)$, $M(9, 8)$, N

10.3 Polar Functions

Alternate Example 2   Graphing with Polar Coordinates

Graph all points in the plane that satisfy the given polar equation

(a) $r = 4$ **(b)** $r = -5$ **(c)** $\theta = \pi/3$

SOLUTION

First, note that we do not label our axes r and θ. We are graphing polar equations in the usual xy-plane, not renaming our rectangular variables.

(a) The set of all points with directed distance 4 units from the pole is a circle of radius 4 centered at the origin (Figure 10.9a).

(b) The set of all points with directed distance –5 units from the pole is a circle of radius 5 centered at the origin (Figure 10.9b).

(c) The set of all points of positive or negative directed distance from the pole in the $\pi/3$ direction is a line through the origin with slope $\tan(\pi/3)$ (Figure 10.9c).

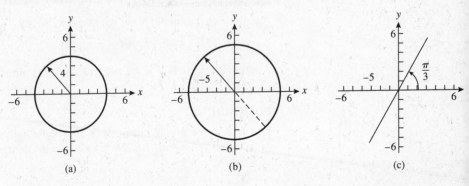

Figure 10.9 Polar graphs of (a) $r = 4$, (b) $r = -5$, and (c) $\theta = \dfrac{\pi}{3}$.

Exercises for Alternate Example 2

In Exercises 1–8, graph all points in the plane that satisfy the given polar equations.

1. $r = 7$ **2.** $r^3 = 8$ **3.** $r^2 + 10 = 7r$ **4.** $r = -4$ **5.** $|\theta| = \dfrac{\pi}{8}$ **6.** $\theta = \dfrac{\pi}{4}$

7. $\theta = -\dfrac{\pi}{5}$ **8.** $\theta = \dfrac{2\pi}{3}$

Alternate Example 4   Converting Polar to Rectangle

Use the polar-rectangular conversion formulas to show that the polar graph of $r = 8 \sin \theta$ is a circle.

SOLUTION

To facilitate the substitutions, multiply both sides of the original equation by r. (This could introduce extraneous solutions with $r = 0$, but the pole is the only such point, and we notice that it is already on the graph.)

$$r = 8\sin\theta$$
$$r^2 = r(8\sin\theta)$$
$$x^2 + y^2 = 8y$$
$$x^2 + y^2 - 8y = 0$$
$$x^2 + y^2 - 8y + 16 = 16$$
$$x^2 + (y - 4)^2 = 16$$

Sure enough, the graph is a circle centered at $(0, 4)$ with radius 4.

Exercises for Alternate Example 4

In Exercises 9–16, replace the polar equation by an equivalent Cartesian (rectangular) equation. Then identify or describe the graph.

9. $r = 10\sin\theta$ **10.** $r = 8\cos\theta$ **11.** $r = -2\csc\theta$ **12.** $r = 6\cos\theta + 6\sin\theta$ **13.** $r^2\sin 2\theta = 6$

14. $r^2 = -2r\cos\theta$ **15.** $2r^4 - r^2 - 1 = 0$ **16.** $r = \dfrac{3}{\cos\theta - 4\sin\theta}$ ■

Alternate Example 6 Finding Area

Find the area of the region in the plane enclosed by the cardioid $r = 4(1 + \cos\theta)$.

SOLUTION

We graph the cardioid (Figure 10.10) and determine that the radius OP sweeps out the region exactly once as θ runs from 0 to 2π.

Solve Analytically The area is therefore

$$\int_0^{2\pi} \frac{1}{2} r^2\, d\theta = \int_0^{2\pi} \frac{1}{2}(4(1 + \cos\theta))^2\, d\theta$$

$$= \int_0^{2\pi} \frac{16}{2}(1 + \cos\theta)^2\, d\theta$$

$$= \int_0^{2\pi} 8(1 + 2\cos\theta + \cos^2\theta)\, d\theta$$

$$= \int_0^{2\pi} 8\left(1 + 2\cos\theta + \frac{1 + \cos 2\theta}{2}\right) d\theta$$

$$= \int_0^{2\pi} 4\left(2 + 4\cos\theta + 2\frac{1 + \cos 2\theta}{2}\right) d\theta$$

$$= \int_0^{2\pi} 4(2 + 4\cos\theta + 1 + \cos 2\theta)\, d\theta$$

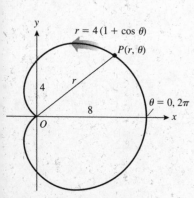

Figure 10.10 The cardioid
$r = 4(1 + \cos\theta)$

$$= \int_0^{2\pi} (8 + 16\cos\theta + 4 + 4\cos 2\theta)d\theta$$

$$= \left[12\theta + 16\sin\theta + 2\sin 2\theta\right]_0^{2\pi}$$

$$= 24\pi - 0$$

$$= 24\pi.$$

Support Graphically NINT $(8(1 + \cos\theta)^2, \theta, 0, 2\pi) = 75.39822369$, which agrees with 24π to eight decimal places.

Exercises for Alternate Example 6

In Exercises 17–22, find the area of the region described.

17. $r = 6(1 + \cos\theta)$ **18.** $r = 4\sin(8\theta)$ **19.** $r = 10(1 + \sin\theta)$ **20.** $r = 5 - 3\sin\theta$ **21.** $r = 2 + \cos\theta$

22. $r = 14(1 + \cos\theta)$ ■

Alternate Example 8 Finding the Area Between Curves

Find the area of the region that lies inside the circle $r = 3$ and outside the cardioid $r = 3(1 - \cos\theta)$.

SOLUTION

The region is shown in Figure 10.11. The outer curve is $r_2 = 3$, the inner curve is $r_1 = 3(1 - \cos\theta)$, and θ runs from $-\pi/2$ to $\pi/2$. Using the formula for the area between polar curves, the area is

$$A = \int_{-\pi/2}^{\pi/2} \frac{1}{2}\left(r_2{}^2 - r_1{}^2\right)d\theta$$

$$= 2\int_0^{\pi/2} \frac{1}{2}\left(r_2{}^2 - r_1{}^2\right)d\theta \qquad \text{By x-axis symmetry}$$

$$= \int_0^{\pi/2} \left(r_2{}^2 - r_1{}^2\right)d\theta$$

$$= \int_0^{\pi/2} \left(3^2 - (3(1 - \cos\theta))^2\right)d\theta$$

$$= \int_0^{\pi/2} \left(9 - (9 - 18\cos\theta + 9\cos^2\theta)\right)d\theta$$

$$= \int_0^{\pi/2} (9 - 9 + 18\cos\theta - 9\cos^2\theta)d\theta$$

$$= \int_0^{\pi/2} 9(2\cos\theta - \cos^2\theta)d\theta$$

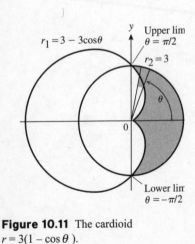

Figure 10.11 The cardioid $r = 3(1 - \cos\theta)$.

$$= \int_0^{\pi/2} 9\left(2\cos\theta - \frac{1 + \cos 2\theta}{2}\right) d\theta$$

$$= \int_0^{\pi/2} 9\left(2\cos\theta - \frac{1}{2} - \frac{\cos 2\theta}{2}\right) d\theta$$

$$= 9\left[-\frac{1}{2}\theta + 2\sin\theta - \frac{\sin 2\theta}{4}\right]_0^{\frac{\pi}{2}}$$

$$= 9\left(-\frac{\pi}{4} + 2\right)$$

$$\approx 10.9314.$$

Exercises for Alternate Example 8

In Exercises 23–28, find the area of the region described.

23. Inside the circle $r_1 = 2$ and outside the cardiod $r_2 = 2(1 - \cos\theta)$

24. Inside the circle $r_1 = 4$ and outside the circle $r_2 = 2\sin\theta$

25. Inside the circle $r_1 = 8$ and outside the circle $r_2 = 8\cos\theta$

26. Outside the cardiod $r_1 = 3(1 + \sin\theta)$ and inside the circle $r_2 = 6$

27. Outside the four-petal rose $r_1 = 3\cos 2\theta$ and inside the circle $r_2 = 3$

28. Inside the circle $r_1 = 12$ and outside the cardiod $r_2 = 12(1 - \cos\theta)$

Answers to Exercises

Chapter 1
Prerequisites for Calculus

1.1 Lines

1. $y = -2x + 4$ **2.** $y = -5x + 1$ **3.** $y = 3x - 11$

4. $y = 3x + 3$ **5.** $y = \dfrac{3}{11}x + 2$ **6.** $y = -5x - 2$

7. $y = -\dfrac{4}{3}x - 7$ **8.** $y = -5x - 11$ **9.** $y = -3x - 9$

10. $y = -5x + 1$ **11.** $y = 3x - 17$ **12.** $y = x - 5$

13. $y = 5x - 1$ **14.** $y = -3x + 9$ **15.** $y = -x + 11$

16. $y = -2x + 1$ **17.** (a) $y = x + 2$ **18.** (a) $y = -x + 4$

                                    (b) $y = -x + 4$ (b) $y = x + 2$

19. (a) $y = 4x - 1$ **20.** (a) $y = 7x - 4$

    (b) $y = -\dfrac{1}{4}x + \dfrac{13}{4}$ (b) $y = -\dfrac{1}{7}x + \dfrac{22}{7}$

21. (a) $y = -2x + 5$ **22.** (a) $y = 2x + 1$

    (b) $y = \dfrac{1}{2}x + \dfrac{5}{2}$ (b) $y = -\dfrac{1}{2}x + \dfrac{7}{2}$

23. (a) $y = -3x + 6$ (b) $y = \dfrac{1}{3}x + \dfrac{8}{3}$

24. $m = 3$ and $b = -11$ **25.** $m = -1$ and $b = 9$

26. $m = 5$ and $b = -1$ **27.** $m = 1$ and $b = -5$

28. $m = -1$ and $b = -2$ **29.** $m = 3$ and $b = -12$

30. $m = 5$ and $b = -1$

1.2 Functions and Graphs

1. (a) Domain: $[-1, 1]$, Range: $[0, 1]$

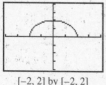

$[-2, 2]$ by $[-2, 2]$

(b) Domain: $(-\infty, \infty)$, Range: $(-\infty, 0)$

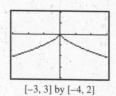

$[-3, 3]$ by $[-4, 2]$

2. (a) Domain: $[-\sqrt{3}, \sqrt{3}\,]$, Range: $[0, \sqrt{3}\,]$

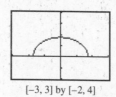

$[-3, 3]$ by $[-2, 4]$

(b) Domain: $(-\infty, \infty)$, Range $= (-\infty, \infty)$

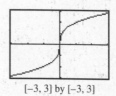

$[-3, 3]$ by $[-3, 3]$

3. (a) Domain: $[-7, 7]$, Range: $[0, 7]$

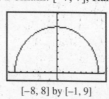

$[-8, 8]$ by $[-1, 9]$

(b) Domain: $(-\infty, \infty)$, Range: $(-\infty, \infty)$

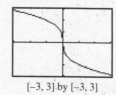

$[-3, 3]$ by $[-3, 3]$

4. (a) Domain: $[-2\sqrt{3}, 2\sqrt{3}]$, Range: $[0, 2\sqrt{3}]$

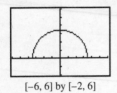

[-6, 6] by [-2, 6]

(b) Domain: $(-\infty, \infty)$, Range: $[0, \infty)$

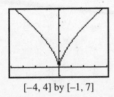

[-4, 4] by [-1, 7]

5. (a) Domain: $[-4, 4]$, Range: $[0, 4]$

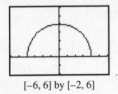

[-6, 6] by [-2, 6]

(b) Domain: $[0, \infty)$, Range: $(-\infty, 0]$

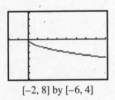

[-2, 8] by [-6, 4]

6. (a) Domain: $[-6, 6]$, Range: $[0, 6]$

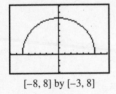

[-8, 8] by [-3, 8]

(b) Domain: $[0, \infty)$, Range: $[0, \infty)$

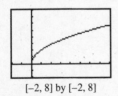

[-2, 8] by [-2, 8]

7. (a) Domain: $[-4\sqrt{3}, 4\sqrt{3}]$, Range: $[0, 4\sqrt{3}]$

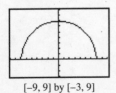

[-9, 9] by [-3, 9]

(b) Domain: $[0, \infty)$, Range: $(-\infty, 0]$

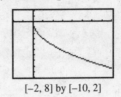

[-2, 8] by [-10, 2]

8. even	**9.** neither	**10.** odd	**11.** even
12. odd	**13.** neither	**14.** even	

15. $\begin{cases} y = 3x & 0 < x < 1 \\ y = 3x - 3 & 1 < x < 2 \end{cases}$

16. $\begin{cases} y = \dfrac{1}{2}x & 0 < x < 2 \\ y = \dfrac{1}{2}x - 1 & 2 < x < 4 \end{cases}$

17. $\begin{cases} y = 2x & -1 < x < 0 \\ y = 2x + 2 & -2 < x < -1 \end{cases}$

18. $\begin{cases} y = -2x & 0 < x < 1 \\ y = -2x + 2 & 1 < x < 2 \end{cases}$

19. $\begin{cases} y = -x & 0 < x < 1 \\ y = -x + 1 & 1 < x < 2 \end{cases}$

20. $\begin{cases} y = \dfrac{1}{2}x & -2 < x < 0 \\ y = \dfrac{1}{2}x + 1 & -4 < x < -2 \end{cases}$

21. $f(g(x)) = 15x^3 + 1, f(g(-1)) = -14$

22. $f(g(x)) = 36x^2 - 48x + 16, \ f(g(0)) = 16$

23. $f(g(x)) = 6x^5 - 3, f(g(-1)) = -9$

24. $f(g(x)) = -6x^3 + 3, f(g(-2)) = 51$

25. $f(g(x)) = 25x^2 - 1, f(g(-2)) = 99$

26. $f(g(x)) = -64x^3, \ f(g(1)) = -64$

27. $f(g(x)) = -x^4 - 3, f(g(5)) = -628$

1.3 Exponential Functions

1. Domain: $(-\infty, \infty)$, Range: $(-1, \infty)$

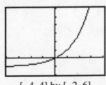

[-4, 4] by [-2, 6]

2. Domain: $(-\infty, \infty)$, Range: $(-3, \infty)$

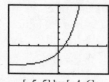

$[-5, 5]$ by $[-4, 6]$

3. Domain: $(-\infty, \infty)$, Range: $(-1, \infty)$

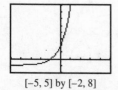

$[-5, 5]$ by $[-2, 8]$

4. Domain: $(-\infty, \infty)$, Range: $(-\infty, 4)$

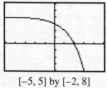

$[-5, 5]$ by $[-2, 8]$

5. Domain: $(-\infty, \infty)$, Range: $(-6, \infty)$

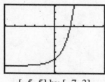

$[-5, 5]$ by $[-7, 3]$

6. Domain: $(-\infty, \infty)$, Range: $(-\infty, -5)$

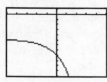

$[-5, 5]$ by $[-12, 1]$

7. 3.802   **8.** 0   **9.** 6.213

10. 4.923   **11.** 1.985   **12.** 9.919

13. 11.70 days   **14.** 63.40 days   **15.** 26.44 days

16. 46.44 days   **17.** 60 days   **18.** 54.74 days

1.4 Parametric Functions

1. right half of parabola $y = \dfrac{3}{4}x^2$

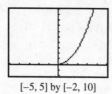

$[-5, 5]$ by $[-2, 10]$

2. right half of parabola $y = -x^2$

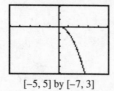

$[-5, 5]$ by $[-7, 3]$

3. top half of parabola $x = 2y^2$

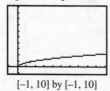

$[-1, 10]$ by $[-1, 10]$

4. right half of parabola $y = 5x^2$

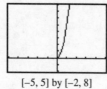

$[-5, 5]$ by $[-2, 8]$

5. left half of parabola $y = \dfrac{2}{3}x^2$

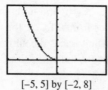

$[-5, 5]$ by $[-2, 8]$

6. bottom half of parabola $x = \dfrac{y^2}{2}$

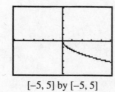

$[-5, 5]$ by $[-5, 5]$

7. The Cartesian equation of the graph is $\left(\dfrac{x}{6}\right)^2 + \left(\dfrac{y}{2}\right)^2 = 1$.

The parameterized curve lies along an ellipse with major axis endpoints $(\pm 6, 0)$ and minor axis endpoints $(0, \pm 2)$. As t increases from 0 to 2π, the point $(6\cos t, 2\sin t)$ starts at $(6, 0)$ and traces the entire ellipse once counterclockwise. Thus $(6, 0)$ is the initial point and the terminal point.

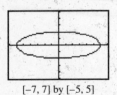

[−7, 7] by [−5, 5]

8. The Cartesian equation of the graph is $\left(\dfrac{x}{3}\right)^2 + \left(\dfrac{y}{4}\right)^2 = 1$.

The parameterized curve lies along an ellipse with major axis endpoints $(0, \pm 4)$ and minor axis endpoints $(\pm 3, 0)$. As t increases from 0 to 2π, the point $(3\cos t, 4\sin t)$ starts at $(3, 0)$ and traces the entire ellipse once counterclockwise. Thus $(3, 0)$ is the initial point and the terminal point.

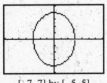

[−7, 7] by [−5, 5]

9. The Cartesian equation of the graph is $\left(\dfrac{x}{-5}\right)^2 + \left(\dfrac{y}{1}\right)^2 = 1$. The parameterized curve lies along

an ellipse with major axis endpoints $(\pm 5, 0)$ and minor axis endpoints $(0, \pm 1)$. As t increases from 0 to 2π, the point $(-5\sin t, \cos t)$ starts at $(0, 1)$ and traces the entire ellipse once counterclockwise. Thus $(0, 1)$ is the initial point and the terminal point.

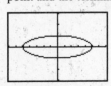

[−7, 7] by [−3, 3]

10. The Cartesian equation of the graph is $\left(\dfrac{x}{5}\right)^2 + \left(\dfrac{y}{-2}\right)^2 = 1$. The parameterized curve lies along

an ellipse with major axis endpoints $(\pm 5, 0)$ and minor axis endpoints $(0, \pm 2)$. As t increases from 0 to 2π, the point $(5\cos t, -2\sin t)$ starts at $(5, 0)$ and traces the entire ellipse once clockwise. Thus $(5, 0)$ is the initial point and the terminal point.

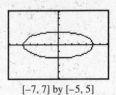

[−7, 7] by [−5, 5]

11. The Cartesian equation of the graph is $\left(\dfrac{x}{3}\right)^2 + \left(\dfrac{y}{-1}\right)^2 = 1$.

The parameterized curve lies along an ellipse with major axis endpoints $(\pm 3, 0)$ and minor axis endpoints $(0, \pm 1)$. As t increases from 0 to 2π, the point $(3\cos t, -\sin t)$ starts at $(3, 0)$ and traces the entire ellipse once clockwise. Thus $(3, 0)$ is the initial point and the terminal point.

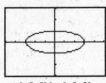

[−5, 5] by [−3, 3]

12. The Cartesian equation of the graph is $\left(\dfrac{x}{2}\right)^2 + \left(\dfrac{y}{3}\right)^2 = 1$.

The parameterized curve lies along an ellipse with major axis endpoints $(0, \pm 3)$ and minor axis endpoints $(\pm 2, 0)$. As t increases from 0 to 2π, the point $(2\sin t, 3\cos t)$ starts at $(0, 3)$ and traces the entire ellipse once clockwise. Thus $(0, 3)$ is the initial point and the terminal point.

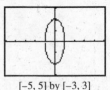

[−5, 5] by [−3, 3]

13. $y = \dfrac{5}{3}x + 1,\ 0 \le x \le 3$

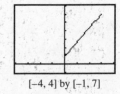

[−4, 4] by [−1, 7]

14. $y = \dfrac{3}{4}x - 3,\ 0 \le x \le 4$

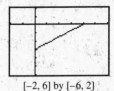

[−2, 6] by [−6, 2]

15. $y = \dfrac{x}{2} - 1,\ 0 \le x \le 6$

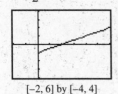

[–2, 6] by [–4, 4]

16. $y = -\dfrac{x}{2} + 1,\ 0 \le x \le 2$

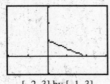

[–2, 3] by [–1, 3]

16.

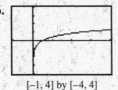

[–1, 4] by [–4, 4]

17.

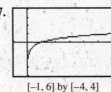

[–1, 6] by [–4, 4]

17. $y = \dfrac{x}{4} - \dfrac{13}{4},\ -1 \le x \le 5$

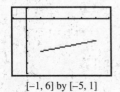

[–1, 6] by [–5, 1]

18. $y = \dfrac{x}{2} + \dfrac{13}{2},\ -5 \le x \le 3$

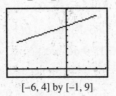

[–6, 4] by [–1, 9]

18.

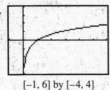

[–1, 6] by [–4, 4]

19.

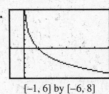

[–1, 6] by [–6, 8]

19. $x = 3 + 3t,\ y = 7 - 9t,\ \text{and } 0 \le t \le 1$

20. $x = 2 - 5t,\ y = 5 + t,\ \text{and } 0 \le t \le 1$

21. $x = 2 - t,\ y = 1 + 2t,\ \text{and } 0 \le t \le 1$

22. $x = 3 + t,\ y = 1 + 4t,\ \text{and } 0 \le t \le 1$

23. $x = 3 - 6t,\ y = -1 + 3t,\ \text{and } 0 \le t \le 1$

24. $x = 2 + 3t,\ y = -5 + 11t,\ \text{and } 0 \le t \le 1$

25. $x = 2 + t,\ y = 6 - 4t,\ \text{and } 0 \le t \le 1$

20.

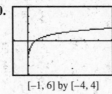

[–1, 6] by [–4, 4]

21.

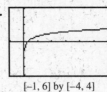

[–1, 6] by [–4, 4]

22. $t = 5.86$ years   **23.** $t = 1.95$ years

24. $t = 3.16$ years   **25.** $t = 4.66$ years

26. $t = 8.97$ years   **27.** $t = 8.31$ years

1.5 Functions and Logarithms

1. $f^{-1}(x) = 11 - x$

2. $f^{-1}(x) = \dfrac{1}{3}x + 5$

3. $f^{-1}(x) = -\dfrac{1}{11}x + \dfrac{6}{11}$

4. $f^{-1}(x) = \sqrt[3]{x - 1}$

5. $f^{-1}(x) = \sqrt{\dfrac{x + 15}{3}}$

6. $f^{-1}(x) = \sqrt{x} + 3$

7. $f^{-1}(x) = \sqrt[4]{\dfrac{1}{x}}$

8. (a) $x = e^{t-11}$ (b) $x = -0.90$

9. (a) $x = e^{11t+12}$,
(b) $x = 2.64$

10. (a) $x = e^{t+11}$
(b) $x = -1.763$

11. (a) $x = e^{-11t-12}$
(b) $x = 0.497$

12. (a) $x = e^{3t-6}$
(b) $x = 2.89$

13. (a) $x = e^{2t+14}$
(b) $x = 0.77$

14.

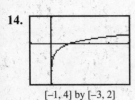

[–1, 4] by [–3, 2]

15.

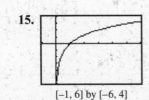

[–1, 6] by [–6, 4]

1.6 Trigonometric Functions

1. $\sin \theta = -\dfrac{2\sqrt{6}}{5}$, $\tan \theta = 2\sqrt{6}$,

$\cot \theta = \dfrac{\sqrt{6}}{12}$, $\csc \theta = -\dfrac{5\sqrt{6}}{12}$, and $\sec \theta = -5$

2. $\cos \theta = -\dfrac{3\sqrt{5}}{7}$, $\tan \theta = \dfrac{2\sqrt{5}}{15}$,

$\cot \theta = \dfrac{3\sqrt{5}}{2}$, $\csc \theta = -\dfrac{7}{2}$, and $\sec \theta = -\dfrac{7\sqrt{5}}{15}$

3. $\sin \theta = \dfrac{2\sqrt{6}}{5}$, $\tan \theta = 2\sqrt{6}$, $\cot \theta = \dfrac{\sqrt{6}}{12}$,

$\csc \theta = \dfrac{5\sqrt{6}}{12}$, and $\sec \theta = 5$

4. $\cos \theta = -\dfrac{2\sqrt{6}}{7}$, $\tan \theta = \dfrac{5\sqrt{6}}{12}$, $\cot \theta = \dfrac{2\sqrt{6}}{5}$,

$\csc \theta = -\dfrac{7}{5}$, and $\sec \theta = -\dfrac{7\sqrt{6}}{12}$

5. $\sin \theta = -\dfrac{\sqrt{7}}{4}$, $\tan \theta = \dfrac{\sqrt{7}}{3}$, $\cot \theta = \dfrac{3\sqrt{7}}{7}$,

$\csc \theta = -\dfrac{4\sqrt{7}}{7}$, and $\sec \theta = -\dfrac{4}{3}$

6. $\cos = \dfrac{12}{13}$, $\tan \theta = \dfrac{5}{12}$, $\cot \theta = \dfrac{12}{5}$, $\csc \theta = \dfrac{13}{5}$, and

$\sec \theta = \dfrac{13}{12}$

7. (a) $\dfrac{2\pi}{5}$ (b) $(-\infty, \infty)$ (c) $[-8, 0]$

(d)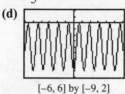

$[-6, 6]$ by $[-9, 2]$

8. (a) $\dfrac{\pi}{3}$ (b) $(-\infty, \infty)$ (c) $[-3, 1]$

(d)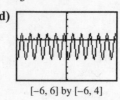

$[-6, 6]$ by $[-6, 4]$

9. (a) $\dfrac{\pi}{2}$ (b) $(-\infty, \infty)$ (c) $[-8, -4]$

(d)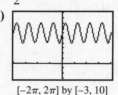

$[-2\pi, 2\pi]$ by $[-3, 10]$

10. (a) $\dfrac{2\pi}{3}$ (b) $(-\infty, \infty)$ (c) $[1, 3]$

(d)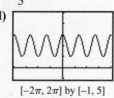

$[-2\pi, 2\pi]$ by $[-1, 5]$

11. (a) π (b) $(-\infty, \infty)$ (c) $[-11, -1]$

(d)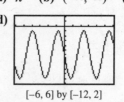

$[-6, 6]$ by $[-12, 2]$

12. (a) 4π (b) $(-\infty, \infty)$ (c) $[0, 6]$

(d)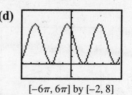

$[-6\pi, 6\pi]$ by $[-2, 8]$

13. 138.59 degrees, 2.42 radians

14. 71.56 degrees, 1.25 radians

15. −40.54 degrees, −0.708 radian

16. 2.86 degrees, 0.05 radian

17. 31.79 degrees, 0.555 radian

18. −85.24 degrees, −1.488 radians

19. −61.64 degrees, −1.076 radians

20. −66.04 degrees, −1.153 radian

21. (a) 0.12, $\pi - 0.12$ **22.** (a) 1.13, -1.13

(b) $0.14 + k\pi$ (b) $1.37 + k\pi$

23. (a) 0.58, $\pi - 0.58$ **24.** (a) 0.59, $\pi - 0.59$

(b) $-0.12 + k\pi$ (b) $1.41 + k\pi$

25. (a) 0.27, $\pi - 0.27$ **26.** (a) 0.57, -0.57

(b) $-0.32 + k\pi$ (b) $0.08 + k\pi$

27. (a) 0.98, -0.98 (b) $1.32 + k\pi$

Chapter 2
Limits and Continuity

2.1 Rates of Change and Limits

1. 32 ft/sec **2.** 96 ft/sec **3.** 160 ft/sec

4. 192 ft/sec **5.** 224 ft/sec **6.** 256 ft/sec

7. 288 ft/sec **8.** 320 ft/sec **9.** −2

10. $\dfrac{1}{4}$ **11.** 0 **12.** 12

13. $\dfrac{7}{4}$ **14.** 1 **15.** $\dfrac{1}{4}$

16. $\dfrac{a}{b}$ **17.** 11 and 10 **18.** 7 and 6

19. 9 and 8   **20.** 21 and 20   **21.** −5 and −6
22. −21 and −22   **23.** 14 and 13   **24.** 0
25. 3   **26.** 0   **27.** 0
28. 1   **29.** 7

2.2 Limits Involving Infinity

1. 1   **2.** 0   **3.** 0   **4.** −4   **5.** $\dfrac{1}{6}$

6. 0   **7.** $x = \ldots, -4\pi, \ -2\pi, 0, \ 2\pi, \ 4\pi,$

8. $x = 2$ **9.** $x = \ldots, \ -5\pi, \ -3\pi, \ -\pi, \ \pi, 3\pi, 5\pi, \ldots$

10. $x = \ldots, -\dfrac{17\pi}{6}, -\dfrac{13\pi}{6}, -\dfrac{7\pi}{6}, \dfrac{\pi}{6}, \dfrac{5\pi}{6}, \dfrac{13\pi}{6}, \dfrac{17\pi}{6}, \ldots$

11. $x = -\dfrac{1}{2}, \dfrac{1}{2}$ **12.** $x = \ldots, \ -\dfrac{7\pi}{2}, \ -\dfrac{3\pi}{2}, \dfrac{\pi}{2}, \dfrac{5\pi}{2}, \ldots$

13. $x = -\dfrac{1}{2}$ **14.** $x = -1, 1$

15. $\displaystyle\lim_{x \to \pm\infty} \frac{f(x)}{g(x)} = \lim_{x \to \pm\infty} \frac{11x^7 - 6x^6 - 7x^3 + 11x^2 - 3x + 14}{11x^7}$
$$= \lim_{x \to \pm\infty}\left(1 - \frac{6}{11x} - \frac{7}{11x^4} + \frac{11}{x^5} - \frac{3}{11x^6} + \frac{14}{11x^7}\right)$$
$$= 1$$

16. $\displaystyle\lim_{x \to \pm\infty} \frac{f(x)}{g(x)} = \lim_{x \to \pm\infty} \frac{-3x^6 - x^3 + 8x^2 - x + 4}{-3x^6}$
$$= \lim_{x \to \pm\infty}\left(1 + \frac{1}{3x^2} - \frac{8}{3x^4} + \frac{1}{3x^5} - \frac{4}{3x^6}\right)$$
$$= 1$$

17. $\displaystyle\lim_{x \to \pm\infty} \frac{f(x)}{g(x)} = \lim_{x \to \pm\infty} \frac{2x^5 - 3x^4 - x^3 + x^2 - 7x + 21}{2x^5}$
$$= \lim_{x \to \pm\infty}\left(1 - \frac{3}{2x} - \frac{1}{2x^2} + \frac{1}{2x^3} - \frac{7}{2x^4} + \frac{21}{2x^5}\right)$$
$$= 1$$

18. $\displaystyle\lim_{x \to \pm\infty} \frac{f(x)}{g(x)} = \frac{\dfrac{x^2 - 3}{2x + 4}}{\dfrac{x}{2}}$
$$= \lim_{x \to \pm\infty} \frac{2x^2 - 6}{2x^2 + 4x}$$
$$= \lim_{x \to \pm\infty}\left(1 - \frac{4x + 6}{2x^2 + 4x}\right)$$
$$= 1$$

19. $\displaystyle\lim_{x \to \pm\infty} \frac{f(x)}{g(x)} = \lim_{x \to \pm\infty} \frac{\dfrac{x^3 - x^2 + 10}{3x^2 - 4x}}{\dfrac{x}{3}}$
$$= \lim_{x \to \pm\infty} \frac{3x^3 - 3x^2 + 10}{3x^3 - 4x^2}$$
$$= \lim_{x \to \pm\infty}\left(1 + \frac{x^2 + 10}{3x^3 - 4x^2}\right)$$
$$= 1$$

20. $\displaystyle\lim_{x \to \pm\infty} \frac{f(x)}{g(x)} = \lim_{x \to \pm\infty} \frac{\dfrac{x + 2}{x^2 + 6x + 4}}{\dfrac{1}{x}}$
$$= \lim_{x \to \pm\infty} \frac{x^2 + 2x}{x^2 + 6x + 4}$$
$$= \lim_{x \to \pm\infty}\left(1 - \frac{4x + 4}{x^2 + 6x + 4}\right)$$
$$= 1$$

21. $g(x) = -2x, \ h(x) = -e^{-x}$ **22.** $g(x) = -x, \ h(x) = 2e^{-x}$
23. $g(x) = -3e^{-x}, \ h(x) = x^2$ **24.** $g(x) = x^3, \ h(x) = x^3$
25. $g(x) = e^x, \ h(x) = -3x^2$ **26.** $g(x) = ax, \ h(x) = be^{-x}$

2.3 Continuity

1. continuous at every point of its domain (1, 9] except at $x = 3, 6$

2. continuous at every point of its domain (1, 6) except at $x = 3$

3. continuous at every point of its domain [0, 9] except at $x = 1, 7$

4. continuous at every point of its domain [0, 8] except at $x = 2, 5, 7$

5. continuous at every point of its domain [0, 9] except at $x = 3, 6$

6. continuous at every point of its domain [0, 9) except at $x = 2.5, 5$

7. The function f is discontinuous at $x = -3$.

8. The function f is discontinuous at $x = \pm 1$.

9. The function f is discontinuous at $x = 0$.

10. The function f is discontinuous at multiples of $\dfrac{\pi}{2}$.

11. The function f is discontinuous at $x = 0$.

12. The function f is discontinuous at $x = 1$.

13.

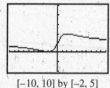

[−10, 10] by [−2, 5]

$g(x) = |x|$, $f(x) = \dfrac{x^2 + 4x + 4}{x^2 + 4}$. Both are continuous

functions, so $g \circ f$ is also continuous.

14.

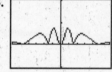

[−6, 6] by [−0.25, 0.5]

$g(x) = |x|$, $f(x) = \dfrac{-x^2 \cos x}{x^4 + 2}$. Both are continuous

functions, so $g \circ f$ is also continuous.

15.

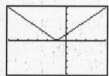

[−6, 4] by [−5, 5]

$g(x) = \sqrt{x}$, $f(x) = x^2 + 2x + 1$. Both are continuous

functions, so $g \circ f$ is also continuous.

16.

[−5, 5] by [−5, 5]

$g(x) = \cos x$, $f(x) = x^2 + 1$. Both are continuous

functions, so $g \circ f$ is also continuous.

17.

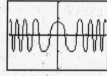

[−5, 5] by [−2, 2]

$h(x) = \sqrt[3]{x}$, $g(x) = \cos x$, $f(x) = x^2 + 1$. All three are

continuous functions, so $h \circ g \circ f$ is also continuous.

18.

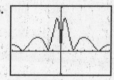

[−6, 6] by [−0.5, 1]

$g(x) = |x|$, $f(x) = \dfrac{-3x \cos x}{3x^2 + 1}$. Both are continuous

functions, so $g \circ f$ is also continuous.

19. A real number exists.
$y = x^6 - x - 6$

[−2, 2] by [−10, 10]

20. A real number exists.
$y = x^2 - x - 4$

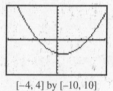

[−4, 4] by [−10, 10]

21. A real number exists.
$y = x^8 - x - 8$

[−4, 4] by [−10, 10]

22. No real number exists.
$y = x^{10} - x + 10$

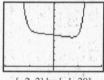

[−2, 2] by [−1, 20]

23. A real number exists.
$y = x^7 - x - 7$

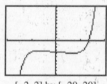

[−2, 2] by [−20, 20]

24. A real number exists.
$y = x^3 - x + 5$

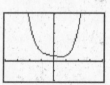

[−4, 4] by [−10, 25]

25. No real number exists.
$y = x^4 - x + 3$

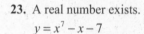

[−4, 4] by [−10, 25]

2.4 Rates of Change and Tangent Lines

1. $m = 6$ and $y = 6x + 10$

2. $m = 8$ and $y = 8x - 9$

3. $m = 6$ and $y = 6x - 5$

4. $m = 16$ and $y = 16x + 21$

5. $m = -2$ and $y = -2x - 8$

6. $m = 4$ and $y = 4x + 1$

7. $m = -2$ and $y = -2x + 5$

8. $m = 6$ and $y = 6x + 13$

9. (a) $m = -\dfrac{6}{5a^2}$, **(b)** $a = \pm 5$, **(c)** The slope of the tangent is always negative. Tangents are nearly horizontal as a moves away from the origin.

10. (a) $m = \dfrac{1}{2a^2}$, **(b)** $a = \pm 7$ **(c)** The slope of the tangent is always positive. Tangents are nearly horizontal as a moves away from the origin.

11. (a) $m = 2a$, **(b)** $a = 2$, **(c)** The slope of the tangent increases as a increases.

12. (a) $m = 3a^2$, **(b)** $a = \pm 3$, **(c)** The slope of the tangent is always positive except at $a = 0$, where the slope $= 0$. The slope decreases as $a \to 0^-$ and increases as a goes from 0 to ∞.

13. (a) $m = 2x + 2$, **(b)** $a = -1$, **(c)** The slope of the tangent increases as a increases.

14. (a) $m = \dfrac{-6}{a^3}$, **(b)** $a = 2$, **(c)** The slope of the tangent is positive when $a < 0$ and negative when $a > 0$.

15. $y = \dfrac{1}{2}x + \dfrac{7}{2}$ **16.** $y = -\dfrac{1}{8}x + \dfrac{29}{4}$

17. $y = 2x + \dfrac{3}{2}$ **18.** $y = \dfrac{1}{12}x - \dfrac{31}{6}$

19. $y = -\dfrac{1}{6}x + \dfrac{17}{6}$ **20.** $y = -\dfrac{1}{2}x + 1$

21. $y = \dfrac{5}{6}x - \dfrac{11}{30}$ **22.** $y = \dfrac{1}{8}x - \dfrac{49}{8}$

23. 64 ft/sec   **24.** 128 ft/sec   **25.** 160 ft/sec

26. 192 ft/sec   **27.** 224 ft/sec   **28.** 256 ft/sec

29. 288 ft/sec   **30.** 320 ft/sec

Chapter 3
Derivatives

3.1 Derivative of a Function

1. $f'(x) = 3$ **2.** $f'(x) = 2x$

3. $f'(x) = -12x^2 - 5$ **4.** $f'(x) = 3x^2$

5. $f'(x) = 10x$ **6.** $f'(x) = 2 + 2x$

7. $f'(x) = 18x^2$ **8.** $f'(x) = 2x + 2$

9. $f'(x) = -\dfrac{1}{2x^2}$ **10.** $f'(x) = \dfrac{x}{\sqrt{x^2 - 1}}$

11. $f'(x) = 2x + 5$ **12.** $f'(x) = 3x^2 - 1$

13. $f'(x) = -2x$

14. $f'(x) = -\dfrac{6}{x^3}$

15. $f'(x) = \dfrac{-3}{\sqrt{2x - 1}}$

16. $f'(x) = -3$

17.

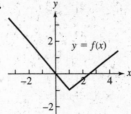

18.

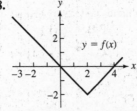

19.

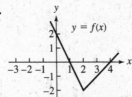

20.

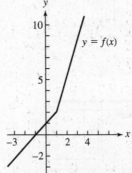

21.

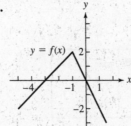

22.

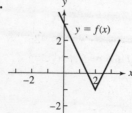

23. Left-hand derivative: –4; right-hand derivative: 1

24. Left-hand derivative: –2; right-hand derivative: 1

25. Left-hand derivative: 0; right-hand derivative: 3

26. Left-hand derivative: 2; right-hand derivative: 3

27. Left-hand derivative: 0; right-hand derivative: 1

28. Left-hand derivative: 2; right-hand derivative: –3

3.2 Differentiability

1. at $x = 3$ **2.** at $x = 2$ **3.** at $x = -4$

4. at $x = 2$ **5.** at $x = -7$ **6.** at $x = 0$

7. at $x = -1, 0, 3$ **8.** $x = -2, 2$ **9.** 9

10. –8   **11.** –1425.00059   **12.** –47

13. 12   **14.** 0.3333333951

15. $f(x) = \dfrac{1}{x-3}$

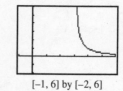 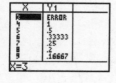

[–1, 6] by [–2, 6]

16. $f(x) = \cos x$

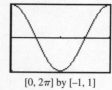 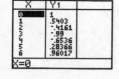

[0, 2π] by [–1, 1]

17. $f(x) = \dfrac{1}{x}$

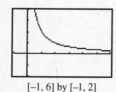 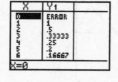

[–1, 6] by [–1, 2]

18. $f(x) = x^2$

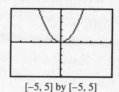 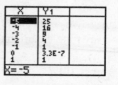

[–5, 5] by [–5, 5]

19. $f(x) = \begin{cases} -1 & x < 0 \\ 0 & x = 0 \\ 1 & x > 0 \end{cases}$

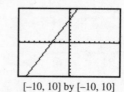 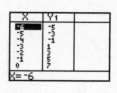

[–5, 5] by [–5, 5]

Note: NDER gives $f'(0) = 0$; however, $|x|$ is not differentiable at $x = 0$.

20. $f(x) = 2x + 7$

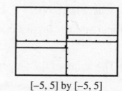

[–10, 10] by [–10, 10]

3.3 Rules for Differentiation

1. $20t^4 - 8t^3 + 18t^2 + 5$ **2.** $-24t^3 + 3t^2 + 22t + 1$

3. $5t^4 - 4t^3 + 3t^2 - 2t + 3$ **4.** $55t^4 - 8t^3 + 33t^2 + 28t + 1$

5. $60t^4 - 56t^3 + 27t^2 + 12t + 1$

6. $65t^4 - 8t^3 + 18t^2 + 10t + 5$

7. $95t^4 - 8t^3 + 18t^2 + 10t + 8$

8. $5t^4 - 8t^3 + 18t^2 + 10t + 11$

9. $3x^2 + 42x - 1$ **10.** $7x^6 - 16x^3 - 9x^2$

11. $9x^2 - 6x + 6$ **12.** $6x^5 - 15x^4 + 8$

13. $48x^5 + 8x^3 - 16x$ **14.** $36x^5 + 24x^3 - 4x$

15. $6x - 6$ **16.** $12x^2 - 10x + 1$

17. $y = -\dfrac{1}{2}x - 2$ **18.** $y = -\dfrac{2}{9}x - \dfrac{1}{6}$

19. $y = \dfrac{3}{5}x - \dfrac{2}{5}$ **20.** $y = 9x + 12$

21. $y = 4x - 2$ **22.** $\dfrac{1}{5}x + \dfrac{3}{5}$

23. 120   **24.** $2160x$

25. $2520x^2$

26. 480

27. $2520x^2$

28. $6720x^3$

29. $-720x^{-7}$

30. $-1440x^{-7}$

3.4 Velocity and other Rates of Change

1. (a) 12.57 and 25.13
   (b) square centimeters per centimeter

2. (a) 18.85 and 31.42
   (b) square yards per yard

3. (a) 37.70 and 50.27
   (b) square miles per mile

4. (a) 43.98 and 56.55
   (b) square inches per inch

5. (a) 62.83 and 69.12
   (b) square millimeters per millimeter

6. (a) 75.40 and 87.96
   (b) square kilometers per kilometer

7. (a) 100.53 and 106.81
   (b) square meters per meter

8. (a) 138.23 and 157.08
   (b) square feet per foot

9. (a) 324 ft   **(b)** 80 ft/sec
   (c) -32 ft/sec^2 **(d)** $t = 9$ sec

10. (a) 256 ft   **(b)** 55.43 ft/sec
   (c) -32 ft/sec^2 **(d)** $t = 8$ sec

11. (a) 361 ft   **(b)** 88 ft/sec
   (c) -32 ft/sec^2 **(d)** $t = 9.5$ sec

12. (a) 320 m   **(b)** 16 m/sec
   (c) -1.6 m/sec^2 **(d)** $t = 40$ sec

13. (a) 720 m   **(b)** 32 m/sec
   (c) -1.6 m/sec^2 **(d)** $t = 60$ sec

14. (a) 845 m   **(b)** 28 m/sec
   (c) -1.6 m/sec^2 **(d)** $t = 65$ sec

15. (a) -2 m   **(b)** 1 m/sec
   (c) 11 m/sec   **(d)** $a(7) = 2$ m/sec^2
   (e) The particle starts at the point 1, moves left for $0 \le t < 1.5$, changes direction at $t = 1.5$, and then moves right for $t > 1.5$.

16. (a) -8 m   **(b)** -2 m/sec
   (c) 8 m/sec   **(d)** $a(7) = 2$ m/sec^2
   (e) The particle starts at the point 5, moves left for $0 \le t < 3$, changes direction at $t = 3$, and then moves right for $t > 3$.

17. (a) 14 m   **(b)** 5 m/sec
   (c) -5 m/sec   **(d)** $a(7) = -2$ m/sec^2
   (e) The particle starts at the point -4, moves right for $0 \le t < 4.5$, changes direction at $t = 4.5$, and then moves left for $t > 4.5$.

18. (a) 18 m   **(b)** 7 m/sec
   (c) -3 m/sec   **(d)** $a(7) = -2$ m/sec^2
   (e) The particle starts at the point -9, moves right for $0 \le t < 5.5$, changes direction at $t = 5.5$, and then moves left for $t > 5.5$.

19. (a) 8 m   **(b)** 2 m/sec
   (c) 63 m/sec   **(d)** $a(7) = 28$ m/sec^2
   (e) The particle starts at the point -8, moves right for $0 \le t < 1.451$, changes direction at $t = 1.451$ and moves left for $1.451 < t < 3.215$, changes direction at $t = 3.215$ and moves right for $t > 3.215$.

20. (a) -16 m   **(b)** -4 m/sec
   (c) -55 m/sec   **(d)** $a(7) = -26$ m/sec^2
   (e) The particle starts at the point 16, moves left for $0 \le t < 2$, changes direction at $t = 2$ and moves right for $2 < t < 3.33$, changes direction at $t = 3.33$ and moves left for $t > 3.33$.

21. $c'(x) = 118$ dollars and $r'(x) = 156$ dollars

22. $c'(x) = 78$ dollars and $r'(x) = 172$ dollars

23. $c'(x) = 39$ dollars and $r'(x) = 114$ dollars

24. (a)

[0, 10] by [100, 210]

In this problem situation, $x \ge 1$ makes sense.

(b) $r'(x) = \dfrac{200x}{\left(x^2 + 1\right)^2}$

(c) $r'(2) = \$16.00$

(d) $\lim\limits_{x \to \infty} r'(x) = 0$

This means that, after a point, there is very little increase in revenue no matter how many items are sold each week.

25. (a)

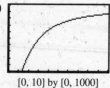

[0, 10] by [0, 1000]

In this problem situation, $x \geq 2$ makes sense.

(b) $r'(x) = \dfrac{1000(x^4 + 6x^3 + 2x^2 + 8)}{(x^3 + 4x)^2}$

(c) $r'(2) = \$312.50$

(d) $\lim\limits_{x \to \infty} r'(x) = 0$ This means that, after a point, there is very little increase in revenue no matter how many items are sold each week.

26. (a)

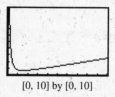

[0, 10] by [0, 10]

In this problem situation, $x \geq 1$ makes sense.

(b) $r'(x) = \dfrac{50(200x^4 - 191x^2 - 400x + 3)}{(200x^2 + 3)^2}$

(c) $r'(2) \approx \$0.13$

(d) $\lim\limits_{x \to \infty} r'(x) = \dfrac{1}{4}$. This means that the revenue continues to increase without bound as more items are sold.

3.5 Derivatives of Trigonometric Functions

1. $y' = x^3(4\cos x - x\sin x)$ **2.** $y' = -\sec^2 x$

3. $y' = 3x(x\sin x - 2\cos x)$ **4.** $y' = \dfrac{3 - 9\cos x}{(\cos x - 3)^2}$

5. $y' =$

$\dfrac{x + 6x^2\sec x - x^3\sec^2 x - \sec x\tan^2 x + 3x^2\tan x - 2x^3\sec x\tan x}{(\sec x - x^3)^2}$

6. $y' = \dfrac{\cos x + \cos x\cot x + \sin x\csc^2 x}{(1 + \cot x)^2}$

7. $j(t) = -\sin t$ **8.** $j(t) = -\cos t - 3\sin t$

9. $j(t) = 3\sin t$ **10.** $j(t) = -\cos t - \sin t$

11. $j(t) = -3\sin t$ **12.** $j(t) = -3\sin t$

13. $j(t) = -2\sin t$ **14.** $j(t) = 4\sin t$

15. $y - \dfrac{3\sqrt{3}}{2} = \dfrac{3}{2}\left(x - \dfrac{\pi}{3}\right)$ and $y - \dfrac{3\sqrt{3}}{2} = -\dfrac{2}{3}\left(x - \dfrac{\pi}{3}\right)$

16. $y = -\dfrac{2}{\pi}x + 1$ and $y = \dfrac{\pi}{2}x - \dfrac{\pi^2}{4}$

17. $y = -\left(x - \dfrac{\pi}{2}\right)$ and $y = x - \dfrac{\pi}{2}$

18. $y = x - \pi$ and $y = -(x - \pi)$

19. $\left(y - \dfrac{2}{3\pi}\right) = -\dfrac{4}{3\pi^2}\left(x - \dfrac{\pi}{2}\right)$ and

$\left(y - \dfrac{2}{3\pi}\right) = \dfrac{3\pi^2}{4}\left(x - \dfrac{\pi}{2}\right)$

20. $\left(y - \dfrac{3}{4\pi}\right) = -\dfrac{3(\sqrt{3}\pi + 3)}{4\pi^2}\left(x - \dfrac{\pi}{3}\right)$ and

$\left(y - \dfrac{3}{4\pi}\right) = \dfrac{4\pi^2}{3(\sqrt{3}\pi + 3)}\left(x - \dfrac{\pi}{3}\right)$

21. $y'' = \sec^3 x + \sec x\tan^2 x$

22. $2\sec^2 x\tan x$ **23.** 0 **24.** $\dfrac{\sin x}{(1 + \cos x)^2}$

25. $2\tan x + (4x + 2x^2\tan x)\sec^2 x$

26. $\dfrac{-x^2\cos x + 2x\sin x + 2\cos x}{x^3}$

3.6 Chain Rule

1. $y' = 6x^2(x^3 + 5)$ **2.** $y' = 30x^2(5x^3 - 1)$

3. $y' = -3\cos^2 x\sin x$ **4.** $y' = -3x^2\sin(x^3)$

5. $y' = 6x\cos(3x) + 2\sin(3x)$ **6.** $y' = \dfrac{3x + 1}{\sqrt{3x^2 + 2x + 1}}$

7. $y' = 30\left(x + \dfrac{1}{x}\right)^{29}\left(1 - \dfrac{1}{x^2}\right)$

8. $y' = -\sec^2(\cos x)\sin x$ **9.** $v(t) = -2t\sin(t^2 + 8)$

10. $v(t) = 4t\cos(2t^2 + 1)$

11. $v(t) = -(2t + 1)\sin(t^2 + t)$

12. $v(t) = -12\sin(3t) + 3\sin(4)$

13. $v(t) = 2\sec^2\left(\dfrac{\pi}{4} + 2t\right)$

14. $v(t) = -(\pi + \sec t\tan t)(\csc^2(\pi t + \sec t))$

15. $v(t) = 2(t^2 + t)(\sin t\cos t) + (2t + 1)\sin^2 t$

16. $v(t) = 6\cos(6t)\cos(\sin(6t))$

17. $g'(t) = -3t(3t^2 + 1)^{-3/2}$

18. $g'(t) = -30(2t + 1)^2 \cot^4(2t + 1)^3 \csc^2(2t + 1)^3$

19. $g'(t) = -96t^3 \cot(t^4) \csc^{24}(t^4)$

20. $g'(t) = \left(2\sqrt{1 + \sqrt{1 + \sqrt{t}}}\right)^{-1} \left(2\sqrt{1 + \sqrt{t}}\right)^{-1} \left(2\sqrt{t}\right)^{-1}$

21. $g'(t) = \left[t^2\left(1 + \dfrac{1}{t}\right)^2\right]^{-1}$

22. $g'(t) = \dfrac{2\pi}{3}\tan(\pi t)\sec^2(\pi t)(1 + \tan^2(\pi t))^{-2/3}$

23. $g'\big(t\big) = 36\cos(3 + \sin 6t)(\cos 6t)$

24. $g'(t) = \dfrac{2(-2t^2 + \pi\sec^2(\pi/t))}{(2t + \tan(\pi/t))^3 t^2}$

25. (a) $m = 0$

  (b) $y' = \dfrac{3}{(5 - x)^4}$ is a quotient of positive numbers

26. (a) $m = \sqrt{3}$

  (b) $y' = \dfrac{15}{(1 - 3x)^6}$ is a quotient of positive numbers

27. (a) $m = 0$

  (b) $y' = \dfrac{20}{(2 - x)^6}$ is a quotient of positive numbers

28. (a) $m = \dfrac{3\sqrt{3}}{2}$

  (b) $y' = \dfrac{-4}{(1 - x)^2}$ is a quotient of a positive and a negative number

29. (a) $m = -2\sqrt{2}$

  (b) $y' = \dfrac{24}{(1 - 2x)^4}$ is a quotient of positive numbers

30. (a) $m = 0$

  (b) $y' = \dfrac{30}{(1 - 5x)^2}$ is a quotient of positive numbers

3.7 Implicit Differentiation

1. $\dfrac{dy}{dx} = \dfrac{-3}{2y}$ **2.** $\dfrac{dy}{dx} = \dfrac{8x}{3y^2}$ **3.** $\dfrac{dy}{dx} = \dfrac{-25x}{y}$

4. $\dfrac{dy}{dx} = \dfrac{-(32 + y^3)}{3xy^2}$ **5.** $\dfrac{dy}{dx} = \dfrac{7 - 2y}{2x}$

6. $\dfrac{dy}{dx} = \dfrac{2y}{x^2 + 2x + 4xy + 4y^2}$

7. $\dfrac{dy}{dx} = \dfrac{4x^3 - y - 2x^2 y}{2x^3}$ **8.** $\dfrac{dy}{dx} = \dfrac{y + x\cos x}{\cot x - x^2}$

9. $y' = \dfrac{-10x}{3 + \cos y}$ and $3 + \cos y \neq 0$ for every y.

10. $y' = \dfrac{-8x}{11 + 3\cos y}$ and $11 + 3\cos y \neq 0$ for every y.

11. $y' = \dfrac{-2x}{5 - 3\sin y}$ and $5 - 3\sin y \neq 0$ for every y.

12. $y' = \dfrac{-8x}{7 - 2\cos y}$ and $7 - 2\cos y \neq 0$ for every y.

13. $y' = \dfrac{-2x}{4 - 3\sin y}$ and $4 - 3\sin y \neq 0$ for every y.

14. $y' = \dfrac{-4x}{4 - 3\sin y}$ and $4 - 3\sin y \neq 0$ for every y.

15. $\dfrac{d^2 y}{dx^2} = \dfrac{4y^2 - 16x^2}{y^3}$ **16.** $\dfrac{d^2 y}{dx^2} = \dfrac{48xy^2 - 9x^4}{64y^3}$

17. $\dfrac{d^2 y}{dx^2} = -\dfrac{40}{3}x^3$ **18.** $\dfrac{d^2 y}{dx^2} = \dfrac{-25}{64y^3}$

19. $\dfrac{d^2 y}{dx^2} = \dfrac{12xy^2 - 9x^4}{4y^3}$ **20.** $\dfrac{d^2 y}{dx^2} = -\dfrac{1}{y^3}$

21. $\dfrac{2}{\sqrt{4x - 1}}$ **22.** $-\dfrac{5}{3}\sin^{2/3} x\cos x$

23. $\dfrac{3}{2}\sqrt{x}$ **24.** $\dfrac{-2x + 2}{(3x^2 - 2x + 1)^{3/2}}$

25. $\dfrac{-3\csc^2(2x)}{4\cot^{5/8}(2x)}$ **26.** $\dfrac{x^2}{2\sqrt{x + 1}} + 2x\sqrt{x + 1}$

27. $\dfrac{-8x\sin(x^2 + \pi)}{5\cos^{1/5}(x^2 + \pi)}$ **28.** $\dfrac{-9x^2}{5\sqrt[5]{(6 - x^3)^2}}$

3.8 Derivatives of Inverse Trigonometric Functions

1. $y' = \dfrac{2}{\sqrt{1 - 4t^2}}$ **2.** $y' = \dfrac{-8}{|x|\sqrt{x^2 - 1}}$

3. $y' = \sin^{-1} t^2 + \dfrac{2t^2}{\sqrt{1 - t^4}}$ **4.** $y' = \dfrac{1}{2\sqrt{-x^2 + x}}$

5. $y' = \dfrac{2}{\sqrt{-4x^2 + 10x - 6}}$

6. $y' = \dfrac{-3}{\sqrt{-9x^2 + 30x - 24}}$

7. $\dfrac{3}{82}$ **8.** $\dfrac{1}{2}$ **9.** $\dfrac{2}{\sqrt{3}}$ **10.** $\dfrac{1}{\sqrt{5}}$ **11.** $\dfrac{8}{3\sqrt{65}}$

12. $\dfrac{\sqrt{2}}{72}$ **13.** $\dfrac{dy}{dx} = \dfrac{2}{|x|\sqrt{49x^4 - 1}}$

14. $\dfrac{dy}{dx} = \dfrac{-64}{x\sqrt{x^8 - 256}}$, $|x| < 2$

15. $\dfrac{dy}{dx} = \dfrac{-2x}{2x^4 - 2x^2 + 1}$

16. $\dfrac{dy}{dx} = \dfrac{1}{(2x+4)\sqrt{x+1}} + \dfrac{1}{\sqrt{4 - x^2}}$, $-1 < x < 2$

17. $\dfrac{dy}{dx} = \dfrac{x(4x^2 + 4)}{(x^4 + 2x^2)\sqrt{(x^4 + 2x^2)^2 - 1}}$

18. $\dfrac{dy}{dx} = \dfrac{x}{|x|\sqrt{1 - x^2}}$, $|x| < 2$

19. $y - 0.11 = -\dfrac{3}{82}(x - 3)$

20. $y + \dfrac{\pi}{3} = \dfrac{1}{4}(x + \sqrt{3})$

21. $y - 1.772 = \dfrac{1}{2\sqrt{6}}(x + 1)$

22. $y - \dfrac{\pi}{3} = -\dfrac{1}{2}\left(x - \dfrac{6}{\sqrt{3}}\right)$

23. $y - \dfrac{\pi}{6} = \dfrac{2}{\sqrt{3}}\left(x + \dfrac{1}{2}\right)$

24. $y - 0.17 = -\dfrac{6}{37}(x - 1)$

3.9 Derivatives of Exponential and Logarithmic Functions

1. $\dfrac{dy}{dx} = (3 - 2x)\,e^{(3x - x^2)}$ **2.** $\dfrac{dy}{dx} = \pi(e^{\pi x} + 1)$

3. $\dfrac{dy}{dx} = x^2 e^x + 2x e^x + 1$ **4.** $\dfrac{dy}{dx} = \dfrac{-1}{2\sqrt{x+1}\,e^{\sqrt{x+1}}}$

5. $\dfrac{dy}{dx} = 6e^x (e^x + 1)^5$ **6.** $\dfrac{dy}{dx} = -\sin x\, e^{\cos x}$

7. $\dfrac{dy}{dx} = -ex^{-(e+1)} - e^{-x}$ **8.** $\dfrac{dy}{dx} = (1 - 14x)\,e^{(x - 7x^2)}$

9. $f'(x) = \dfrac{8}{8x - 1}, \left(\dfrac{1}{8}, \infty\right)$

10. $f'(x) = \dfrac{1}{2(x - 9)}, (9, \infty)$

11. $f'(x) = \dfrac{-\sin x}{1 + \cos x}$, $x \neq n\pi$ where n is an odd integer

12. $f'(x) = \dfrac{2x}{x^2 - 1}, |x| > 1$ **13.** $f'(x) = \dfrac{3}{x \ln \pi}, x > 0$

14. $f'(x) = 1 + \dfrac{2}{x}, x \neq 0$ **15.** $f'(x) = 1, (-\infty, \infty)$

16. $f'(x) = \dfrac{1}{x - 2}, (2, \infty)$

17. $y' = x^{\sin x}\left(\dfrac{\sin x}{x} + \cos x \ln x\right)$

18. $y' = (\ln x)^x \left(\dfrac{1}{\ln x} + \ln(\ln x)\right)$

19. $y' = -x^{-x}(\ln x + 1)$

20. $y' = (\cos x)^{2x+1}\big(2\ln(\cos x) - (2x + 1)\tan x\big)$

21. $y' = \sqrt[3]{\dfrac{(x-2)^3(2x^2 + 3)}{(x+1)^2}}\left(\dfrac{1}{x - 2} + \dfrac{4x}{3(2x^2 + 3)} - \dfrac{2}{3(x + 1)}\right)$

22. $y' = (x^2 + 1)^{\ln x}\left(\dfrac{2x \ln x}{x^2 + 1} + \dfrac{\ln(x^2 + 1)}{x}\right)$

Chapter 4
Applications of Derivatives

4.1 Extreme Values of Functions

1. maximum: 1 (once); minimum: −1 (twice)
2. maximum: 3 (once); minimum: −3 (twice)
3. maximum: 2 (twice); minimum: 0 (once)
4. maximum: 2 (once); minimum: 0 (once)
5. maximum: 33 (once); minimum: −31 (once)
6. maximum: $-e^{-3}$ (once); minimum: $-e^5$ (once)
7. maximum: 2 ln 9 (once); minimum: 0 (once)
8. maximum: 10 (once); minimum: 10/81 (once)
9. Maximum values of 5 at $x = -1$ and $x = 1$, minimum value of 0 at $x = 0$

10. Minimum values of –6.96 at $x = -2$ and $x = 2$, maximum value of 0 at $x = 0$

11. Maximum value of 1 at $x = \pi$, minimum value of –1 at $x = -\pi$

12. Maximum values of $\ln\sqrt{21}$ at $x = 10$, minimum value of 0 at $x = 0$

13. Maximum values of 4.18 at $x = -5$ and $x = 5$, minimum value of 0 at $x = 0$

14. Minimum values of $-1/e$ at $x = -1$, maximum value of $2e^2$ at $x = 2$

15. Absolute maximum of –7 at $x = 0$

16. Absolute minimum of $\dfrac{5\sqrt{21}}{21}$ at $x = 0$

17. No absolute maximum or minimum

18. No absolute maximum or minimum

19. Absolute minimum of $\dfrac{11\sqrt{7}}{7}$ at $x = 0$

20. Absolute minimum of 1 at $x = 0$

21. Local maximum of $\left(\dfrac{4}{5}, \dfrac{6}{5}\sqrt[3]{\dfrac{16}{25}}\right)$ and local minimum at $(0, 0)$

22. Local maximum at $(0, 6)$ and local minimum at $(2, 2)$

23. Local maximum at $(0, 5)$ and local minimum at $(1, 4)$

24. Local maximums at $(-4, 0)$ and $(2\sqrt{2}, 16)$ and local minimums at $(4, 0)$ and $(-2\sqrt{2}, -16)$

25. Local maximum at $\left(-\dfrac{4}{5}, \dfrac{16}{25\sqrt{5}}\right)$ and local minimums at $(-1, 0)$ and $(0, 0)$

26. Local maximum at $\left(-\dfrac{1}{\sqrt{7}}, \left(\dfrac{1}{\sqrt{7}}\right)^{1/3}\cdot\dfrac{6}{7}\right)$ and local minimum at $\left(\dfrac{1}{\sqrt{7}}, \left(-\dfrac{1}{\sqrt{7}}\right)^{1/3}\cdot\dfrac{6}{7}\right)$

4.2 Mean Value Theorem

1. $c = \dfrac{9}{2}$ **2.** $c = 5$ **3.** $c = \dfrac{7}{2}$ **4.** $c = \dfrac{9}{2}$

5. $c = 3$ **6.** $c = \dfrac{\sqrt{\pi^2-4}}{\pi}$ **7.** $c = \dfrac{2}{\ln 3} - 3$ **8.** $c = 5$

9. Decreasing on $(-\infty, 6]$; increasing on $[6, \infty)$

10. Increasing on $(-\infty, 0]$; decreasing on $[0, 1]$, increasing on $[1, \infty)$

11. Increasing on $[-2\sqrt{2}, 2\sqrt{2}]$; decreasing on $[-4, -2\sqrt{2}]$ and $[2\sqrt{2}, 4]$

12. Increasing on $\left[\dfrac{n\pi}{2}, \dfrac{(n+1)\pi}{2}\right]$, where n is any odd integer, decreasing on $\left[\dfrac{n\pi}{2}, \dfrac{(n+1)\pi}{2}\right]$, where n is any even integer

13. Increasing on $\left(\infty, -\dfrac{5}{6}\right]$, decreasing on $\left[-\dfrac{5}{6}, \infty\right)$

14. Increasing on $[-1, \infty)$, decreasing on $(-\infty, -1]$

15. Increasing on $\left(-\infty, -\dfrac{1}{3}\right]$, decreasing on $\left[-\dfrac{1}{3}, \dfrac{1}{3}\right]$, increasing on $\left[\dfrac{1}{3}, \infty\right)$

16. Increasing on $\left[6+2\sqrt{10}, \infty\right)$, decreasing on $\left(-\infty, 6-2\sqrt{10}\right]$, decreasing on $\left[6+2\sqrt{10}, \infty\right)$

17. $f(x) = x^2 - 3x + 4$ **18.** $f(x) = 2x^3 - 3x + 1$

19. $f(x) = \dfrac{1}{x^2} + 3$ **20.** $f(x) = -2\sin x + 0.41$

21. $f(x) = -\dfrac{3}{2}\ln(2x+1)$ **22.** $f(x) = -\cos x - \sin x + 2$

23. $v(t) = 9.8t + 4$ **24.** $v(t) = 9.8t + 9$

25. $v(t) = \dfrac{t^2}{2} + 4$ **26.** $v(t) = -\cos t + 4$

27. $v(t) = -e^t + 8$ **28.** $v(t) = \ln(t+1)$

29. $v(t) = \sec t + 2$ **30.** $v(t) = \tan t + 6$

4.3 Connecting f' and f'' with the Graph of f

1. (a) Concave down (b) Concave up on $(0, \pi)$ and concave down on $(\pi, 2\pi)$

2. (a) Concave up (b) Concave down on $\left(\pi, \dfrac{3\pi}{2}\right)$ and concave up on $\left(\dfrac{3\pi}{2}, 2\pi\right)$

3. (a) Concave up on $(0, 6)$, concave down on $(6, 10)$ (b) Concave up on $(0, \pi)$ and concave down on $(\pi, 2\pi)$

4. (a) Concave down on $\left(\dfrac{1}{\sqrt{2}}, 1\right)$, concave up on $\left(0, \dfrac{1}{\sqrt{2}}\right)$ (b) Concave up on entire interval

5. **(a)** Concave down **(b)** Concave up on $\left(0, \dfrac{\pi}{4}\right)$ and

concave down on $\left(\dfrac{\pi}{4}, \pi\right)$

6. **(a)** Concave up **(b)** Concave up on $\left(0, \dfrac{\pi}{2}\right)$ and

$\left(\dfrac{3\pi}{2}, 2\pi\right)$ and concave down on $\left(\dfrac{\pi}{2}, \dfrac{3\pi}{2}\right)$

7. $x = -\dfrac{\sqrt{2}}{2}$ and $x = \dfrac{\sqrt{2}}{2}$ **8.** $x = -\dfrac{\sqrt{2}}{2}$ and $x = \dfrac{\sqrt{2}}{2}$

9. $x = 0$ **10.** no inflection points

11. $x = \pm\dfrac{3\pi}{4}$ and $x = \pm\dfrac{\pi}{4}$ **12.** $x = 0$

13. Local minimum at $x = -\dfrac{2}{\sqrt{3}}$; local maximum at $x = \dfrac{2}{\sqrt{3}}$

14. Local minimum at $x = 1$; local maximum at $x = -1$

15. Local minimum at $x = -1$; local maximum at $x = 1$

16. Local maximum at $x = -\dfrac{\sqrt{2}}{2}$; local minimum at

$x = \dfrac{\sqrt{2}}{2}$

17. Local maximum at $x = 2$; local minimum at $x = 0$

18. No local minimums or maximums

19. **(a)** Local minimum at $x = 2$ **(b)** Decreasing on $(-\infty, 0]$
and $[0, 2]$, and increasing on $[2, \infty)$ **(c)** Concave up on

$(-\infty, 0]$ and $\left[\dfrac{4}{3}, \infty\right)$, concave down on $\left[0, \dfrac{4}{3}\right]$

(d)

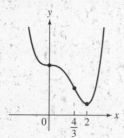

20. **(a)** Local maximum at $x = -\dfrac{1}{4}$ **(b)** Increasing on

$\left(-\infty, -\dfrac{1}{4}\right]$ and decreasing on $[0, \infty)$ and $\left[-\dfrac{1}{4}, 0\right]$

(c) Concave down on $\left(-\infty, -\dfrac{1}{6}\right]$ and $\left[0, -\dfrac{1}{6}\right)$, and

concave up on $\left[-\dfrac{1}{6}, 0\right]$

(d)

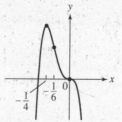

21. **(a)** Local minimum at $x = -\dfrac{1}{5}$ **(b)** Decreasing on

$\left(-\infty, -\dfrac{1}{5}\right]$ and increasing on $\left[-\dfrac{1}{5}, 0\right]$ and $[0, \infty)$

(c) Concave up on $\left(-\infty, -\dfrac{2}{15}\right]$ and $[0, \infty)$, concave

down on $\left[-\dfrac{2}{15}, 0\right]$

(d)

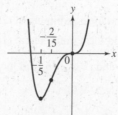

22. **(a)** Local minimum at $x = -2$,
(b) Decreasing on $(-\infty, -2]$, and increasing on $[-2, 0]$
and $[0, \infty)$,

(c) Concave up on $(-\infty, -3]$, and $\left[-\dfrac{7}{3}, \infty\right)$, concave

down on $\left[-3, -\dfrac{7}{3}\right]$

(d)

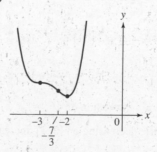

23. (a) Local minimum at $x = -3$ and $x = 1$, local maximum at $x = -2$,

(b) Decreasing on $(-\infty, -3]$ and $[-2, 1]$, and increasing on $[-3, -2]$ and $[1, \infty)$

(c) Concave up on

$$\left(-\infty, -\frac{4}{3} - \frac{\sqrt{13}}{3}\right] \text{ and } \left[-\frac{4}{3} + \frac{\sqrt{13}}{3}, \infty\right), \text{ concave down}$$

on $\left[-\frac{4}{3} - \frac{\sqrt{13}}{3}, -\frac{4}{3} + \frac{\sqrt{13}}{3}\right]$

(d)

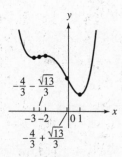

24. (a) Local maximum at $x = -2$; local minimum at $x = -1$

(b) Increasing on $(-\infty, -3]$ and $[-3, -2]$; decreasing on $[-2, -1]$; increasing on $[-1, \infty)$,

(c) Concave down on $(-\infty, -3]$ and

$$\left[-\frac{15}{8} - \frac{\sqrt{17}}{8}, -\frac{15}{8} + \frac{\sqrt{17}}{8}\right]; \text{ concave up on}$$

$$\left[-3, -\frac{15}{8} - \frac{\sqrt{17}}{8}\right] \text{ and } \left[-\frac{15}{8} + \frac{\sqrt{17}}{8}, \infty\right)$$

(d)

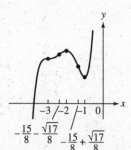

4.4 Modeling and Optimization

1. 12 and 12   **2.** 14 and 14   **3.** 16 and 16

4. 18 and 18   **5.** 1   **6.** 6 ft by 6 ft

7. $A = 20{,}000$ sq ft; 100 ft by 200 ft

8. $A = 25$ cm^2; the legs are $5\sqrt{2}$ and $5\sqrt{2}$

9. $x = 1$ and $V = 18$ **10.** $x = 1.84$ and $V = 102.57$

11. $x = 3$ and $V = 486$ **12.** $x = 2$ and $V = 128$

13. $x = 0.74$ and $V = 6.56$ **14.** $x = 2.21$ and $V = 177.13$

15. $x = 4.44$ **16.** $x = 3.73$ **17.** $x = 5.14$

18. $x = 17/3$ **19.** $x = 1$ **20.** none

21. $x = 2.5$ **22.** $x = 3.5$ **23.** $x = 4$

24. none   **25.** $x = 1$ **26.** $\pi/2 + 2n\pi$

4.5 Linearization and Newton's Method

1. $\sin(0.5) \approx \frac{1}{2} + \frac{\sqrt{3}}{2}\left(0.5 - \frac{\pi}{6}\right) \approx 0.48$

2. $\sin(1) \approx \frac{\sqrt{3}}{2} + \frac{1}{2}\left(1 - \frac{\pi}{3}\right) \approx 0.84$

3. $\sin(0.8) \approx \frac{\sqrt{2}}{2} + \frac{\sqrt{2}}{2}\left(0.8 - \frac{\pi}{4}\right) \approx 0.72$

4. $\cos(1.6) \approx -\left(1.6 - \frac{\pi}{2}\right) \approx -0.03$

5. $\cos(0.1) \approx 1$

6. $\cos(-2) \approx -\frac{1}{2} + \frac{\sqrt{3}}{2}\left(-2 + \frac{2\pi}{3}\right) \approx -0.42$

7. -0.5641 **8.** -0.0908 **9.** 0.2235

10. 1.8794 **11.** -1.4960 **12.** 1.5106

13. $dy = 0.06$ **14.** $dy = 0.20$ **15.** $dy = 0$

16. $dy = -0.24$ **17.** $dy = -0.03$ **18.** $dy = 0.0016$

19. $dy = 0.415$ **20.** $dy = 0.103$

21. (a) $\Delta f = 1.292$ **22. (a)** $\Delta f = 0.122$

(b) $df = 1.2$ **(b)** $df = 0.100$

(c) $|\Delta f - df| = 0.092$ **(c)** $|\Delta f - df| = 0.022$

23. (a) $\Delta f = -0.0194$ **24. (a)** $\Delta f = 2.333$

(b) $df = -0.020$ **(b)** $df = 2.25$

(c) $|\Delta f - df| = 0.000586$ **(c)** $|\Delta f - df| = 0.0827$

25. $dS = 2\pi r\, dh$ **26.** $dS = (2b\pi + 2\pi h)dr$

4.6 Related Rates

1. $\dfrac{dA}{dt} = \dfrac{1}{2}\left(b\dfrac{dh}{dt} + h\dfrac{db}{dt}\right)$ **2.** $\dfrac{dA}{dt} = \dfrac{1}{2}\left(m\dfrac{dh}{dt} + h\dfrac{dm}{dt}\right)$

3. $\dfrac{dV}{dt} = A\dfrac{dh}{dt} + h\dfrac{dA}{dt}$ **4.** $\dfrac{dA}{dt} = r\theta\dfrac{dr}{dt} + \left(\dfrac{r^2}{2}\right)\dfrac{d\theta}{dt}$

5. $\dfrac{dK}{dt} = \pi\left(\dfrac{da}{dt} + \dfrac{db}{dt}\right)$ **6.** $\dfrac{dA}{dt} = \dfrac{dh}{dt} + \dfrac{db}{dt}$

7. $\dfrac{dh}{dt} = 222.87$ ft/min   **8.** $\dfrac{dh}{dt} = 183.93$ ft/min

9. $\dfrac{dh}{dt} = 92.39$ ft/min   **10.** $\dfrac{dh}{dt} = 183.34$ ft/min

11. $\dfrac{dh}{dt} = 3250.02$ ft/min   **12.** $\dfrac{dh}{dt} = 339.96$ ft/min

13. $\dfrac{dx}{dt} = 110.76$ **14.** $\dfrac{dx}{dt} = 83.33$

15. $\dfrac{dx}{dt} = 111.34$ **16.** 339.20 mph

17. 350.07 mph   **18.** 246.23 mph

19. $\dfrac{dx}{dt} = 0.102$ ft/min   **20.** $\dfrac{dx}{dt} = 0.055$ ft/min

21. $\dfrac{dx}{dt} = 0.064$ ft/min   **22.** $\dfrac{dr}{dt} = 0.056$ ft³/min

23. $\dfrac{dr}{dt} = 0.055$ ft³/min   **24.** $\dfrac{dr}{dt} = 0.039$ ft³/min

Chapter 5
An Introduction to Calculus:
The Definite Integrals

5.1 Estimating with Finite Sums

1. $x = 12$ **2.** $x = -45$ **3.** $x = \dfrac{75}{2}$ **4.** $x = 36$

5. $x = 965.25$ **6.** $x = 359.375$ **7.** $x = 56.91$ **8.** $x = 101$

9. 2.1666667   **10.** 1.2238   **11.** 0.300306

12. 2025.0914   **13.** 6.111097   **14.** 5908.7553

15. 5.12 L/min   **16.** 4.84 L/min   **17.** 581.50 feet

18. 682.5 feet   **19.** 527.0 feet   **20.** 729.0 feet

5.2 Definite Integrals

1. $\displaystyle\int_{-3}^{3} (x^4 - x^3 + 4x)\,dx$ **2.** $\displaystyle\int_{-3}^{3} (-4x^2 + 3x - 8)\,dx$

3. $\displaystyle\int_{-3}^{3} \dfrac{4x^2 - 4x + 24}{x^2 + 1}\,dx$ **4.** $\displaystyle\int_{-3}^{3} (\sin^2(2x) + x)\,dx$

5. $\displaystyle\int_{-3}^{3} \sqrt{2x + 10}\,dx$ **6.** $\displaystyle\int_{-3}^{3} x^2 e^{2x}\,dx$ **7.** $\displaystyle\int_{-3}^{3} \ln(2x + 10)\,dx$

8. $\displaystyle\int_{-3}^{3} 2^{-x}\,dx$ **9.** $\dfrac{\pi}{2}$ **10.** 8π

11. $\dfrac{5}{2}$ **12.** $\dfrac{17}{2}$ **13.** 18

14. 12   **15.** $72\pi + 24$ **16.** 96

17. $\displaystyle\int_{0}^{4/3} 12\,dx$, 16 inches   **18.** $\displaystyle\int_{0}^{31} 200\,dx$, \$6,200

19. $\displaystyle\int_{0}^{8} 6\,dx$, 48 gallons   **20.** $\displaystyle\int_{0}^{900} 3\,dx$, 2700 megabytes

21. $\displaystyle\int_{0}^{7} 10{,}000\,dx$, 70,000 gallons   **22.** $\displaystyle\int_{0}^{30} 0.5\,dx$, 15 quart

23. $\displaystyle\int_{0}^{9/4} 1.2\,dx$, 2.7 inches   **24.** $\displaystyle\int_{0}^{16} 20\,dx$, 320 plate

25. **(a)** $x = -1$ **26.** **(a)** $x = 3/2$
       (b) 3   **(b)** 10

27. **(a)** $x = 0$ **28.** **(a)** $x = -1/3$

       (b) 2π **(b)** $4\dfrac{2}{3}$

29. **(a)** $x = -4$ **30.** **(a)** $x = 1$
       (b) 17.5   **(b)** 4

5.3 Definite Integrals and Antiderivatives

1. -14 **2.** -24 **3.** -17 **4.** Not possible

5. -126 **6.** Not possible

7. $\displaystyle\int_{\pi/4}^{\pi/2} (\sin x - \cos x)\,dx \le 1 \cdot \left(\dfrac{\pi}{2} - \dfrac{\pi}{4}\right) = \dfrac{\pi}{4}$

8. $\displaystyle\int_{-2}^{2} e^{-x}\,dx \le e^2(2 - (-2)) = 4e^2 < 4\pi^2$

9. $\displaystyle\int_{2}^{6} \sqrt{4 + \cos x}\,dx \le \sqrt{5}(6 - 2) < 3 \cdot 4 = 12 < 32$

10. $\displaystyle\int_{1}^{4} \ln x\,dx \le \ln 4 \cdot (4 - 1) < \ln(e^2) \cdot 3 = 6$

11. $\displaystyle\int_{0}^{6} \sqrt{6 - 5\sin x}\,dx \le \sqrt{11} \cdot (6 - 0) < 20$

12. $\displaystyle\int_{0.01}^{0.02} \dfrac{1}{x^2 dx} \le (100)^2 \cdot (0.02 - 0.01) = 100$

13. $av(f) = 3$; $c =$ any point in $[0, 3]$

14. $av(f) = -4$; $c = 2$ **15.** $av(f) = \dfrac{47}{2}$; $c = \dfrac{5}{2}$

16. $av(f) = 0$; $c = \dfrac{\pi}{2}$ **17.** $av(f) = 64$; $c = 2\sqrt{3}$

18. $av(f) = \dfrac{91}{3}$; $c = \dfrac{5\sqrt{3}}{3}$ **19.** 0   **20.** 0

21. 26   **22.** $\sqrt{2} - 1$ **23.** $e - \dfrac{1}{e}$

24. 10   **25.** -624 **26.** $1 - \ln 2$

5.4 Fundamental Theorem of Calculus

1. $\dfrac{dy}{dx} = 3\sin(3x)$ 2. $\dfrac{dy}{dx} = (3x^2+1)(x^3+x)e^{x^3+x}$

3. $\dfrac{dy}{dx} = \dfrac{2x^5+2x^3+2x}{x^2-1}$

4. $\dfrac{dy}{dx} = \dfrac{(2x+3)\ln(2x^2+6x)}{x^2+3x}$

5. $\dfrac{dy}{dx} = -\dfrac{1}{2x^2}\cos\left(\dfrac{1}{x}\right)$

6. $\dfrac{dy}{dx} = 5\tan(25x^2-10x+1)$ 7. $-36x\sin 3x$

8. $4x^3\ln\sqrt{2x^4+3} - 2x\ln\sqrt{2x^2+3}$

9. $-297x^2\cos 3x$ 10. $\dfrac{2}{5-e^{-2x}}$ 11. $\dfrac{8x-7}{x+1}$

12. $3-\tan^{-2/3}x\sec^2 x$ 13. -12 14. $14-\ln 4$

15. $5-7/\sqrt{2}$ 16. -16 17. $\dfrac{e^2-1}{3}$ 18. $\dfrac{81}{4}$

19. 4   20. $6\sqrt{3}$ 21. $\dfrac{56}{3}$ 22. 56

23. 34   24. 4   25. $\dfrac{1}{2}$ 26. $\dfrac{59}{2}$

5.5 Trapezoidal Rule

1. (a) 6   2. (a) 5.671875   3. (a) 9.272362
   (b) 6   (b) 5.25   (b) 9.259029

4. (a) 0.987116   5. (a) −9.28125
   (b) 1   (b) −9

6. (a) 57.991950   (b) 53.59815

7. −35.25   8. −32.775   9. −32.1375

10. −15   11. −8.25   12. −6.25

13. $\dfrac{1}{6}\left(1\cdot 1+4\cdot\sqrt[3]{\dfrac{31}{32}}+2\cdot\sqrt[3]{\dfrac{7}{8}}+4\cdot\sqrt[3]{\dfrac{23}{32}}+1\cdot\sqrt[3]{\dfrac{1}{2}}\right)$

$\approx 1.8746;\ 1.8747$

14. $\dfrac{1}{12}(1\cdot(-1)+4\cdot(-e^{-1/6})+2\cdot(-e^{-1/4})+4\cdot(-e^{-9/16})$

$+1\cdot(-e^{-1}))\approx -0.74686;\ -0.74682$

15. $\dfrac{1}{12}\left(1\cdot 3+4\cdot\dfrac{192}{65}+2\cdot\dfrac{8}{3}+4\cdot\dfrac{192}{91}+2\cdot\dfrac{3}{2}+4\cdot\dfrac{192}{189}\right.$

$\left.+2\cdot\dfrac{24}{35}+4\cdot\dfrac{192}{407}+1\cdot\dfrac{1}{3}\right)\approx 3.2703;\ 3.2700$

16. $\dfrac{1}{12}\left(1\cdot 0+4\cdot 2\sqrt{\dfrac{3}{16}}+2\cdot 2\sqrt{\dfrac{1}{4}}+4\cdot 2\sqrt{\dfrac{3}{16}}+1\cdot 0\right)$

$\approx 0.7440;\ 0.7854$

17. $\dfrac{2}{9}\left(1\cdot 2+4\cdot\dfrac{3}{2}+2\cdot\dfrac{6}{5}+4\cdot 1+2\cdot\dfrac{6}{7}+4\cdot\dfrac{3}{4}+1\cdot\dfrac{2}{3}\right)$

$\approx 4.3958;\ 4.3944$

18. $\dfrac{1}{12}\left(1\cdot 5+4\cdot 4+2\cdot\dfrac{10}{3}+4\cdot\dfrac{20}{7}+1\cdot\dfrac{5}{2}\right)\approx 3.4663;\ 3.4657$

Chapter 6
Differential Equations and Mathematical Modeling

6.1 Slope Fields and Euler's Method

1. $y=\dfrac{1}{3}x^3+2x^2+x+C$ 2. $y=-2x^3-\sec x+C$

3. $y=\dfrac{(u^2-1)^2}{2}+C$ 4. $y=x^6+\ln x+C$

5. $y=-3\cos x+5\sin x+C$ 6. $y=3^x-\sin^{-1}x+C$

7. $y=x+\sin x+4$ 8. $y=-\dfrac{1}{t}+\dfrac{t^2}{2}-\dfrac{1}{2}$

9. $y=\cos(\pi x)-1$ 10. $v=t^3+t^2+t-3$

11. $y=10x+2x^{3/2}+4$ 12. $y=\dfrac{2}{1+x^2}-1$

13. e   14. b   15. a   16. f
17. c   18. d   19. 0.977   20. 1.355
21. 1.08   22. 1.72102   23. 1.8371   24. 1.13

6.2 Antidifferentiation by Substitution

1. $\dfrac{x^4}{4}+C$ 2. $\dfrac{x^6}{6}+2x^3+\dfrac{x^2}{2}-x+C$

3. $\sin x+C$ 4. $-\cot x+x^3+C$

5. e^u+C 6. $3\tan^{-1}t+C$

7. $-\dfrac{1}{4}\sqrt{1-4x^2}+C$ 8. $\dfrac{2}{3}(t^2+1)^{3/2}+C$

9. $-\dfrac{1}{4}\cos(4x)+C$ 10. $\dfrac{1}{7}\sin(7t+5)+C$

11. $\dfrac{1}{6}(\ln x)^2+C$ 12. $\dfrac{1}{6}e^{3x^2}+C$

13. $-\dfrac{1}{5}\cos^5 x + \dfrac{2}{3}\cos^3 x - \cos x + C$

14. $\dfrac{1}{5}\tan^5 x + \dfrac{1}{3}\tan^3 x + C$

15. $\dfrac{1}{9}\sin^9 x - \dfrac{2}{7}\sin^7 x + \dfrac{1}{5}\sin^5 x + C$

16. $\tan x - x + C$ **17.** $\sec x + C$

18. $-\sin x - \csc x + C$ **19.** $2 - \ln 2$

20. 410 **21.** $2\left(-2 + \csc\left(\dfrac{\pi}{8}\right)\right)$

22. $-\dfrac{1}{2} - \dfrac{\pi}{4}$ **23.** $2(\sqrt{2} - 1)$

24. $1 - \dfrac{\sqrt{3}}{2}$

6.3 Antidifferentiation by Parts

1. $\dfrac{-1}{x}(\ln x + 1) + C$ **2.** $x\ln(1 + x^2) - 2x + 2\tan^{-1} x + C$

3. $x\tan^{-1} x - \dfrac{1}{2}\ln(1 + x^2) + C$ **4.** $\dfrac{1}{2}e^{x^2}(x^2 - 1) + C$

5. $\dfrac{1}{4}(2x^2 \sin 2x + 2x\cos 2x - \sin 2x) + C$

6. $\dfrac{1}{2}(x^2 \tan^{-1} x - x + \tan^{-1} x) + C$

7. $\dfrac{e^x}{2}(\sin x - \cos x) + C$

8. $\dfrac{t}{2}[\sin(\ln t) - \cos(\ln t)] + C$

9. $\dfrac{1}{2}x^3 e^{2x} - \dfrac{3}{4}x^2 e^{2x} + \dfrac{3}{4}xe^{2x} - \dfrac{3}{8}e^{2x} + C$

10. $\dfrac{1}{3}x^2 e^{3x} - \dfrac{2}{9}xe^{3x} + \dfrac{2}{27}e^{3x} + C$

11. $x(\ln x)^2 - 2x\ln x + 2x + C$

12. $t(\ln t)^3 - 3t(\ln t)^2 + 6t\ln t - 6t + C$

13. $x^2 \sin x + 2x\cos x - 2\sin x + C$

14. $\dfrac{1}{4}x^2 \sin 4x + \dfrac{1}{8}x\cos 4x - \dfrac{1}{32}\sin 4x + C$

15. $e^x(x^3 - 3x^2 + 6x - 6) + C$

16. $-\dfrac{1}{8}e^{-2x}(4x^3 + 6x^2 + 6x + 3) + C$

17. $\dfrac{1}{13}e^{3x}(3\sin 2x - 2\cos 2x) + C$

18. $\dfrac{1}{5}e^{2x}(\sin x + 2\cos x) + C$

6.4 Exponential Growth and Decay

1. $y = 2e^{x^2/2}$

2. $y = \ln 2 - \ln(3 - t^2)$, valid for $-\sqrt{3} < t < \sqrt{3}$

3. $y = \dfrac{1}{\sqrt{1 - x^2}}$, valid for $-1 < x < 1$

4. $y = -1 - \sqrt{4 - x^2}$, valid for $-2 < x < 2$

5. $y = -\dfrac{1}{\sqrt{3 - 2\sqrt{1 + x^2}}}$, valid for $-\dfrac{\sqrt{5}}{2} < x < \dfrac{\sqrt{5}}{2}$

6. $y = 4e^{0.02t}$

7. (a) 2837.62   **8.** (a) 2133.93
   (b) 2828.09   (b) 2131.73

9. (a) 3175.50   **10.** (a) 29,679.75
   (b) 3160.77   (b) 27,621.31

11. (a) 2019.73   **12.** (a) 1768.21
   (b) 2018.67   (b) 1767.92

13. (a) 2128.60   **14.** (a) 6040.37
   (b) 2127.05   (b) 5971.76

15. 83 years   **16.** 166 years   **17.** 5700 years

18. 11,400 years   **19.** 32,170 years   **20.** 37,870 years

6.5 Logistic Growth

1. $f(x) = \dfrac{1}{4(x - 2)} - \dfrac{1}{4(x + 2)}$

2. $f(x) = \dfrac{-7}{(x + 4)} + \dfrac{8}{(x + 5)}$

3. $f(x) = \dfrac{2}{(x + 1)} + \dfrac{3}{(x - 3)}$

4. $f(x) = \dfrac{2}{x} - \dfrac{3}{(x + 1)}$ **5.** $f(x) = \dfrac{5}{(x + 2)} - \dfrac{2}{(x + 3)}$

6. $f(x) = \dfrac{2}{(x - 1)} - \dfrac{1}{(x + 2)}$ **7.** $\dfrac{1}{6}\ln\left|\dfrac{(x - 3)}{(x + 3)}\right| + C$

8. $\dfrac{4}{13}\ln\left|\dfrac{(x - 2)}{(3x + 7)}\right| + C$

9. $-\dfrac{5}{22}\ln|2x+1|+\dfrac{8}{11}\ln|x-5|+C$

10. $\dfrac{1}{5}\ln|(x+1)(x-4)^4|+C$

11. $x+\dfrac{1}{2}\ln\left|\dfrac{(x-1)}{(x+1)}\right|+C$

12. $\dfrac{1}{3}x^3+\dfrac{1}{2}x^2+3x+3\ln|x-1|+C$

13. $-\dfrac{1}{6}\ln|x|+\dfrac{1}{2}\ln|x-2|-\dfrac{1}{3}\ln|x+3|+C$

14. $\ln\left|\dfrac{(x+2)(x-1)}{x}\right|+C$

15. $-\dfrac{1}{2}\ln x+\dfrac{9}{10}\ln(2x-1)+\dfrac{1}{10}\ln(x+2)+C$

16. $\dfrac{1}{2}\ln\left|\dfrac{(x-1)^3(x-3)^{19}}{(x-2)^{18}}\right|+C$

17. $\dfrac{1}{8}\ln\left|\dfrac{(x-1)^6(x-3)^5}{(x+1)^3}\right|+C$

18. $-2\ln|x|+\dfrac{9}{4}\ln|x-1|-\dfrac{1}{4}\ln|x+3|+C$

Chapter 7
Applications of Definite Integrals

7.1 Integral As Net Change

1. **(a)** stops at $t=2$, moves to the left before and to the right after
   (b) net displacement $=-12+12=0$, $s(4)=8$
   (c) distance traveled $=|-12|+12=24$
2. **(a)** stops at $t=2$, moves to the left before and to the right after
   (b) net displacement $=-5+8=3$, $s(4)=8+3=11$
   (c) distance traveled $=|-5|+8=13$
3. **(a)** stops at $t=\pi/4$, moves to the right before and to the left after
   (b) net displacement $=2-2=0$, $s(4)=8$
   (c) distance traveled $=2+|-2|=4$
4. **(a)** stopped at start, moves to the right throughout interval
   (b) net displacement $=2$, $s(4)=8+2=10$
   (c) distance traveled $=2$
5. **(a)** stops at $t=3$ and $t=4$, moves to the right before $t=3$ and to the left between $t=3$ and $t=4$

(b) net displacement $=13\dfrac{1}{2}-\dfrac{1}{6}=13\dfrac{1}{3}$,

$s(4)=8+13\dfrac{1}{3}=21\dfrac{1}{3}$

(c) distance traveled $=13\dfrac{1}{2}+\left|-\dfrac{1}{6}\right|=13\dfrac{2}{3}$

6. **(a)** stopped at endpoints and at $\pi/2$, moves to the right throughout interval
   (b) net displacement $=2+2=4$, $s(4)=8+4=12$
   (c) distance traveled $=2+2=4$
7. $v(4)=34$ mph, $s(4)=0.020$ mi
8. $v(2)=26$ mph, $s(2)=0.078$ mi
9. $v(3)=29.1$ mph, $s(3)=0.013$ mi
10. $v(4)=12.5$ mph, $s(4)=0.0013$ mi
11. $v(\pi/2)=11$ mph, $s(\pi/2)=0.0046$ mi
12. $v(\pi)=14.3$ mph, $s(\pi)=0.011$ mi
13. 55.68   **14.** 10.28   **15.** 13.99   **16.** 17.35
17. 84.98   **18.** 6291.67   **19.** 18.02   **20.** 7.72
21. 128   **22.** 64   **23.** 216   **24.** 640
25. 68.4   **26.** 2115

7.2 Areas in the Plane

1. 0.17   **2.** 0.33   **3.** 21.33   **4.** 0.5
5. 0.11   **6.** 4   **7.** 6.5   **8.** 18.67
9. 1   **10.** 0.92   **11.** 1.17   **12.** 0.41
13. 1.5   **14.** 14.17   **15.** 1   **16.** 0.97
17. 0.83   **18.** 0.59   **19.** 8.68   **20.** 1.73
21. 4.5   **22.** 1.33   **23.** 2.17   **24.** 0.27

7.3 Volumes

1. 170.67   **2.** 576   **3.** 2.67   **4.** 136.53
5. 1.15   **6.** 59.12   **7.** 1.05   **8.** 53.62
9. 6.28   **10.** 3431.46   **11.** 19.2684   **12.** 25.13
13. 944.36   **14.** 335.103   **15.** 18π **16.** 32π
17. 50.27   **18.** 1.12   **19.** 137.39   **20.** 27.97
21. 9.87   **22.** 43.53   **23.** 157.08   **24.** 13.40
25. 18.04   **26.** 157.08

7.4 Lengths of Curves

1. 10.54   **2.** 21.39   **3.** 8.63   **4.** 7.72
5. 19.14   **6.** 5.04   **7.** 49.62   **8.** 15.79
9. 12.41   **10.** 4.03   **11.** 1.43   **12.** 1.22
13. 24.77   **14.** 78.94   **15.** 64.05   **16.** 54.05
17. 10.41   **18.** 38.30   **19.** 42.70   **20.** 41.93
21. 20.30   **22.** 9.75   **23.** 7.64   **24.** 4.04

7.5 Applications from Science and Statistics

1. $\frac{1}{5\pi}$ J 2. 0.45 J 3. 0.05 J 4. 23.65 J

5. 2.60 J 6. 4.24 J 7. 0.62 J 8. 0.92 J

9. (a) 264 J 10. (a) 336 J 11. (a) 288 J

(b) 330 J (b) 350 J (b) 520 J

(c) 43.20 J (c) 58.80 J (c) 76.80 J

(d) 637.2 J (d) 744.8 J (d) 884.8 J

12. 495 J 13. 525 J 14. 780 J

15. 34,850.73 ft • lb 16. 32,169.91 ft • lb

17. 40,317.43 ft • lb 18. 37,216.09 ft • lb

19. 1,197,653 ft • lb 20. 1,206,371 ft • lb

21. 15.87% 22. 73.33% 23. 11.75%

24. 2.3% 25. 59.53% 26. 4.78%

Chapter 8
Sequences, L'Hôpital's Rule, and Improper Integrals

8.1 Sequences

1. $b_1 = 5$, $b_2 = 0$, $b_3 = -5$, and $b_7 = -25$
2. $b_1 = 1$, $b_2 = 3$, $b_3 = 7$, and $b_7 = 127$
3. $b_1 = 2$, $b_2 = 2$, $b_3 = 2$, and $b_7 = 2$
4. $b_1 = 1$, $b_2 = 5$, $b_3 = 13$, and $b_7 = 253$
5. $b_1 = 11$, $b_2 = 20$, $b_3 = 38$, and $b_7 = 578$
6. $b_1 = 4$, $b_2 = 10$, $b_3 = 16$, and $b_7 = 40$
7. $b_1 = -4$, $b_2 = -12$, $b_3 = -36$, and $b_7 = -2916$
8. $b_1 = 7$, $b_2 = 18$, $b_3 = 29$, and $b_7 = 73$
9. **Sequence 1:**
   (a) The ratio between the successive terms is 5.
   (b) $a_8 = 78125$
   (c) The sequence is defined by $a_1 = 1$ and $a_n = 5a_{n-1}$ for $n \geq 2$.
   (d) The sequence is defined explicitly by $a_n = 5^{n-1}$.

   Sequence 2:
   (a) The ratio between the successive terms is $(-2)^{-1}$
   (b) $a_8 = (-2)^{-9}$
   (c) The sequence is defined by $a_1 = (-2)^{-2}$ and $a_n = (-2)^{-1}a_{n-1}$ for $n \geq 2$.
   (d) The sequence is defined explicitly by $a_n = (-2)^{-n-1}$.
10. **Sequence 1:**
    (a) The ratio between the successive terms is -1.
    (b) $a_8 = -11$
    (c) The sequence is defined by $a_1 = 11$ and $a_n = -a_{n-1}$ for $n \geq 2$.

(d) The sequence is defined explicitly by $a_n = 11(-1)^{n-1}$.

Sequence 2:
(a) The ratio between the successive terms is 3^{-3}
(b) $a_8 = 3^{-24}$
(c) The sequence is defined by $a_1 = 3^{-3}$ and $a_n = (3^{-3})a_{n-1}$ for $n \geq 2$.
(d) The sequence is defined explicitly by $a_n = 3^{-3n}$.

11. **Sequence 1:**
    (a) The ratio between the successive terms is -3.
    (b) $a_8 = 6561$
    (c) The sequence is defined by $a_1 = -3$ and $a_n = -3a_{n-1}$ for $n \geq 2$.
    (d) The sequence is defined explicitly by $a_n = (-3)^n$.

    Sequence 2:
    (a) The ratio between the successive terms is 7^4.
    (b) $a_8 = 7^{31}$
    (c) The sequence is defined by $a_1 = 7^3$ and $a_n = 7^4 a_{n-1}$ for $n \geq 2$.
    (d) The sequence is defined explicitly by $a_n = 7^{4n-1}$.

12. **Sequence 1:**
    (a) The ratio between the successive terms is -2.
    (b) $a_8 = -1280$
    (c) The sequence is defined by $a_1 = 10$ and $a_n = -2a_{n-1}$ for $n \geq 2$.
    (d) The sequence is defined explicitly by $a_n = 10(-2)^{n-1}$.

    Sequence 2:
    (a) The ratio between the successive terms is 11^2
    (b) $a_8 = 11^{17}$
    (c) The sequence is defined by $a_1 = 11^3$ and $a_n = 11^2 a_{n-1}$ for $n \geq 2$.
    (d) The sequence is defined explicitly by $a_n = 11^{1+2n}$.

13. **Sequence 1:**
    (a) The ratio between the successive terms is 5.
    (b) $a_8 = 312500$
    (c) The sequence is defined by $a_1 = 4$ and $a_n = 5a_{n-1}$ for $n \geq 2$.
    (d) The sequence is defined explicitly by $a_n = 4(5^{n-1})$.

    Sequence 2:
    (a) The ratio between the successive terms is 55^{-10}
    (b) $a_8 = 55^{-75}$
    (c) The sequence is defined by $a_1 = 55^{-5}$ and $a_n = 55^{-10} a_{n-1}$ for $n \geq 2$.
    (d) The sequence is defined explicitly by $a_n = 55^{5-10n}$.

14. **Sequence 1:**
    (a) The ratio between the successive terms is 4.
    (b) $a_8 = 98304$

(c) The sequence is defined by $a_1 = 6$ and $a_n = 4a_{n-1}$ for $n \geq 2$.

(d) The sequence is defined explicitly by $a_n = 6(4^{n-1})$.

Sequence 2:

(a) The ratio between the successive terms is 2^{11}.

(b) $a_8 = 2^{88}$

(c) The sequence is defined by $a_1 = 2^{11}$ and $a_n = 2^{11}a_{n-1}$ for $n \geq 2$.

(d) The sequence is defined explicitly by $a_n = 2^{11n}$.

5. $\dfrac{5}{7}$	**16.** $-\dfrac{3}{2}$	**17.** $-\dfrac{1}{11}$	**18.** 0
9. $\dfrac{1}{11}$	**20.** diverges	**21.** 0	**22.** 3
3. 0	**24.** 0	**25.** 0	**26.** 0

8.2 L'Hôpital's Rule

1. $-1/3072$	**2.** $\sqrt{2}$	**3.** $1/3$	**4.** 1
5. $1/2$	**6.** 0	**7.** diverges	**8.** $1/6$
9. diverges	**10.** 0	**11.** 1	**12.** 0
3. 0	**14.** 0	**15.** e^{-25}	**16.** e^{-14}
7. e^{-12}	**18.** e	**19.** e^{-1}	**20.** e^2
1. 1	**22.** 1	**23.** $e^{1/2}$	**24.** e
5. 2	**26.** 3		

8.3 Relative Rates of Growth

1. $\displaystyle\lim_{x\to\infty}\frac{9e^x}{x^3} = \infty$

2. $\displaystyle\lim_{x\to\infty}\frac{-2e^{4x}}{4x^5} = \infty$

3. $\displaystyle\lim_{x\to\infty}\frac{4e^{4x}}{x^3+10^6x^2} = \infty$

4. $\displaystyle\lim_{x\to\infty}\frac{e^{8x}}{x^{100,000}} = \infty$

5. $\displaystyle\lim_{x\to\infty}\frac{e^{6x}}{e^{\sin x}} = \infty$

6. $\displaystyle\lim_{x\to\infty}\frac{e^{3x}}{1/x^2} = \infty$

7. $\displaystyle\lim_{x\to\infty}\frac{e^{5x}}{(\pi/2)^x} = \infty$

8. $\displaystyle\lim_{x\to\infty}\frac{e^{2x}}{2x^2+3x+1} = \infty$

9. $\displaystyle\lim_{x\to\infty}\frac{\ln 7x}{3x} = 0$

10. $\displaystyle\lim_{x\to\infty}\frac{\ln 5x}{x^4} = 0$

1. $\displaystyle\lim_{x\to\infty}\frac{4\ln x}{0.00002x} = 0$

12. $\displaystyle\lim_{x\to\infty}\frac{\ln 6x^2}{\sqrt[3]{6x+1}} = 0$

3. $\displaystyle\lim_{x\to\infty}\frac{\ln(11x+1)}{7x(\sin^2 x+1)} = 0$

14. $\displaystyle\lim_{x\to\infty}\frac{\ln(65x^{85})}{x} = 0$

5. $0 \neq \displaystyle\lim_{x\to\infty}\frac{g(x)}{f(x)} = \frac{11}{3} < \infty$

16. $0 \neq \displaystyle\lim_{x\to\infty}\frac{g(x)}{f(x)} = 1 < \infty$

7. $0 \neq \displaystyle\lim_{x\to\infty}\frac{g(x)}{f(x)} = \frac{7}{5} < \infty$

18. $0 \neq \displaystyle\lim_{x\to\infty}\frac{g(x)}{f(x)} = 3 < \infty$

9. $0 \neq \displaystyle\lim_{x\to\infty}\frac{g(x)}{f(x)} = \frac{2}{3} < \infty$

20. $0 \neq \displaystyle\lim_{x\to\infty}\frac{g(x)}{f(x)} = \frac{1}{3} < \infty$

21. $\displaystyle\lim_{x\to\infty}\frac{f(x)}{g(x)} = 1 < \infty$

22. $\displaystyle\lim_{x\to\infty}\frac{f(x)}{g(x)} = 1 < \infty$

23. $\displaystyle\lim_{x\to\infty}\frac{f(x)}{g(x)} = \frac{1}{2} < \infty$

24. $\displaystyle\lim_{x\to\infty}\frac{f(x)}{g(x)} = \sqrt{\frac{7}{2}} < \infty$

25. $\displaystyle\lim_{x\to\infty}\frac{f(x)}{g(x)} = 3 < \infty$

26. $\displaystyle\lim_{x\to\infty}\frac{f(x)}{g(x)} = 3 < \infty$

8.4 Improper Integrals

1. $4\ln(5/6)$	**2.** $11(\ln 2)$		**3.** diverges
4. $-8(\ln 2)$	**5.** $-\dfrac{7\ln 3}{2}$		**6.** $\dfrac{-5\ln(7/9)}{2}$
7. $\dfrac{6e^{-5}}{25}$	**8.** $\dfrac{-9e^{-8}}{8}$		**9.** diverges
10. $\dfrac{-7e^{-6}}{36}$	**11.** diverges		**12.** diverges
13. $3\sqrt[3]{9}$	**14.** $6\sqrt[3]{3}$		**15.** diverges
16. $\dfrac{3}{2}\left(9^{2/3}-7^{2/3}\right)$	**17.** diverges		**18.** $2(e^3-1)$

19. One quarter of the circle has arc length

$$L = \int_0^4 \sqrt{1+\left(-\frac{x}{\sqrt{16-x^2}}\right)^2}\, dx = 2\pi\,.$$ Thus the circumference is $4L = 8\pi$.

20. One quarter of the circle has arc length

$$L = \int_0^7 \sqrt{1+\left(-\frac{x}{49-x^2}\right)^2}\, dx = \frac{7\pi}{2}\,.$$ The circumference is $4L = 14\pi$.

21. One quarter of the circle has arc length

$$L = \int_0^{12} \sqrt{1+\left(-\frac{x}{144-x^2}\right)^2}\, dx = 6\pi\,.$$ The circumference is $4L = 24\pi$.

22. One quarter of the circle has arc length

$$L = \int_0^5 \sqrt{1+\left(-\frac{x}{25-x^2}\right)^2}\, dx = \frac{5\pi}{2}\,.$$ The circumference is $4L = 10\pi$.

23. One quarter of the circle has arc length

$$L = \int_0^{11} \sqrt{1+\left(-\frac{x}{\sqrt{121-x^2}}\right)^2}\, dx = \frac{11\pi}{2}\,.$$ The circumference is $4L = 22\pi$.

24. One quarter of the circle has arc length

$$L = \int_0^6 \sqrt{1+\left(-\frac{x}{\sqrt{36-x^2}}\right)^2}\, dx = 3\pi\,.$$ The circumference is $4L = 12\pi$.

Chapter 9
Infinite Series

9.1 Power Series

1. Diverges
2. Converges
3. Converges
4. Diverges
5. Diverges
6. Diverges
7. Converges
8. Converges
9. Diverges
10. Converges
11. Converges
12. Diverges

13. $f'(x) = \dfrac{1}{x}; \displaystyle\sum_{n=0}^{\infty} (-1)^n (x-1)^n$

14. $f'(x) = \dfrac{1}{x+1}; \displaystyle\sum_{n=1}^{\infty} (-1)^{n-1} x^{n-1}$

15. $f'(x) = \dfrac{1}{(x+2)^2}; \dfrac{1}{2}\displaystyle\sum_{n=0}^{\infty} \dfrac{n}{2}\left(-\dfrac{x}{2}\right)^{n-1}$

16. $f'(x) = \dfrac{1}{(x+1)^4}; -\dfrac{1}{3}\displaystyle\sum_{n=1}^{\infty} \dfrac{n(n^2-1)(-1)^{n+1}}{2} x^{n-2}$

17. $f'(x) = \dfrac{x-(x+1)\ln(x+1)}{x^2(x+1)} \displaystyle\sum_{n=1}^{\infty} \dfrac{(-1)^{n+1}(n-1)}{n} x^{n-2}$

18. $f'(x) = \dfrac{1}{(1-x^2)^2}; \displaystyle\sum_{n=0}^{\infty} nx^{2n-1}$

19. $-\left(1 - \dfrac{x^2}{2!} + \dfrac{x^4}{4!} - \cdots\right)$ 20. $1 + x + x^2 + x^3 + \ldots$

21. $x - \dfrac{x^3}{3!} + \dfrac{x^5}{5!} - \dfrac{x^7}{7!} + \ldots$

22. $x - x^2 + \dfrac{4x^3}{3} - \dfrac{8x^4}{4} + \dfrac{16x^5}{5} - \ldots$

23. $-x + \dfrac{x^3}{3} - \dfrac{x^5}{5} + \dfrac{x^7}{7} - \ldots$

24. $\dfrac{-1}{2} + x^2 - \dfrac{8x^4}{4!} + \dfrac{32x^6}{6!} - \dfrac{128x^8}{8!} + \ldots$

9.2 Taylor Series

1. $P(x) = 1 - x + x^2 - x^3 + x^4$ 2. $P(x) = x^2$

3. $P(x) = x - \dfrac{x^3}{3!}$ 4. $P(x) = x + \dfrac{x^3}{3}$

5. $P(x) = 1 + \dfrac{x}{3} - \dfrac{x^2}{9} + \dfrac{5}{81}x^3 - \dfrac{10}{243}x^4$

6. $P(x) = 1 - \dfrac{9}{2}x^2 + \dfrac{27}{8}x^4$

7. $1 + x + \dfrac{1}{2!}x^2 + \dfrac{1}{3!}x^3 + \dfrac{1}{4!}x^4 + \dfrac{1}{5!}x^5 + \dfrac{1}{6!}x^6; \displaystyle\sum_{0}^{\infty} \dfrac{1}{n!}x^n$

8. $1 - x + \dfrac{1}{2!}x^2 - \dfrac{1}{3!}x^3 + \dfrac{1}{4!}x^4 - \dfrac{1}{5!}x^5 + \dfrac{1}{6!}x^6;$

$\displaystyle\sum_{n=0}^{\infty} \dfrac{(-1)^n}{n!}x^n$

9. $-1 + 2x^2 - \dfrac{2}{3}x^4 + \dfrac{4}{45}x^6; \displaystyle\sum_{n=0}^{\infty} \dfrac{(-1)^{n+1}2^{2n}}{(2n)!}x^{2n}$

10. $1 + x + x^2 + x^3 + x^4 + x^5 + x^6; \displaystyle\sum_{n=0}^{\infty} x^n$

11. $1 + 3x + \dfrac{9}{2!}x^2 + \dfrac{27}{3!}x^3 + \dfrac{81}{4!}x^4 + \dfrac{243}{5!}x^5 + \dfrac{729}{6!}x^6;$

$\displaystyle\sum_{n=0}^{\infty} \dfrac{3^n}{n!}x^n$

12. $1 - x + x^2 - x^3 + x^4 - x^5 + x^6; \displaystyle\sum_{n=0}^{\infty} (-1)^n x^n$

13. $1 - \dfrac{x}{2!} + \dfrac{x^2}{4!} - \dfrac{x^3}{6!} + \dfrac{x^4}{8!}$

14. x^3 15. 1 16. $1 + 2x + \dfrac{4x^2}{2!} + \dfrac{8x^3}{3!} + \dfrac{16x^4}{4!}$

17. $2 - 25x^2 + \dfrac{625x^4}{12}$ 18. $1 - \dfrac{x^3}{2!} + \dfrac{x^6}{4!} - \dfrac{x^9}{6!}$

19. $25 + 25(x-3) + 9(x-3)^2 + (x-3)^3$

20. $x - x^2 + x^3 - x^4 + \cdots = \displaystyle\sum_{n=0}^{\infty} (-1)^n x^{n+1}$

21. $e^6 + e^6(x-6) + \dfrac{e^6}{2!}(x-6)^2 + \ldots + \dfrac{e^6}{n!}(x-6)^n + \ldots$

$= \displaystyle\sum_{n=0}^{\infty} \dfrac{e^6}{n!}(x-6)^n$

22. $1 + 2(x+1) + 3(x+1)^2 + 4(x+1)^3 + 5(x+1)^4 + \cdots$

$= \displaystyle\sum_{n=0}^{\infty} (n+1)(x+1)^n$

23. $3 + 3\ln 3(x-1) + \dfrac{3}{2}(\ln 3)^2(x-1)^2 + \dfrac{1}{2}(\ln 3)^3(x-1)^3$

$+ \dfrac{1}{8}(\ln 3)^4(x-1)^4 + \cdots = \displaystyle\sum_{n=0}^{\infty} \dfrac{3(\ln 3)^n (x-1)^n}{n!}$

24. $(x-1) - \dfrac{(x-1)^2}{2} + \dfrac{(x-1)^3}{3} - \dfrac{(x-1)^4}{4} + \dfrac{(x-1)^5}{5} - \cdots$

$= \displaystyle\sum_{n=0}^{\infty} (-1)^{n-1}\dfrac{(x-1)^n}{n!}$

9.3 Taylor's Theorem

1. P_{15} **2.** P_{11} **3.** P_9 **4.** P_2 **5.** P_9 **6.** P_8

7. $\dfrac{x^7}{1-x}$ **8.** $\dfrac{x^{10}}{1+x}$ **9.** $\dfrac{2^6 x^6}{1-2x}$ **10.** $\left|\dfrac{-3^3 x^3}{1+3x}\right|$

11. $\left|\dfrac{-x^{11}}{1+x}\right|$ **12.** $\dfrac{x^4}{128(4+x)}$

13. Verify that the hypotheses of the Remainder Estimation Theorem are met by $f(x)$ as follows:

$$S(x) = \sum_{n=0}^{\infty} \frac{(-1)^n (2x)^{2n}}{(2n)!} \qquad f(x) = \cos(2x)$$

Notice that $f^{(n)}(x) = \pm 2^n \sin(2x)$ or

$f^{(n)}(x) = \pm 2^n \cos(2x)$ for all n. Thus

$\left|f^{(n+1)}(t)\right| \le 2^{n+1}$ for all t. Setting $M = 1$ and $r = 2$ in the

Remainder Theorem assures us of convergence.

14. Verify that the hypotheses of the Remainder Estimation Theorem are met by $f(x)$ as follows:

$$S(x) = \sum_{n=0}^{\infty} (-1)^{n+1} \frac{2(3x)^{2n+1}}{(2n+1)!} \qquad f(x) = -2\sin(3x)$$

Notice that $f^{(n)}(x) = \pm 2 \cdot 3^n \sin(3x)$ or

$f^{(n)}(x) = \pm 2 \cdot 3^n \cos(3x)$ for all n. Thus

$\left|f^{(n+1)}(t)\right| \le 2 \cdot 3^{n+1}$ for all t. Setting $M = 2$ and $r = 3$ in

the Remainder Theorem assures us of convergence.

15. Verify that the hypotheses of the Remainder Estimation Theorem are met by $f(x)$ as follows:

$$S(x) = \sum_{n=0}^{\infty} (-1)^n (x-1)^n \quad f(x) = \frac{1}{x}, \, x > 0$$

Notice that $\left|f^{(n+1)}(t)\right| = \dfrac{1}{t^{n+1}}$ for all n and $S(x)$ is the

Taylor Series for f at $x = 1$. By the Remainder

Estimation Theorem, it suffices to show that

$\dfrac{1}{t^{n+1}} \le M r^{n+1}$ for all t between 1 and an arbitrary x.

Since $\left|f^{(n+1)}(t)\right|$ is decreasing for each n, we know that it

attains its maximum value at the left hand endpoint of

any closed interval. Thus, if the interval is $[x, 1]$ the

maximum is $\dfrac{1}{x^{n+1}}$ and we can set $M = 1, r = 1/x$ in the

Remainder Theorem. If the interval is $[1, x]$ the

maximum is 1 and we set $M = 1, r = 1$ in the Remainder

Theorem. Either way, convergence is assured.

16. Verify that the hypotheses of the Remainder Estimation Theorem are met by $f(x)$ as follows:

$$S(x) = \sum_{n=0}^{1} \frac{(-1)^{n+1}(2x-1)^n}{n} \quad f(x) = \ln(2x)$$

Note that $S(x)$ is the Taylor's Series for f at $x = 1$ and

that $\left|f^{(n+1)}(t)\right| = \dfrac{1}{t^{n+1}}$, which is a decreasing function for

$t > 0$ so that a maximum is reached at the left hand

endpoint of any closed interval. For an arbitrary $x > 0$,

consider each interval, $[x, 1]$ and $[1, x]$. $1/t^{n+1}$ attains a

maximum value of $1/x^{n+1}$ on $[x, 1]$ so that setting

$M = 1, r = 1/x$ in the Remainder Theorem will suffice.

On the interval $[1, x]$, $1/t^{n+1}$ attains a maximum value of

1 so that setting $M = r = 1$ in the Remainder Theorem

will suffice. In either case, convergence is assured.

17. Verify that the hypotheses of the Remainder Estimation Theorem are met by $f(x)$ as follows:

$$S(x) = \sum_{n=0}^{\infty} \frac{x^n}{n!} \qquad f(x) = e^x$$

Note that $S(x)$ is the Taylor's Series for f at

$x = 0$. Notice that $\left|f^{(n+1)}(t)\right| = e^t$ for all n. Since this is an

increasing function, it attains its maximum value on a

closed interval at the right hand endpoint. Thus for an

arbitrary x, the maximum value on the interval $[0, x]$ is

e^x and we can set $M = e^x, r = 1$ in the Remainder

Theorem. If the interval is $[x, 0]$, then the maximum is

$e^0 = 1$ so that we can set $M = r = 1$ in the Remainder

Theorem. Either way, convergence is assured.

18. Verify that the hypotheses of the Remainder Estimation Theorem are met by $f(x)$ as follows:

$$S(x) = \sum_{n=0}^{\infty} \frac{(-1)^{n+1}(x-1)^n}{n} \qquad f(x) = \ln x$$

Notice that $\left|f^{(n+1)}(t)\right| = 1/t^{n+1}$ is a decreasing function for

all t so that its maximum on any closed interval is

attained at the left hand endpoint. The series $S(x)$ is

centered at 1 so we consider, for any arbitrary $x > 0$, the

two intervals $[x, 1]$ and $[1, x]$. For t in $[x, 1]$, the

maximum of $1/t^{n+1}$ is $1/x^{n+1}$ and so we can set $M = 1$ and

$r = 1/x$ in the Remainder Theorem. For t in $[1, x]$, the

maximum of $1/t^{n+1}$ is 1 so that both $M = 1$ and $r = 1$. In

either case, convergence is assured.

19. 5.21×10^{-3} **20.** 2.84×10^{-6} **21.** 2.63×10^{-2}

22. 9.87×10^{-6} **23.** 9.88×10^{-2} **24.** 2.42×10^{-5}

9.4 Radius of Convergence

1. Follows by the logic of example 2 by replacing x^4 by x^6 throughout.

2. Note that $\displaystyle\sum_{n=4}^{\infty} \frac{1}{(n-3)^2} = \sum_{n=1}^{\infty} \frac{1}{n^2}$, which is known to

converge.

3. $\dfrac{1}{3^n + 3n} \le \dfrac{1}{3^n}$ for all n and $\displaystyle\sum_{n=1}^{\infty} \dfrac{1}{3^n}$ is known to converge.

4. For n sufficiently large, we have that

$\dfrac{1}{n^2} \le \dfrac{1}{n(n-11)} \le \dfrac{1}{(n-11)^2}$ and $\displaystyle\sum_{n=1}^{\infty} \dfrac{1}{(n-11)^2}$ must

converge since it is just a shift of $\displaystyle\sum_{n=1}^{\infty} \dfrac{1}{n^2}$ which

converges.

5. Follows by the logic of Example 2 by replacing x^4 by x^{12} throughout.

6. Follows by the logic of Example 2 by replacing x^4 by x^8 throughout.

7. Use the logic given in Example 3 in the text replacing $\sin x$ by $\cos x$ and noting that since $(5n!) \ge n!$ we have

that $\dfrac{1}{(5n)!} \le \dfrac{1}{n!}$.

8. Use the logic given in Example 3 in the text noting that

since $n^n \ge n!$ for all n we have that $\dfrac{1}{n^n} \le \dfrac{1}{n!}$.

9. Use the Direct Comparison Test and the fact that

$\left| \dfrac{(\sin x)^n}{n^2} \right| \le \dfrac{1}{n^2}$.

10. Use the Direct Comparison Test and the fact that

$\left| \dfrac{(\cos x)^n}{n^2} \right| \le \dfrac{1}{n^2}$.

11. Use the logic given in Example 3 in the text replacing $\sin x$ by $\cos x$ and noting that since $(2n!) \ge n!$ we have

that $\dfrac{1}{(2n)!} \le \dfrac{1}{n!}$.

12. Use the logic given in Example 3 in the text noting that

since $(2n)! \ge n!$ for all n we have that $\dfrac{1}{(2n)!} \le \dfrac{1}{n!}$.

13. Use the logic given in Example 3 in this manual replacing $\cos x$ by $\sin x$ throughout.

14. Converges   15. Converges   16. Converges

17. Diverges   18. Converges   19. Converges

20. Diverges   21. Converges   22. 1

23. $\dfrac{3}{4}$ 24. $-\dfrac{21}{4}$ 25. 2

26. 5   27. 8   28. $-\dfrac{1}{4}$

29. -1

1. Converges to 2   2. Diverges

3. Diverges   4. Converges to $\dfrac{12}{11}$

5. Diverges   6. Converges to $\dfrac{2}{7}$

7. 55   8. 8,104   9. 59,875

10. 2.649×10^{10} 11. 5.835×10^{14} 12. 8.660×10^{16}

13. Converges   14. Converges   15. Converges

16. Diverges   17. Diverges   18. Converges

19. Converges absolutely for all x 20. $-8 < x < 6$

21. Converges only at $x = 0$ 22. $-4 < x < 2$

23. $-11 < x < 1$ 24. Converges absolutely for all x

Chapter 10
Parametric, Vector, and Polar Functions

10.1 Parametric Functions

1. (a)
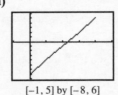
[−1, 5] by [−8, 6]
(b) yes
(c) $y = 3x - 7$

2. (a)
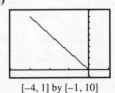
[−4, 1] by [−1, 10]
(b) yes
(c) $y = -3x$

3. (a)

[−14.1, 14.1] by [−9.3, 9.3]
(b) no
(c) $x^2 + y^2 = 36$

4. (a)

[−4.7, 4.7] by [−3.1, 3.1]
(b) no
(c) $x^2 + 4y^2 = 4$

5. (a)
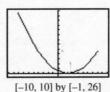
[−10, 10] by [−1, 26]

6. (a)
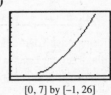
[0, 7] by [−1, 26]

(b) yes

(c) $y = \left(\dfrac{x}{2} - 1\right)^2$

(b) yes

(c) $y = (x-1)^2$

7. (a)

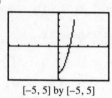

[-5, 5] by [-5, 5]

(b) yes

(c) $y = 3x^2 - 4$

8. (a)

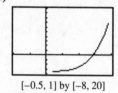

[-0.5, 1] by [-8, 20]

(b) yes

(c) $y = 25x^4 - 7$

9. (a)

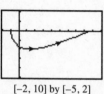

[-2, 10] by [-5, 2]

(b) lowest point: (1.4649, -2), highest points at (-1, 0) and $(\pi^2 - 1, 0)$

(c) (6.831, -0.673)

0. (a)

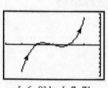

[-6, 0] by [-7, 7]

(b) highest point: (-1, 6), lowest point (-5, -6)

(c) (-3, 0)

1. (a)

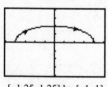

[-1.25, 1.25] by [-1, 1]

(b) highest point: (0, 1), lowest points (-1, 0) and (1,0)

(c) None

2. (a)

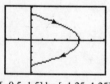

[-0.5, 1.5] by [-1.25, 1.25]

(b) highest point: (0, 1), lowest point: (0, -1)

(c) (1, 0)

13. (a)

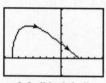

[-8, 6] by [-2, 6]

(b) highest point: (-4.5326, 4), lowest points: (-7, 0) and $(\pi^2 - 7, 0)$

(c) (0.831, 1.346)

14. (a)

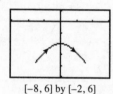

[-8, 6] by [-2, 6]

(b) highest point: (0, -2), lowest points: $(\tan(\pm1), -2\sec(\pm1))$

(c) none

15. π **16.** 8   **17.** 18   **18.** 45.23

19. 9.417   **20.** 8.04   **21.** 60.35739   **22.** 0.771

23. 32   **24.** 16   **25.** 88   **26.** 24

27. 48   **28.** 72

10.2 Vectors in the Plane

1. $|\mathbf{v}| = 4$, $\theta = 75.52°$ **2.** $|\mathbf{v}| = \sqrt{11}$, $\theta = 37.09°$

3. $|\mathbf{v}| = 4$, $\theta = 255.52°$ **4.** $|\mathbf{v}| = 4$, $\theta = 138.60°$

5. $|\mathbf{v}| = 4$, $\theta = 318.59°$ **6.** $|\mathbf{v}| = \sqrt{39}$, $\theta = 16.10°$

7. $|\mathbf{v}| = 2$, $\theta = 240°$ **8.** $|\mathbf{v}| = \sqrt{19}$, $\theta = 336.59°$

9. $\langle 9, 28 \rangle$ **10.** $\langle 12, 32 \rangle$ **11.** $\langle 57, -132 \rangle$

12. $\langle 66, -152 \rangle$ **13.** $30 - 6\sqrt{17}$ **14.** $5 - \sqrt{17}$

15. $|\mathbf{u} + \mathbf{v}| = 670.48$ and $\theta = 3.42°$

16. $|\mathbf{u} + \mathbf{v}| = 433.83$ and $\theta = 5.07°$

17. $|\mathbf{u} + \mathbf{v}| = 654.30$ and $\theta = 84.63°$

18. $|\mathbf{u} + \mathbf{v}| = 689.28$ and $\theta = 271.85°$

19. $|\mathbf{u} + \mathbf{v}| = 965.74$ and $\theta = 3.78°$

20. $|\mathbf{u} + \mathbf{v}| = 758.11$ and $\theta = 46.17°$

21. $\langle t^3 + 2t + 1, -t^2 + 8 \rangle; 1 \le t \le 2$

22. $\left\langle t^2 - \sin \pi t + 2, \quad t^2 + \cos \pi t + 4 \right\rangle$; $1 \le t \le 5$

23. $\left\langle te^t, 2e^{-2t} \right\rangle$; $2 \le t \le 3$

24. $\left\langle \dfrac{1}{1+t}, (t+1)^{-1/2} \right\rangle$; $2 \le t \le 8$

25. $\left\langle t^2 - \sin \pi t + 2, \; 2t^2 + \cos \pi t + 3 \right\rangle$; $2 \le t \le 4$

26. $\left\langle 2t^2 - \sin \pi t + 1, \; \dfrac{3}{2}t^2 + \cos \pi t + 1 \right\rangle$; $2 \le t \le 3$

12. $(x-3)^2 + (y-3)^2 = 18$, a circle centered at (3, 3) of radius $3\sqrt{2}$

13. $xy = 3$, a hyperbola

14. $(x+1)^2 + y^2 = 1$, a circle centered at (–1, 0) of radius 1

15. $(2x^2 + 2y^2 + 1) \cdot (x^2 + y^2 - 1) = 0$, the unit circle

16. $4y = x - 3$, a line   **17.** 54π **18.** 8π **19.** 150π

20. $\dfrac{59}{2}\pi$ **21.** $\dfrac{9}{2}\pi$ **22.** 294π **23.** $8 - \pi$

24. 15π **25.** 48π **26.** $\dfrac{45\pi}{2}$ **27.** $\dfrac{9\pi}{2}$

28. $228 - 36\pi$

10.3 Polar Functions

1.

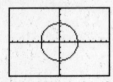

[–18.8, 18.8] by [–12.1, 12.1]

2.

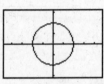

[–4.7, 4.7] by [–3.1, 3.1]

3.

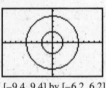

[–9.4, 9.4] by [–6.2, 6.2]

4.

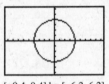

[–9.4, 9.4] by [–6.2, 6.2]

5.

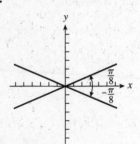

6.

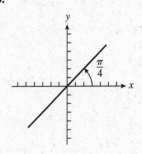

7.

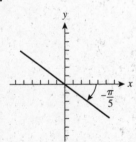

8.

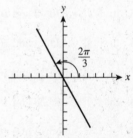

9. $x^2 + (y-5)^2 = 25$, a circle centered at (0, 5) of radius 5

10. $(x-4)^2 + y^2 = 16$, a circle centered at (4, 0) of radius 4

11. $y = -2$, a horizontal line